JOSEPH (JOE) DUVERNAY

TWELVE
AMERICAN
DANCES

POEMS NEW AND SELECTED

Library of Congress Control Number 2021924316
ISBN HARDCOVER Number 979-8-9852907-4-5

Joseph Duvernay, Publisher
Frazier Park, CA

AFTER W. BLAKE

Twelve American Dances
Poems New and Selected

Knowing you want to go home gets you there. The Eumenides will follow. Knowing mind could describe a box where there is no box only shadow, should sober. Need Dimension be mentioned ... or is captured-perspective alone here spoken of... it that flairs vector ray-like; all aware of each at a distance, gravity, while Fibonacci, arithmetic, hop-scotch recurring, a slice of realities, and are many? A woman and a sonogram of her baby in her womb ferried thought of baby's perspective, its cave like world, alien from that outside, and perceived not least, a few or 'n' dimensions there. Baby's, the space between, mine—since dimension concerns time—the Mother, doctor, fly on window, ant somewhere in or out ... so many that show the magnificence! And ever is there prayer for happy accident!

Folly, and likely too far self-effacing, to suppose any but the author and some few readers will find the ongoing paintable, singable, danceable or of much importance. But this work tries, in select, to gather as much of the early part, with some latest—photo sits in the middle of—the past twenty-three or so years' 'unpublished in book form' work to a single volume as stuff and pack did allow. And though I doubt it, if the reader will find a phrase or more similar to a past volume, or some correlate, I apologize. Twenty plus years of attempted going-fore, with over the years' revisits and keep of document, breed, or may breed omission and overlap.

JOSEPH (JOE) DUVERNAY

TWELVE
AMERICAN
DANCES

POEMS NEW AND SELECTED

II
When ...Chinese dancers enwound/ A shining web,
a floating ribbon of cloth,/ It seemed that a dragon of air/
Had fallen among dancers.../All men are dancers and their
tread/ Goes to the barbarous clangour of a gong...

III
Some moralist or mythological poet/ Compares the solitary
soul to a swan;/ I am satisfied with that,/ Satisfied if
a troubled mirror show it,/ Before that brief gleam
of its life be gone...

Nineteen Hundred Nineteen
William Butler Yeats

"Ἴτε, ὦ ποιηταί, ταυτί γάρ ὑμετερα,
και ῥαψῳδῖτε πρός τούτους τούς ἀθύμους..."
δέ οῦκ σκοτῷ φής ηέλιος αγλαῷ.

Philostratus Apollonius of Tyana Bk. VII, 6

"Come, poets for this is yours,
and stitch-together for those the despondent..."
but (do) not you say in darkness the sun it shines,
uncūö hū longe unsure how long.

The racist or fundamentalist parents of our students say that in a truly democratic society the students should not be forced to read books by Black people, Jewish people, homosexual people. They will protest that these books are being jammed down their children's throats. I cannot see how to reply to this charge without saying something like: "There are credentials for admission to our democratic society, credentials which we liberals have been making steadily more stringent by doing our best to excommunicate racists, male chauvinists, homophobes, and the like. You have to be educated to be a citizen of our society, a participant in our conversation, someone with whom we can envision merging our horizons. So we are going to go right on trying to discredit you in the eyes of your children, trying to strip your fundamentalist religious community of dignity, trying to make your views seem silly rather than discussable. We are not so inclusivist as to tolerate intolerance such as yours."

Pragmatism as Anti-Authoritarianism
Universality and Truth (1993/1996)
8-Communicating or Educating?
Richard Rorty

"How do you live a life that is one and the same with your art? A life that improvises music cannot run by another's rules. This may bring problems if based on an ordinary observer's rules for behavior in a society that does not always understand what art is, or what an artist is, or why there is nothing without music."

On The Eckstine Bus Notes For A Screenplay
Dexter Gordon and Maxine Gordon, 1987

A light in the window, Love! Hello Oldowan! Hello San!
Under sign of kind dragon, carrying water,
he will add, the young brave from the trees.
Liparos—gentle to the gentle, wide awake in his wideawake,
earlier born and further seeing, he is epichthonios (living on
the Earth) still and
ÀNHP, man, real man, warrior, hero, while too
ÀNΘΡΟΠΟΣ, mere man! and huddles darkle.
Bought unguent acorn pages have stratosphere.
He will Sufi swirl. Pantagruelize, man his zeibekiko,
and curled straight in-meditative, wait, as they circle round dance
exorcising Ajun-Kpa. So tracks respondent the mambo,
bomba and rumba with cakewalk, fox-trot, jitterbug, swing,
jig and clog so the charleston break true.
But we have seen black bottoms do their enriching war dance
among the evil, harm leaden, and we wish them well.
Myrobalan = myron + balanos: dried astringent East Indian
fruit used in tanning, and ink is there too, as mention, so
he can get his rueful referral proctor supervisor, to monitor
in the examination; supra, super, soprano,
Quels son les plus beaux—highest!
'À la meilleure proposition. Hubble constant, expansion.
Brisance, break rub, explosive, crushes; clothes of argaman?
Sonar—sound. Soufflé, puffed up. God: Atom, all the rest,
Viracocha and Waheguru too.
Lidar—laser light. Catchpenny arcades and amusements:
The five, or ten thousand things. Edema—swelling,
Forward! rubus mow of mindful thought.

[Gk.] oidein, to swell. Oidema! Edel—[G.] noble.
Edaphos [Gk.] edaphic, bottom, ground, of the soil.
Old notes steer! [Old Norse] edda, norse, eddic—edacious, edac, edax
[L.] edere, to eat voracious.
Ecru: raw, beige.
Ect. Ecto—Outside, external.
Quondam, former, sometime.
Recurrence. Knock-on effect of Bais management of African Elephants,
as well, themselves; greet man like the whale in his
whale road. Asking if we'll love them.

CONTENTS

SEC. I: TROUBLED MIRROR

CH. 1
STARTING-BACK ROUND DANCE

CH. 2
IN-MEMORY-OF FLAT-FOOT STOMP

CH. 3
HOW-TO-WALK SALSA

CH. 4
EARTH-FIRST SUN DANCE

CH. 5
THE-UNIVERSE-AT-DAWN JARABE TAPATIO

SEC. II: SUCH A SKY AS THIS

CH. 6
BRING-ME-WORKERS CUMBIA

CH. 7
A COMMENTS CAPER

CH. 8
A TRANSLATIONS HOP

CH. 9
BOOK REVIEW SQUARE DANCE

SEC. III: MURMURACIONS

CH. 10
THE-LIGHT-OF-PROMISE GHOST DANCE

CH. 11
KING-FOR-A-DAY MOONWALK

CH. 12
MEETING-WHISTLER BREAKDANCE

SEC. I
TROUBLED MIRROR

CH. 1
STARTING-BACK ROUND DANCE

STARTING BACK

Press it as far as possible. See how much you can understand!
Mr. Prof. Noam Chomsky on Knowledge and Understanding
On AMA—you tube 12-21-2020

(A writers instructions.) Back from Hiatus.
Ready to defend; wane, whisk cup of tea.

Be prepared on that mnonsters back
while each engines machinations
triple time needed to weigh things out,
scoots along floor on hind,
wiping hind gambol, as if.

Now! We must step up.
Raise hand and volunteer
%^##$@!&*!

See how that's done now?
—Got out of car,
actually pulled-off highway this time
and took a look; closer, way back
seemed slanted some.
Don't ask!

What instruction rendered, will be valued
to large degree, when Big Guy says 'go!'
and instructs instructions for achieving to flow.

God I hear a trumpet! Sax's phones
call out names on a list captured, named,
you lend landscape to the others.

Thanking for chore!
Sun on canvas; ripped-up more.

When tacking to other than pendantry
try pendantry on.
Fits! Ah! As I thought.
Too many and too much.

Note: See Endnotes.

NON-KNOWING

—further in the study!...

This world, vigorously displayed
Less yours. There were days could ride on the back boards
And laugh; believe for a while, so wanted to.
It belongs to the shapers and well-healers, clapping,
Of which you too live in some level, where
Another sees you favored when viewed from there,
And meaning scares itself off. But what
Can even great literature hold good of its own doing that lasts?
Can any art or science realm him up so he is comfy?
When is it to be? When was it and how long did it last?
Was in those times when non-knowing laid stage
And you could believe the earth flat, till Copernicus
Annotated his ancients to steer round, show clearer.
I would, if you reader, abandon this migrant
He works like a lazy ****, of which there could never be any,
In company his morrows, thoughts of them and the bull-whip,
Against wall of despair, sits the stick he walks and carries
out of that house, For snakes, madmen and such, but it's all talk!
'I'll eat an alligator!' dunk habit in strangest dissolving fluid,
Eat where Helen Thomas eats; sit where she's been relegated,
Catch whiff of free-based people's initiative And remember
what she and others have been saying, 'We (The People) are paying
For that, them—President, Press Secretary and all government
Inhabitants'.
Now it seems shadows have been invited.
Cause loss of sight and mis-steps on stair, so falling
Invite ourselves to the ball, might, some say must,
Carry in kindred gifts left by these in the mud,
Stepping from shinning coaches: horror at war,
Smiles turned toward fear, envy let out to run the yard, recover it.
All the crimes I've committed in my un-knowing states:
Some lifting from my retention at all costs of power, prestige, privilege,
"This will be the best for them!"
Others growing wildly from barn doors I've cut open,
The flocks and herds misused and the ones betrayed by my greedy farming,
"Get off! Clear this county by sundown and don't look back!"
Ranchers that never inhaled a fresh sage day, but in their lost initiatives for
Good reason, that abandoned them and us, 'cause no good in it,
Went on to do Madison Ave. theatre, and suggested.
It seems the truth in this, under these barrages,
Waits quiet to be judged, to recite, but can't.

ON THE STAGE

Friends to trust.
    Hair all mussed-up as a must.
    "Somewhere in my mind, I think I'm moving."
    Poetry stands blind to: 'You can't do that here.'
    Says, "#$@* off" to bending a dearest's ear...
That's why submitted to...
Unwilling to submit. Says come closer story listeners,
Stories told here.
    Russian and I same.
    Tibetan, San, and I.
    Your views and mine.
Hey mate! You's walking this trail for a reason?

Who's taking meals-festive to heights unadorned?
Who's banking on 'deamons to see through to angels?'
Taken directly, Wes Craven ends.
Another name bends all to its wishes.

    Light-up!
    Left, wind-up.
    Hands wave, "I'm fine, just breathing."
    Stooped over, coughing.
    Says, "#$@* off' to 'tending some dearest's garden...'
Willing to submit to you angel eyes!
Says show us your ass,
Those glistening thighs.

Easy virtue housed here.
Kidnapper and I same.
Murderer and I 'wave our hands in the air like we just don't care.'
Tremulous, slink to our goal,
Slither to and fro and...whoosh!
Washed away,
Make way for another show.

WIDE-EYED

Is there a chance perception will
Link lines of formula
Once handling all the equations?
There is!
Is there, in there, sums totaled
That grouped in two's the calculations?
There are!
Will opinion create a mess
And leave the driving to us?
It will!
If in this scientific afterglow,
Man sees only the possible
And the probable gets scant attention,
Is it inevitable we will perish?
Is! Because right answers often
Are gleaned from an archaic
And the possible
Needs remember the probable—
Cause and effect,
Where all the good went down,
Was not counted among,
Best crowned, but abandoned.
He, the sage of yesterdays'
Opines on relationships between
Man and forest, man and wetlands,
Man and sea-shore—route come sooner—
Light lend prohibition,
Posterity listens and wide-eyed
Pins hopes to us.

THE WORK

In turns our treatise;
Hot flashes of insight,
Labored over,
Lived with constantly
Dressed and unclothed,
Then expounded,
Given reception or no.
Colleagues clap,
Some angered.
Are denounced, praised
Given review and words.
Families indignant,
Friends afraid they
'May be spoken of next.'
Some say, 'what an idiot',
Others unearth some past indiscretion
Say lays light on character.
All this the faith-giver
Goes through, days in phase and out.
Blame she'll take and then time slips
Knots it's cared much of
Slides past decades and
'We think special was!'
But too late for you.
Your reward in the thing done.
Paint
Sculpt
What script is this?
A book? From you?
Ah so! There
'Fun' is to be seen only
In the first five,
The later are not of you.

LEGACY

Translating Marvell's
'Edmundi Trotii Epitaphium'
and after first verse stopped—Italian,
A Latin legacy with commencements and convention
saying, "enough, enough, already enough!"
So, as the four sons are named, wave goodby
from this shore to retackle at later date.

But before go, let it be said
appreciate more each year
our fortune here with whom came from, even if
"Legite Parentes, vanissimus hominum ordo,"
and must in ways abundant pass on,
that which saints, scholar and philosophe
labored overtime on—your "sapite infortunio"
spread out in "forma virili, specie eximic."
And with this, some exuberant aberration
informa pauperis, plays our games cerebral
in our living rooms—exedra redux
and we converse furioso.

MOVING EARTH

Crackle on palisade
Tension blurs
Sea and storm
Run palpable rings,
Actually smash and quaver.
Rocks mud its very splash below,
As the face falls.
This is how many roads are washed-out.
Rarely can cliffs take
The bashing for long.
Sea being strong
And long, lasting longer
Can by a day briefly
Lead portions down,
So over time
Nothing is left.
This is how we men too
Are found at an end to be jaded,
Gravity choose, that all things
Go back to the source is how.
Corf full and leaning,
We find a place to dump the load.

THE WORLD LEFT ITS OWN DEVICES

Whatever do
gain meaning of, will
tool for success, where
endeavor tries answers to
have at table during breakfast.
As perspectives acquire
differing, acute, leaning-in, tiring
glances often executing mad schemes
in protect from evil, in pursuit of.

Noses vary dependent the weather!
It's sweep, vacuum, hose drive,
clean tile, stone and linoleum.
It's too high and too tough for two
of our invited guests: democrat and republican,
singing songs still too lacking any expert,
knowing utilitarian animism,
where rational, rationale could
sneak out and go home.

In questions directed; what of environment now?
     Say touch us, ease-up
     find smiles in your cup
          Times rough-blush
          could worry us how

     May tourist, may Shanghai
     may spam all the stuff
          should stay loose, believe 'um
          grab far less the scruff.

A WOMAN IN THE MILD

Could give you all my salt,
But you'll not like results!?
It's a mess!
Gold, yours
Life and wild, gone!
A decent way to behave as though
Earth could sustain us all indifferently
'Tween seen and what would rock-the-house.
Soon spectacular wreathing array
A spot of spectacular
Frame team expecting some how-the-moist-came.
Claim nothing,
But in evidentiary laying
Line the walls with gifts, prayers even
To her a woman in the mild.

FOR PAULINE AND WILLIAM (To The Drinking Life)

From: William Makepeace Thackery's
'Some Roundabout Papers', 'On Some Carp at Sans Souci', 'De Juventute'
see pagebypagebooks.com, etc.

Now so,
Having read a sheaf of papers some gathering there
Where could find them and spent hours upholding
In the fine ramp-up that is coin, morning study
Some say warms not just the bank of memory,
Too the heart and breath of,
Now slaps awake to ride (I mean write) ancient,
But not ancient enough brougham pulled
By a sidling animal we'll not call horse
For the general fear we'll be laughed at.
A heckling ransom might feed despondent shots around
And screaming in patterns may come finally to terms
With an addling rancor's twine's, tempts and tips
Ribbons into noose, let's have sung her songs by then!

Well, yellow peaks through haze of nights drop,
"It's two o'clock and this century!"
No, two passed some time ago,
More like approaching four and,
'the purple shadows "slant o'er the snowy sward.'"
As proof,
Is maintained as friend, saw hollering,
Entrancing by the east
And soon grapes purple too.

Were, as ambulatory as Thackery made mock of
In days; a pantomime a Duvernay bayadere of lap and lush,
As I read it, how the young men blushed at her feminine.
—Then was the eighteen thirty's—
How rapid the loss, how vapid what hailed, drank muck
And washed down a tank with more of same,
Ale, a mount of red nose, eyes that slant and
Without care,
'The pub is on Tuesday's closed!'

SHEE

Two members move up
Die cast
Shee obtains
Righted permit(s)
Contained in the satchel captured
Among slight careen-crass
Spend-if-you-will-in-days-scattering
a-lot!-we us see the way it might
seen in there yelling
room a-morphed way from
keen scent women sent
sea of gallon grass and sweep-weed
a friend caught some wilder chatter
feeling skin flat offer, off her
wheel the last days light a brilliance
shown
It's always that way with her
Every other allows consumer
Milder-rain fulfillments through window
Factly preen it spent a fortune
She not.

MISSING A LOVE

Don't give a fart
for reasons coming out of malls
and corporate boardrooms.

Let us work through our unpleasantries!
Let's do, rake in every bit of awe,
the wide pupil sag,
lights eating our lunch for us.

Expect salvos from a single spoiled brats' cuts
at anything getting in way.
Not Sandra or Doris. Nothing described as
helpless or putz offered outstretched hand.

Am indeed ma'am! A quiet, wondering handy man.
Am thinking how nice 'twould be,
all your private parts to see.
Put your hands back there and spread um.

Ah! Send um pictures with the fee.
Poetry, easy enough, complete.
Shan't consider talcum, soap, brush or spoon.
Lie here tasting your wonders perfumed.

HERALDRIC

A rise in interest rate
A loan uncompromising
Tooth and plate un-assailed
Reasoned vile attempt
To post and nail the
Anvil-hunted, headmistress
Master-smith a consultant chore,
Mime split with reality
That laughs cannot un-shift
To wash and restore banquet effect.
Tan hides lying rent,
To the gallows a chartreuse season,
A plum cloak and royal blue hem
Easter array, the families crest
And mantle
A Charolais hump
Stag-based ear,
What Forez leaned in to say
How evident your loose coat,
What will! That set of arms magnificent!
Now detain the meaning
Slay the dreaming
It yells and throws own excrement
And the day, with stars, willows while.

CAN MEADOWS SING

Shall we speculate?
Questions bellow
Are belched-up
Tunes deliver a spent us
And the rallying rhyme
Obliterates, otherwise obliges.
Can meadows sing?
They Can!
Do they though?
No friend! Not lately, not now!

GOING TO GROUND

And the marketplace shouldered the load,
As a main contingent excluded
What sacrifice people, the masses endured
To keep the thing afloat.
Surrey not for those stepping back a bit
From the high-times high-living meant
To surround,
They shall cousin each other smaller
Anecdotal pieces of what stripped pie,
Less gluttony, the press of greed,
Salutary in accident and final campaign screening
That altogether wears out, wears down
Will be seen to anchor while uprooting's too
Wince, but slam not our offers to ground,
Untitled, un-fixed.

Say to those encountering along a road,
Some worn path on the ground,
Say why in truth the lot is full
And the 'tub without bottom.'
The lot; full of penitents!
Tub; holds not a drop
And Lord knows the anvil is a dent
In it's solid use, and hammer invents a case
Could extract alembic truth
From whatever is loaded on screen
To sift and sieve lives through
To ground!

ADHERENCE CRAFTED

Move me
You heavens appear
And earth to stand on
And I will take the short route
To a happiness gathers you under sleeve.

Move me
You always turn to pragmatism's
Wily empiricism
And I will open depths to whim.
Allay frowns we fracture.
Lay-in of taxes great for the
Weaning-off of luxurious liberty
Where they have taken dollars from us
And speed justice here.

In the then fine adherence crafted,
say how protistan and extremophile
Are cousin
And the while reign, grab halter
Set, the jab is not a spear.

End with 'Dragon' gone too far afield
Move me and I will,
But send Id driven helms to steer
And run the rivers with.
Do not subject this eerie tale.
Are seen in tandem, fill!

REUNION FANCY

There's a snow in April
What fixes on. What contours landscapes
with wet cure, escapes contention, disturbs
just a bit, then continues coursing through
lean space twixt heaven and this earth here this.

Earth scene, sense can't take home the bacon.
Sense is not quite champion of task,
need what is withheld, social man, held back
not honest show, 'not' due to layers piled-up
over time, that we pray says we are without care.

Heads high from one or two modalities that would
wrestle our limiting selves to the mat and symbolically
wring its less than lover-ly neck, using meanings
left by the ancestors, both man and beast.
Heated up and transient.

It there enters its waiting banquet, shakes sets of hands,
elbows grabbed in delight, as though and ever so
break-neck speed should light the path behind. Hug.
How we got there, where came from, similar smiles,
past usage styles that do line a face

That do set the pace and pre-determine winners outside
marked lanes, the race. Hi Anthony! Hey there's
Deborah, been years. Hello Juan, no we're lacking
specifics and generally don't know the way, but stop
our polonium progress this will not. A many fleeced flock.

HOLY

Finding it most wonderous hey!
How comes the night after day has fed.
What "Blunt truths" nature spikes
And sport a play with men, animal,
of fair grasses too get laid
Down, if not mowed. Suspect no
Evil hand in these rare sights—
Avast! He and Her Rule. Might
achieves that is everywhere, rights itself and
We little angry, potentially if not pliable
Created yaw must reverse trend.
A deminimus encroachment seems all we give
To these altogether God-made things.

NON GUN

Used that old parbuckle to hoist aboard the barrels.
Took sighted aim down two cylinders.
Rounded out my choices in perpetuity
And finally, with archangel authority
Callous your chapped hands here and now.

AND

Two ways drained
From same kettle an drum
Twain leaks and froms. A standard script, lost.
A title twat probest! A flute in ear, birth belch twist
And turn...let them bleed out,
these unexpected turns and twists
and split ear fists, tangled all up with
the following rantour.
In the highlands does by betty reside
In the by-lands near and due.
Back to front when wrestling with you!
Be obscure, if it welcomes your ghosts!
Never demure, as sun cuts in window,
hot saw blade been running all night! My sparrow gist,
My knee deep view to stream bed below, where
tree in grove sits sparkling with the green grass at his/her feet.
And despite call for fame, escape est again had
and no-face in crowd's sustained! Oh yes! The band plays on
And the end searches back so vividly that it runs into
it's own and the others coming!
And this morn-speak at paper wrapped in sound loss...aside,
Works well to walk with hydrogen awareness astride,
Walking those badlands together, welting while melting
into this twenty-first century man-hide and.

POTASH AND COAL DUST

My mordant brackish,
My silly fought.
My ancient back track,
The easy flaunt.
Comes now the term ouch,
Its deadened curve.
The sea is educated,
Their rickets swerve.

O www.
O gracious cow.
Steps of balsa wood,
Am willing now,
To break into song,
Group the bliss found.
Chance fallacious,
Exceed high-strung
See the puss push out.

Lonely in all the right places,
Contained within,
Putrid anecdotes brace.
Exhibit? He knows not how!

Shine, exert in replaying,
Choose restive and restore.
The lengthy undulating,
The boot postulate ascents to abhor.
As rudimentary reddens
And possessive breaks down,
Choose potash and coal dust?
Matter dire now.

BEHAVE

Now finishing,
prepare uplifting demeanor.
Have face washed and teeth gleam
Past hugging pensive: drab,
Loose feel of doom that trains you
On its track—this
Is what men everywhere have always.
Make a sorrow that shaves in the morning no more,
Is not allowed out house, is in closet,
Shut to this world's light—it appreciates not.
Resell foam dispenser,
Get rid of cup and brush no lather
That hoary bearded thing-less.
You may clothe the care in finest drapery though,
Let a cloudy day ferry imagination (the practical relation):
Do a round dance—Vulcan soon to throw
Blue bolts out heaven, if that.
Is dark, forebodes, promises as does fire, life.
Given 'Fubarski's' all your days,
Grow not as jaded as many.
Plan the scanned files, forget revolution,
Delete from him attacking virus.
Say Juniper, a several option:
A mission and missionary be.
This is more than choice. Choice-less,
Only a faith, belief, right action feed?
where are these?
If called on carpet in this,
Mean no harm.

JUDGEMENT
(A Vehicle)

What a bottle of water is a man!
May imagine a maestro saying,
"Part of what's been done lingers, sucks the bold.
Little mind, misfortunes are to overcome.
I will love you matter not your hate for me!"
'Oh yeah! No problem!'

One time, accepted the work of hearts' change,
 disturbed fears veered.
 Now find we've attributed to torture's popularization,
who would've believed such apparitions.

And of apparitions: lately having noticed it on
 Buonarroti's sheet, now see his sack everywhere:
in sweatpants hung over door, just then local
 branches as if flayed don't wave.
 Painter 'alone, silence was blessing'
his vigilance its depiction:
a Last Judgment (one of many) of self.
What of these matchless parts? Never mind!

What's important to the world is
eyes on we polity that will bind shopper wound,
will not pester further still-night, and for the n'th time know:
taking the African out spoils.

TOO SOON

No sun for days,
that's winter: the cold, raucous gent
we entice behind summer heat,
'too brown for a fair praise' too soon.
Now all has this stark fairness, capitalizes
on stuff nose and run out of warmth
too soon.
We spend time with Harper and Angelou,
the masters are among us yet.

This trifle tune may blare enough lack
to tie no concordance, and verification is
a flea that stares from the carpet
into such a dearth too soon.

Because of this wet with cold
injuries taken at their Eden-height seem new—
are the bones that creek and stiff limb
that will not hallelujah!

But, a friend to brethren throughout!
'Engine' somehow, trying all the time
to love the created and that forms
acceptance to make of self,
into plenty 'Hyperion' share,
hammer and short hat—that nail its lover,
Dad, 86
and 'jun kets' 25 forever.
Be sure—the route will soon acquiesce.

NOW IS THE COMING OF THE YEAR

Now is the coming of the year
When executives run and misers weep, their titles showing.
   Where and when
   Crying babes stand, bolt out of cribs,
   Leave off crying, take up plowshares
And cultivate a bit of wee Earth for we...could only see
the folly in our trundled locks and branded chore.
That reach short, breach-snapped baby-caught sore.

Now too smells thought divine show signs of loss,
Incremental clock-switching becomes a familiar tik-tock itch
Here 'neath the quilt of my guilty kilt, a language is old
   And built from some simple example of wishes.

MOVIE MADNESS

As now gather close the trailed obsession,
Now friends as enter tragic arena
let each find traces of the faces once were.

Un-forget sacrifices made and lives lost,
rotate News a little, hit a paywall. Don't go too Oh!wellian!
And when tries gone well ahead, alluvial fields remember
those wet grasses and tall frogs, that stood end on
to get a look at silly, adolescent man were accurate.

Scouted what? Qualia, as you scratched with pine?
With all this said and silently
passed between, with the going-away parties fresh
in ears and on coronas,
clamp crampon a-hide! smiley beast
and start our fishing project!

SEMBLANCE

Cowboy exertion and excrement.
Tie-dyed deadheads and friends said,
"Be fellow and phone person,
Be answered heller".
We ancient balanced mapper.

A quarter part played,
A diminished role found,
A tripped over abundance
a dry western town.

Some pain brought over from yesteryear.
My fumbling, window mind yet near.
My breathing at the fulcrum and at the sweep.
The metered ringing in my silent ear.
All evidence this reside,
All tantamount to this hide.

The rule of society is crucial to our development!
Left ravished.
Found famished.
Consumed of trying.
Ample lost art plying.

ALLNESS

Your life was value even when kicked and devalued most!
It is the best thing you have.
And it's taking away you sometimes long for
Is the stupidest thing you do.

In the light then, of these chlorophyll-full charms
Blood-filled slack arms, stop there and see
The return of you from she as more love song swings up.
Not counting its chances, but allowance given
As fast histories big buck with the smoothness
And rifled agony of top ten hits then

retired toys and learnings from butted storage cabinets
Are to favored hills and common circles taught, whence
Wrapped sacred garments in fleeting moments of realization,
The one allness alls, *adumu*, unhurt. Unhurt and un-bidden by we.

THE ALL ENCOMPASS

In swoop of one full fellness
Enter complete health wellness.

As the mystery of listening goes deeper,
Ear/eye is hone, and what is felt in open air
of incidents through time, there glide reasons
for what does and does not rhyme and why.

It may be waiting in wings for its chance,
This opposite of us thought stream, love dance,
Which, from democracy-like fair interplay
into the dust-born, air worn
And blown back across continents, bows.

With a just twist, so, turn, route.
Open hand, grab, grout.
Innocent angle move your mouth.
With humble gamble the matters' out.

Matter out, matter seen
Leave joy in managed wings.
While other players take the stage
Corporate underwriters nod and wave.

Still blessed goal of taking care of people onward!
And all, in an end, quite surprised, annoyed to see
Life old, life new, life absolutely in between.
Compromises had, agreements found neat,
All at Mother Nature's precipitous teat.

When hired out as best and modest,
Sound argument for education met,
In the bushes as well as the halls,
With slack jaw and blistered feet
On with your good mission for it all.

MADDENED NATURE

Time was, only what was not held was sought.
What could not be had wanted.
Let mountains come to me, on this cloud will I build.
Stand aside!

Leave me never! Ownership, mine!
Think this river belongs to all? Think again.
If you say I can't have it, watch, I'll want it.
Stand aside!

Lean in, crane necks to glimpse what danger.
Wear awe at the dance, feign boredom the table.
Move quarries full and paste the rock.
Ally-oop, stop's the top.
Stand aside!

Looking into the face of the people
One sees just what one wants not,
"Thou art but a man!"

Many hands across many waters,
And the point, missed, when seeing what must be done
One does and is scathed for setting in motion what
only she did nerve and notice. Her chore, her destiny.
Stand aside!

What a fracked tend! Tips and tack it.
Flip some appetite over once lightly.
Cover dead rightly.
Stand aside!

BROUGHT ON BY LORCA

There are things even poets won't touch,
Some anyway,
If doing so, the ire that lurks, inspire,
    As they outside all negatives and positives stand,
    Now welcome.

A dying I speak.
Lastly, twists and turn
Emotings sea the eye.
Rightly done, said, and rightly I.
    You, you are different from me.
    Not me, you. Why?

SOME POETS I

Hardy was rewarded later, but not by Eliot with mention.
Dickinson had to become waiter.
Not then nor now her intention.

Eliot caught the dream with dolor.
Larkin was then, is now—elf.
Rilke Waited his Stormy Night, Solemn Hour.

Wheatley, Dunbar, Du Bois escape attention?
Nor Frost, Lawrence without detection.
Marvel of gardens his spirit spent.

Large numbers move toward Hayden, Thomas.
Evenings latter-day writers clad breath
Grab calamus, laden, squint, churn in seat

Offer lighter fare than we're used to
Where philosophy is gift in art.
How sentences staying power imbue.
Shall we—when mention? What part?

Hopkins' fortuitous portend. Langston's bebop hand.
    Villon ported under veil.
    Rimbaud slipping peal,
With Ginsberg's barks Blake, there to defend himself,
While Bukowski is drunk his dark and feel.
See how words explain empty spaces
Make leap for joy those Milton laces.
It's fast. Shakespearean. Running races.
Weight off shoulders, Rabelais! no limitation.

SYMPATHETIC FIGURE

He dare not....abandon all reason, even though most of that
is handed down. He dare not...accept your high treason,
this is no time for clowns. Thought it easy to stay tied
his pine-yard full, happily clamped the long grass, sewn
into each pine needle, the warranted, fully fine foe accept.
On the rush, show. But no. Two-step.
Not enough. Too quick Ballyhooed dancer. Self, linger, stay,
have another. Stay and shelter? Appear silent side!
Walk in backward. Again—the trying wide.

TO MUM

"Father, Mother has gone below!
She'll birth the Captain soon!"
On uttering those sounds I became
Accessory. And so, this small
Antique story can be told.

Father was of the race of Giants (This is old!)
Mother? Mother belonged to no
Known people or cure.

There then wanderer you come to matters
Crux and closed on off-days, that I tell—
We were without ship for two days.
That is longer any my race has considered,
Yet we three were left of seven on one with seven,
And could see no way toward furtherance
Than to shock the cord and
String some elevate to a new ship
In which
Captains, Commanders, Teammates
And Scholars as Poets are born
To Mum.

> This was accomplished as All that Know
> and Accept Are given means and ends by the wayward
> move, the ether room that is
> the environment!

> Sing then we three and any listening
> for they and it.

CH. 2
IN-MEMORY-OF FLAT-FOOT STOMP

IN MEMORY OF

Oh that's Kafkaesque!
That mere introspection,
That metamorphosing rule.
There's where the sages always hung out.
In the gifted twirling pools
Of the nearest pair of eyes.

"Memories of the love you gave".

DAD

Do our minds know us?
—there were warnings
The way we were going to get there, sitting on a side-board,
Two arms-lengths from us, stringing beads on a pearl wisdom
—so many
Left to rot in a rosary lifted maybe only one.
Not Mary is un-announced, given short ply.
Not She that Mothered Him and that he honors for His holy way,
Wisps of web fragments loosely by on the air, that light,
But the wry continuity of shares that only divide when a lie is hatched
On the waiting, plead in their eyes, county or country folk coming,
That used their feet all day in the sun to get there.
Why be they worthy of a clean break and come out fighting?
—as shall
Did the sound bell tune at different pitch: unheard, ignored, titular
No coins boosting a gloved fist like yours, unfair to height?
Did the child, head down, his early years concentration
A bug crawling—his front stoop—sense you in fifty-share habit
Walking or rolling by?
—the un-evenness went where it could squat!
He or one sees what clothes in a year the child may wear,
How the times goes, where the money will find, how in fact
The fiction of the day's news will be read to a still world.
His Dad, all those pluses banked, announcing. Wanting kindling and faith,
Wanting writers dare anyway, poets fed on the brush off road,
And carpenters hammer gleely.
—Truth owes!
I remember convincing Dad to, "No! Let's go!
They said we won!" one Saturday
And then no prizes for that naked breed,
At least half so in that reveal—a sixties get and long bus ride back
Without the TV, Dad saying, "I told you so!" only once, "Nothing free!"
O well, it couldn't afford us at that!
Our poor so enriched with natural gown, top hats and boot,
Insists the diarist, anything as possible, edges coming round,
That in the others' eyes reflected back,
In his eyes shone.

FIRE AND HAMMER MELDING SCHOOL
(A Study)

Okay! So, of Smithy, of ancestor age.
Grand-père, bottle waits near! Bit of red—Cabernet
opened yesterday. Sauvignon this way! A port stay.
 —Nice slanted-land ups a while ago. Stomp!
Him to Australia, shoe horse. Arm an arc to follow,
core for inner mark we aim.
'Twere well met, slidant! these outings of a soul
many visings of a tool. Welcome—
Fire and hammer melding school. Stomp!

    Up in the mountains. A far way up.
    Scatter all your cries to the four and wily winds,
    cool hand in an oven often not missed!
    Not wished by

    As they
    comfortably cool heels on our terraces,
    concave our ceiling'd doors,
    time, spaced up, ever roar.

Should then hike lower traces,
visualize the traps, being?
Cast bently, monuments to our traitor terrorists?
Keep no found secret, safe,
blast over stations tuned nicely?
Shall we, our efforts, away? Widely?

A CRY FOR HELP

Okay!
The view out *this* window…
Shall we proceed description?

Down the hillside miles,
guardian of freeways, homes, not so much malls late.
This space occupied, green in practice sentry;
long appearing rows of tree stand.
Oaks in a cup. Lined up seven fourteen, reven.

My God, where'll all this heaven lean?
There it lies! Grass bents, Green.

Pay for it when welter come.
Sun that bleeps on purpose,
contorts, clicks on close;
summer skin and fields burn.

Right click here, there, next
Now trans-spy our wicked welty
Raced up 'appy yelp!

A deep rage buts help!
Mantra spoken, as good as high yell.
Heck, why race round obscene,
kicks at first that rap, then this, Stomp!
When massive passive is waist deep
in ace bandage?

A MANY'D VARIETY

As mysteries walk across
all too few moments lived before
rise and save an ancient stand
of tree and forest left in California.

"Put the African back in,"
says a man knows unacceptance put in.
Amiri Baraka at Columbia University
swat-stand trees man, he!
It's a shame—call and response.

Grew up catholic. Seminary bound, thought.
Ma and Pa lived other ideas,
thinking better the expenditure,
and laugh telling saddest of tales of—
'We selling us', as we did to we, initially.
And no Seminary for me.

'Twas best I did not, as said... Was saved.
An Arhully, unpacking some shouting fell! Stomp!
Olado Recreano saved from radio's farcical face. Stomp!
Blues got.
Could capitalize. Ye know.
All seems consequence of. Every has
'waffling in cue' and Columbus, Ohio
February 1998 was what has alive here!
The people must not! Every People must not!
But stand instead! Stomp!

SHE CALLED TO SAY

She called to say it's my voice that's worth hearing
and that hearing did please.
Now, grist for consideration, as though easily
and at whim less than regularly-wracked mind even
could make use of as reason, separations, long absences
and that see? Love is still a-balance.

When perception is elevated to reality, all lose.
As the expected learns it is not chief,
others will have leaned in on, affect absolute,
and that, the same for each, are lights going on
in the most socially conscious heads.
Too much time may have passed to recover from.
Or, we are not all the same
nor should sameness be sought.

Waring men do not easily accept what is different,
let alone what lobbies own way.
Still, no exculpatory meaning hatched on this pallet.
See, not we wrinkled the many miss: times neither forest
nor trees. Not our capoeira, less sting!

Instead, some waltzing Florentine in a bulge-free garden
buried that milieu, not apart from merriment, nutriment,
or excessive work—ruined not our cultured (or not)
angled ways inward. Beautiful day's seen scener, keener.

PRIVILEGE

Soon we'll see where the rest of the disaster lies.
Privilege? Who has it?
          All! But
Have the same taken out their big bites long in this?
To be heard in Washington or your capital—
I've come across talk of revolution out among the people!
It slides unerringly from above,
Where it used to go un-noticed,
Settles it does on heads and
      Interrupts conversations every chance gets,
      It hates you
      never and nonetheless let's
      Incorporate the other in our survival plans
      Initiated, succeeding of, for and by the common ones.

REVOLUTION'S RESOLVE

And it was not what he knew to expect.
But that suggests he should have
smelled the expectation and guessed the dirt,
till at last over-sainted could get to top
and dictate revolution's resolve to know nothing.

It was certain to finagle the best of them.
Reputed to have cost a fortune.
Otherwise, neither man knew the why.

And it was totally expected.

Note: line 3 reminiscent of Hugo's line in his Memoir on Rheims;
full text at: www.fulltextarchive.com.

NOTES ON AN EDUCATION

With allure of detached visions,
oftener in Death's boarder, Sleep,
divide everywhere is crossed,
are tarried mind's tuck.
Aghast, redirect; on quests in company
phantasmal appear.

Like Goethe in his pheasant boat,
Einstein catching relativity
a starry native under charley nature,
dreamer fullstop keys convention
consciousness might never call up.

Off his cloak and lily pad
who seeks will find.
A brace for real, cask and world-born cord
surprises eye's day-heavy cloud.
Bearing invention, maxim is hearing uses,
Jabberwocks shelve themselves,
sweep hands fail to out-chum notion,
so, we further an education.

Note: Tuck: vigor, energy.
Goethe in his peasant boat: Johann Wolfgang von Goethe's 'Italian Journey
(1786—'88),' Trans. by W. H. Auden and Elizabeth Mayer
(Penguin Books (Collins 1962), 1970), 112, 113, 127, 222.

TO PEACE RUN

After Paul Celan

This is root's trunk
It was given me by meaning firm
And the shock of hair and the shinning eyes.

This is branch's root
It tangles dragon and tender how
In coven scripted equals all but hope.

This is sprite's manifest that crunches argument
And slides the hours in huge
'what was meant by whom and why.'

This is mother's pleading
And the death secured by wish
Over the absolute.

And final, this is enemy.
Dump graphic monument there.
Straighten the curl what hair cinches rope.

Over these five scenes
Close with infirmity and exterminate
The it, them, we of war. Stomp!

EDEN IS A GREAT FLUSH

First rain plants surprise on Gaea, but in souls too.
Summer sunned, rang last forebearance,
we noticed the bustle and that's what hide from.

Job's jewel: as kind, dotting mother,
got us thus far through the brown.
Sky yellows, hours smooth.

To the right hearth's harmful scent drifts.
Below, crushed leaf practicing quiet smiles,
points uncle autumn as he harvests new beliefs,
we feel oddly middle-aged, re-freshed.

Great-coats from holdings,
heated speed sol fueled—thicker, had time to get there.
Abreast, warmth: our most prized, falls languid
and that renewal is.

A great flush, sense for us, faith seems:
Eden must be this.

Note: Job (Patience).

GLAD FOR THE VICTORY AND THE DEFEAT

After Cesar Vallejo and Women Writers.
For All True Democracies

I left a tank on deck for you in my hark to decide finds
of accuracy keen, that you might and I might
breathe forward our finds together, passing on:
which waited by a quick boat, initiated love as
more than popular
and that underfed proved self full.
Waves crashed and
the positive shivered with my sweat,
I nearly missed preventing private interests
picking crude schemes to defraud a public:
concentrations of wealth, pride with privilege.
And still, on that rise and mount of heed,
that had to swim those waters,
I dived, circled, did not prevent crush of jaw
and in a single moment, joking: hate went down
unaware its quietus, misinterpreted my smiles.
'Yet even here you reach and arrive at self',
another petition round dance
glad for the victory and the defeat.
Cross a sign, radii a menorah, sword, text and practice
all go with the heartsick down
and still,
as you disappear to depth, I imagine I surface
to a bewilderment paradise answers,
where knowledge and insistent naming
realize they can't do it themselves.
And happy, have learned something.

MS. CHAOS

(Upon Reading Judy Petree's "Strange Attractor in Chaos Theory,
Without the math," 2002) No longer available on-line!?

At long last there is a well meet
for the gypsy seducer she has become.
Her "limit set that collects trajectories"
reveals the smallest movement.
Rough systems tame and illicit
we see gazing twirl her eyes.

Describing a particular subject of study
confined in her system as phase space only,
she, they will have nothing steady state.
Clipped to a pouch, hung from her waist
Posit warms to complexity's vigor,
and butterflies form up,
telling simulated stories in their haste to survive.

And like the rest,
caught in pressures society must dictate,
she is similar, but not identical.
Her self-similarity shows the way
through a Mendelbrot rule or two
to poise noise in recognizable patterns.

Using Feigenbaum numbers, Poincare's precedence,
and super-filial computing, soon predictable turbulence
in its quest to subdue round-head chaos
is clomping fractal geometry's un-limit haunts.
     —Art is not left to back doors, waste hunts,
and comes, late now, with philosophy as fish-in-bowl.

All that, and the metaphor of tiny differences conduct,
at initial, to acquaint into vast remedials,
and though unstable and unable to resist small disturbances,
like ripples on a water, prediction seems, but is not impossible,
and she and we, with Lorentz, institute selves unity
into barely distinct wave patterns on the chimespace,
and Newton's linear paradigm, stealth for its time,
does not reveal the fine detail
that that there chaos-with-complexity can.

TIME TO THINK AN RIDE

If your name be told
Able to speak in every language it Cain happen
and rummage round clock for ticket,
spend Father to Mother in a silvery morn

so the rapsmood decent sunning self
tune our racinates FM intuitively tribal beer.
And let, naked, complain never agin
like the wot am and leak for, just in.

The unease in philosophy's jargon gone gorgon gnosis,
goof proof young gosling.
An it sup with, breaks linen,
and folds glass its longish curly beard.

Are injured in heap, downtrod fumigant initially bent.
Thereat ardor, be read well a minimum in good effect.
Tryun turnbolt and wage truffles out the copse.
Supersized lies cheat payments, intends we blink,

though our cuff and curtsies, late, gone lifeless to falk.
Deception is turncoat ever and marches
fife an drum, its long drive rests less. Go!
Boon when benches near loch with billet we.

*Notes: racinates, from ra·ci·nage !? decorative treatment of leather
with colors and acids to produce a branchlike effect.
French, equivalent to racine root.
Wot: chiefly Brit.: 3rd sing. of wit; know.
See James Joyce's Finnegans Wake (New York, The Viking Press,
Ed. 11, 1971), 137: "... boon when with benches billeted..."*

A CASE FOR REVEALING

H. Taine wrote on French Revolutions' corybant,
after fact, sturdy under decrees, that
caught looking-again! his prose as goodly poem.
Later, Proust-recidivist Bronk agreed his love of Hippolyte;
suggests Joyce, before Joyce, like Rabelais further back,
if reader five to ten one's 'Odysseus' or Gargantuan...
well, you get the picture.
Add Goethe, his 'Affinities,' part shorn a past.

In repeat misery of hell: anger, curse, gossip, rot, irreverent attitude;
fist, spit, kick, slap, push, trip, lay-in-wait; stick, stone, knife, spear,
sword, gun; bomb, missile, tank, and first-fire-jet plain as day
and twice as fast have standing in the rubble of past thought,
too quick made its way through to hiss, nag, cry, gentlepeople!

In navel study, I won't even argue wit-choose!
It's all razzle no dazzle! Id est "The only magic in the world
is Love." New is hug, kiss, sweet whisper,
who knows gifts held in drab sackcloth
from lies flewed in stark wool white.
Lessons of the crowd; learn self, unlock coverlets quite covetous;
forsythia thaumaturge you are folant, as meth estuaries wait.

Notes: Ref: Hippolyte Taine – Fr. (1823-1893) of his last works 1876-1894
Origines de la France contemporaine (t. I : L'ancien régime;
II à IV : La Révolution ; V et VI : Le Régime moderne)
William Bronk – My father's generation!
Corybant: wildly emotional, frenzied.
forsythia: (golden Bells) bloom very early yellow flowers in spring.
Flews: jowls; lips (loose); pendulous lateral parts of a dogs upper lip.
Thaumaturge: trickster, magician.
Folant: strong. Meth: Hebrew = death.

FARTHER FROM THE FIRE

Opposite, sits to chair,
Be elevator,
Slam on break,
A safe ride.
Detach you on highway
To water, grain, fix flats
Tow Sending wishes
For blessings in grave circumstance.

Eyes down the altar, candles light.
And now
Simply want endeavour,
Hold hands round a fire.
Non-confuse, run toward
And thank handout as you let him help.

He receives wealth in these. Flowers
And Tera are softly their own "I Love You Dear!"
We fall to our knees.
Forgiveness: a heady thing. Women
Have spoken of trenchant.
Regain sense masculine, go prostrate!
Column's upright, Visit, stay,
train perception,
Every time recall happy insistence.

Never mind,
Shoe falls farther from the fire
As hearts are spurn to raise hate and fear
And prejudice which is wholly cowardice.
If anything is worth energy: Love of truths—
Which effort completes circles,
Marks spots, snaps a line on the thing called self
And cuts the crap out.

SELF-TEACHING

So everything that came was a scene
Wrought with learned response
Placed chloroform color, rinse azure then bleach
Other entreaties and so spoof
The rest as to slide on
Similar to the line and hedgerow
Always compressed to convey,
Otherwise kind reader holler!

Test me some named Countee Cullen,
Grow the likes of a courageous Amiri Baraka,
(Was not for naught!), Hume me the history of
England and Rousseau tiffs to sleep
When darkness takes her
Gold-tooth and slip-noose
To distinguish the Venerable Bede
Among Nordic horde in the sky of altar,
Or rile-Whitman at field hospital,
Tolstoy—he's not self-annihilating,
But must wave toward cupola.
This a short duration reconnaissance—
Couple years!

GROUP PORTRAITS

Try to keep balance in the desert of being.
Existence offers only what it does and we shine
Like coals in a bank of diamonds,
Or slay our meaning twice in that.

In slanting honors and diverting tales
That hide from every clear talk and flatter,
The poet is and the poet does, because mostly
There is no answer and life in its redos
Flies too loose at and they know they have their
Free in less consistency, less habit,
What happenstance hard by. Get away with that!?

Erroring kindly in this, with your mathematic,
As trending to unveil and nearly can't,
We know too what sacrificial postings
Are the poet's life and truths yield of un-truths' work
Which some say can not example
Real world and hence, are ignorant
And guide unknowing down, where just
Sketches collide with what is material,
Gets in the way. What is learned?

Constitute now a meaning and embark,
The reason for and the trilobite
That walks on stage, gives its monologue,
Creates a picture not far
From tones a dilettante or verser make,
And the same is all there is, not quite,
That emanates, that ochers,
That their removals and voyages
Pen sickly homogeneous and oft south
But that their wish is ever more for man
More felt response
And hoisted round a flag says, 'group portraits
Must not abound.'

WHO BUY

Along, all the matter for populous is decided,
"someone else will do!"
Bought and paid law and press is there fault.

Hu-man's song, though, remains pure,
unforgot in trained hearts,
coursed in etiquette of survival dowers.
Effort and organization into care for all
will swim to top; your lungs will hold.
Look the love and golden rule pocket!

To think Jesus and so many
actually went the distance to help;
and I would be faithful without?

Day dries on the old deception.
I believe some are devoted their covetous.
I believe they are we who buy as acting rite.
In prayer, full responsibility comes in share.
The forward art of philosophy is in there.
Step by step and bag by bag,
let me not, tangled in choice, kill hope.
With life align.

AGAINST THE STUDDED WALL

"My wooing at fifty would engulf the siren"
wrote Lowell finishing a great work
in 1970 You guaranteed yourself a seat
fresh out of secondary,
the serendipity stuttered never in that new back yard
(does now); a cinch for habitat and pay check.

'At fifty my woodshed would coax the muse'
captured in full-lay gown.
Who in young's haste to have and tab it all
you addicted to blinded work.
No cure it was, just slammed innocent disbelieving
against life's studded wall.

SONG

Mook to jugglo in flashes.
My paint enhances,
The throb and the dance are same
In trances claim a new Rage
Call it Rock and slam a friend,
As tutored tempt and trained
Open hand to slap sane
And otherwise be sainted.

"The ages have been
At work on it,
Man can only mar it."
Presidents spoke, speak
Now and when we left
Hear the strain, what sense
To say these things of nature
Ours to ply uncharted waters
Done so long ago and now
Wan waste records on ledger.

I.C.P. (Insane Clown Posse) the band,
Theodore Roosevelt the President
Anatolia the Turkey
Sophia the Church Built by
The emperor of Rome Justinian,
Turned long since Mosque and museum.
Archimedes' wheel,
To inveigh the lot
A shank and leer of spent
Shall quit the spot
So lengthy upending, flap open
Cannot top ours in this time of sweat
You say it's the 'arc of implication'
Can armantrout, may inveigle;
We so much sing songs without.

Notes: Inveigh: from [L.] to carry in; (to protest or complain bitterly).
Inveigle: to blind, hoodwink, win by wiles; entice, etc.

SEPTEMBER 14, 2005

Something of the land.
How dodge and slip, then turn wrong,
never glimpse hands round back:
gift to dullers and paid assassin.
You know your names, coif guise,
we that are but one at a time,
so a we should rarely, and then here do,
foil to trough-feeds at shift Newton
dogged in full-press philter.

War industry sucks air, leagues shots.
Hard to unseat; last to importances parse
Justice, law, States rights?
whose death or that of loved ones will
likely not touch.
The dump we'd officiate,
the counsel would our planets.

"A 'benefit' to expect..."
from same army cresting rise as drove out Lilliputians?
Oh! There is no sign in a lost them finally rover state
of any quick enlighten their eyes.
I require your forgiveness. We move on.

> *Notes: Philter, philter (F.) a potion, a drug, a charm*
> *re: sexual passion and generally magical powers.*
> *Francis Newton—possible execution in Texas 09/14/2005*
> *African-American <u>woman first</u> since 1850's !???*

12, NOV. 2005 & TODAY

Much is made of innocence, its newly retuse edges;
we know that shape, its zero-day beard, sallow pledges.

Your way, there'd be calling out from fallow dockets,
French letters unused in faith-based pockets.

Then who have come from, have distorted,
called everything strange save what Aard threw up?

What was strangest?
Weren't all that extraterrestrial just this bred dense,
spread capture in next-level cares quakes—as now
a 16-year-on beloved cousin Frank from Ireland comes?

Stars are just appreciating Dark energy, matter slump.
She bruit every incidence, he pat living tump,
they fount contemporaine, let the rugose romp;
a little nothing and polished bien? What's for dinner?
"Neither flesh nor foul" (and not so hierarchical).

Talk of the algebra his float, a geometry her form,
re-uptake of dote, the good nation worn.
Time... and Diana comes. Gray placard mist,
paints perennial's upright face. Yeah are!

When we've washed our hands of an injustice,
they may never come clean again.

> Notes: Retuse: blunt.
> French letters (idiomatic!?): condoms.
> Aard: Afrikaans (Dutch) = Earth.
> bruit: to report; to noise around.
> Tump: fertile ground.
> Rugose: wrinkled.
> Diana: sister to Apollo, chariots the moon at night,
> as her brother the sun during day—
> harmless Dear God.
> Gordon Hopkins, contemporary opera.

KITTLE AND KLUDGE

Kittle—tickle, perplex. Kludge—a system
(esp. computers) of poorly matched components.

Rock-wall and branch wave,
not television, gave calm
when rest was sloping mind toward hill's hump,
its saddle this rise.

A warm week, late spring
and heater's fire snuffed.
But like reminder to assume nothing,
the very next day brings winter's much.

Model of kittle and kludge?
What patted judiciously, injusticed by
uniform jumbling of incoherence,
kinesics of the re-direct, bare-faced poker?

In the business we called it A.T.P. when All Tests Passed,
only then was product turned over to customer.
What machine results brought political and actual
A.T.P.s of deception to their 'Hope not!'?

Lengthen harangue; suggest a carry of concern
on sleeve, Wonder—if you've had to live to
the jeers and non-understanding of occupied minds—
it's been your privilege.

As I center, by their faces in the field,
kine example humility not steak.
So clear no path in the forest,
and measure concern like a bag to ventilate in.

FLYING OUT

Midday, ignore hard, bright signs that hovers a cease,
believe all yet is creation,
and just because a thing has never,
its growth from zero could.

Source makes diversions, creation controls!
She willed He'll sit and watch, it had not come to ruin.
Glued how a hero saves, dies and survives in us
and like novitiate's joy in possibility—
just intention, instruct those
who hear what belief and spit can do
for discovery but who say 'we can't stomp with natives,'
to append this honored route.

Foundations are more than filled holes.
Surprises on white-paper? Bouquets on gird, and
in all the square-rigging deception tries
to tie the long weekend into knots.

Still, in created realm, like tardy geese
worried by close dark, but who are flying-out anyway:
faith! And bell shaped head curve no more.

DARK HORIZON

Friends, tireless in laying low: sure mistress
never lags, outstretched in welcome,
prophet obsessed, an inspection of deception:
still living wish for man's life-watching-lives.

Eye out, null nurse feeds munch cow,
that tripped wire getting back.
Renewal—a flash, excites party's boast—
'we may not have NASA, but ideally we've these Burt Rutan,
these Giovanni who too seek horizon!'

There's a copy of Bell's 'The Irish Troubles'
stacked; barely allures from Snoopy kind:
a manifest of broken rims and shattered boards,
toolery till the end!

You'd not expect that to satisfy
till at depth energizes so
flowing serotonin exeunt,
smiles grow the deed good,
sharp pushes back the chair,
recites as linger a doce en doses
and lands um: toe replacing thumb's grip appendage,
even moot court the after-effect,
so days later, like David,
try our quizzical saturnine anyway on.

> *Notes: Poet Nikki Giovanni. Neurotransmitter.*
> *saturnine: astrologically Saturn. Cold and steady in mood,*
> *slow to act or change, of gloomy or surly*
> *disposition, having a sardonic aspect, sullen.*
> *Michelangelo's Statue of David*

UPLAND LOVE

In these tall it's heyday ardor,
all rough, in the sage,
where quail are scratching daybeds
and manzanita plumly welcome lark.

Re-generation be the switch in this garden.
What creature of earth-stuff poet the raveling?
Old, fallen, batten as lay,
oak of kindness is no scrub and
all the sliding silica does not a rock misjudge.
Lost of purpose these ken gird.
Seed-bounty piñon op's stores,
elfin saplings endure and
pageant death promises detail on folded arms.

But millet concerns like:
will these not of their making
and they themselves keep?
Or how an, "...in all of history!" can be
judged by the reference-less
will sink with the top layer
in a few hundred years.
One bolder'd say, Do what intrinsic scolds,
go where remiss
visit and this heaven love.

YEAH YEW

Yeah yew, I guess if you were to pronounce for the world,
you'd say in some wind-rush like a whisper,
forces have more girth than a man,
that even hats won't work.

Small concerns under this lid—
she slips in a rush job and some waiting,
we have two nice evenings,
"I had thought" to invent a double happiness,
but could not find the parts.

Another day, every tool and material
assembled for the heavybreathing
of love gained, of space in the house,
but were taking pictures of the soon thrown out:
an art project.

Saw you and yours taking pictures
as last chance up on the lanes where strained adjustments
ledgered as winds effect only.

Hearts steady-step here where need is gallop.
Fault with age, could be
fault with emperors?

Fine, those who've tried history for us,
very consciousness slows.
Well! the aril of your 'fruitless' will mix
and his steps not stones in a rumored
further walks under yews.

WHEN GOING TO McDONALDS
WAS A DANGEROUS ACT

In that brio for life we finally learned to take it back—
excuse me, we're sorry!
but we weren't. Apologize for breathing?
No! For being seen.

At this late hour, did anticipate
running into Whitman's 'baboon' remark,
Bennett's abortion tricks or as prelude to these
Voltaire's reveal?
Close in the life, writing and off-hand remark
are the brickbats and hurled misjudge.
I'm not stuck!
All here in the hearing and sight of racism:

"the white man's disease" to quote a hero,
not new to siblings and "eye" would have gone
round via the street like others,
but the cop and hot rodders wouldn't have it
So maneuver the one foot pipe
stretched like taunt across a canal your only way back
if back you ever gain.
A thirteen, an eleven and a nine year old—that's fair accurate!
a Mom and Dad's whole tribe at the time.

That's when going to McDonald's was a dangerous act.

Note: Quote Mr. Professor Dr. Albert Einstein
(Lincoln University Commencement Speech, 1946)

ASSIDUOUS THE HERO

It's twelve or it's seven, but it's not five.
Let's not awe at his or her right actions in life,
standings up; surprised we are but let's emulate
and certainly not get in the way.
What one did in life for the billions of
let's copy it, appreciate in the only best—
Do the work giant.
Expose, see fear—forgive—
to actual best practice.

SOUP IN HEAVEN

The mass killer in men, dare they save him?
Society's watermark dries on walls
stained with incredible saint
stolen in daily devotions.

It's easy to see
you're wet and just in
from a cold continent,
find a seat
then crawl about in shadow moments
before it startles
fine fleece majority has
dent and break possibilities.

Shift focus,
rend fits in the world,
hope a fact stream uncoil:
ever situated, largely celebrate.

She bled redder then:
an affirmative dose of spiff.
A splinter needs dangle,
a soup eats in angel heaven.

America, marry me
in my noon apparel!?
Yips cover exit's
roadside facet weal.

I CRY FOR YOU

from too far away!

You wade or holding on
are out of mind at so much water.
I cry for you,
'you are too much with water.
There is no water! Left to disaster,
these tears will not add to that flow',
your need—everywhere mine.

In times less harried I claimed
the world rested on these shoulders,
but it like you is neither mendicant nor host with full basket,
will not support further bruises.

A warning has gone out every day for the last
two hundred and fifty thousand years,
too few have heard the blast
or, hearing, are closing ears and shaking head.

Now, I hail a rescue?
I curse not the water less cursing curse self.
Empty bins of supposed riches for healing.
A new horizon, helicopter sustenance, avoid the fire
and make a further moratorium on indifference
to hold a neighbor by.

WORD IS

You're hopeful of retreating to less ambition.
Hear tell you seek your own way,
outside this glitter with no backing.
"The king and the people have no clothes!"
They want you to call the 800 number for details.
"Stay where you are!"
"You could already be a winner, it's free!"

If nothing else as individuals, we should read
and understand the falsities.
Truths will find us easily, when open,
but falsities will take more to avoid.

"Fill-in the form, answer all the questions,
then we will see if you qualify for our lending program!"
"Your application is with the acceptance committee!"
"No sir! I can't help you with that!"
"Press any key to continue!"
"I'm sorry, that was an incorrect response, please try again!"
"All of our operators are currently busy!"

With animation's touted helpfulness? Up to here!
With Cayman, Delaware accounts and the safe Swiss?
The people can not bear! Their cup over runs with these.
Three eyes explode where there were two.
Any peace and quiet will do.

1 ZWECKGEBUNDENHEIT
(Purpose, tiedness)

cross the waters a-peer
in mode less 'xtravagant
measure fall truancy.
Right as conqueror to clash ship's bell
if capturing?

To guide binary digit
supposed about the mall,
to allay fears of men-at-arms was why
dread lowered us to ask,
"Where are we tracking?"
Pain of lost mystique,
shots not seeking us or our children in latest dream
wend into a hale, a canabinal,
upon a pie-shaped wedge sits a-bloated bile,
we monkey with the Greeks, cut out dolls for Gaia,
show Apollo again where Phaeton came down,
do marvelous
fixing of light on dusky objects.

But as the sun sets our careless eye
sees the referent and relatum capacity, the
reinforced concrete in frowns discern
and we wallop in diversity "we just can't stand
the garden": wanky, wrests mottos,
allows 'no cudgel'.
Then, luxuries appear offense where growth
under breast and cap are meant.
Could a new theogony?

EYES ON THE WATER

Rows an unused boat
on lake of crystal dews
and gets thoughts her stare:
eyes like clear pools after a rain,
that shot meaning; how
she vitaled his human.

Going for an anti-beer, he discovers:
"Truth, be a heart widened
emptied this time for the wife and fishes!
I will: nothing to forestall, hers in fancy,
flagon entire drained,
whole craft put to edge
that ever welcomes her!"

Ill-timed.
his orbs and the vermiculate sea
tell of bonds baffled,
how all slipped easily,
unnoticed out of hands.

KARMA (Part II)

You had some voices,
but they maybe didn't have much to say.

Think like the butterfly:
wild erratic, properly birthed
sin against devil,
dodgeball again,
feinting on the field
with the ball, young.
Memory is injection and
run if you will but you'll come back
like the wobble presence in a star
that throws its light then gathers in swirl.

We believe we're better
When we've tried no treacheries.

A DAY IN LIPETSK

"Do not travel alone!" was warned our build wish.
The country, unstable, safety could not be confirmed.
But off on a site-visit, to breathe the country miles,
hour and a half on the road
with interpreter and driver I gamble my pile.

She, lithe blond of the smiling eyes is guide on arrival,
newly changed Ministry, its wood floors, paneling and drape
coveted cigarette smoke of a century.
Director hurried, proved diffident.
Then to our business tour turned lunch;
we became the ancient little restaurant itself:
snuggled into rock below the boulevard
cozy, comfy, one with booth.
Melt anxiety! Time rest near!

But conditioned with the old reception:
what if kept wary eye and stayed just aft happy;
soon the Black Earth entrusted to Slavs humanizes
and city's lunch-hour streets, riparian views,
feminine company do much to calm, the whole gained.

Can say lunch was a rush of Russian dishes:
borsch, fresh fish, the ready samovar I
and that best Russian Stolichnayan of conversation.
"You like Russian girls?"
"Like a bear that enjoys all the berries!"
cool in rest.

When travel, do the earnest prepare their empathy
noting how every slight or realization at 'home' can clothe
for that prized world-citizenship which returns
persona non grata with sir-patience up-close
and by dunk, are living to promise? Should!

Translator, driver, bonding work done,
Capital's representative comfortable with the focus,
everyone seemed happy,
much so that from that point till end of tour,
light shown on the kind people we all were
and formidable setback with logistics nightmare proved far less,
simply tell it.

TWO WELLS FOR MADELEINE
(An Address)

The broth of life, the crest of legacy
are but a few this monody of you, water.
Let men, calculated, see each patch over the years
and believably garner clue.
Make it, despite caution, when next waterside eyes rises
there be rescue and relief for each.
Also, you water-privilege, stay with populations,
not borne away in commodity's trucks.
Those conscious are not fools;
in places, she's like to let, he may not
and fools are they have love transpositive,
it is not.

Everywhere hear: "there's nothing I'd hide personally,
can't speak for the government, though should,
and its draughts mine."

Perhaps need—longer bowed and shorter greed—
will sweep smear-adaptations, microbial illusions
which seem not bold in any forward sense; and know:
Earth-kin need you now.

Fuller documents defend democracy,
and no saddling by richest:
this, fuller document that currently isn't
full of hold-your-indigent. Show don't tell?

So, sink two wells for Madeleine!
and remind all nationals' crimes done in their name,
like glass broken by the unsupervised,
will have to be paid for.

CH. 3
HOW-TO-WALK SALSA

HOW TO WALK

Arbus' grotesques advert viewers.
hold hand-grenades, lean on and shave off,
like our drab sixties all the best work,
a star monitors its Christmas tree,
is anybody happy?

Were in better time: slower, meaner
wines racked participate.
...When slouched there
secret-server proved betrayal,
forms by fear fancy, you falter,
flirt was touché.

Newly the promise, a ladder,
your heart it soars; to soothe feet
with invested pride, I mull.
—Bathe in no university of nearness
stolen of the fumbling years.

File by shuffle bore, idle life hasn't insisted
every listener like the student is gray
in these frames. Là où sont the smiles?
: notes in books, hair larger than minds,
withered garland, I loved your exhibit!
How life gets lived.

At the park, magnifying sun
saw interested as any; this was their time,
saw your collection and banked it.
Outside—her Penelope to that Odysseus
—in gender mutiny: you win the bread,
he the apron;
now loose in the manor:
that big foot stumbling toe.

Note: Là où sont—where are?

JEAN FOUQUET

La fantasia?
Confused, consulting all of it, wondered just where was he.
He worked in enamel and looking closely we may see
same as blackma(i)led today.
Living in a garden of France, one branch were
from older capitals where lion and elephant,
though in all backgrounds royal, who exceeds?
Près du fleuve de Loire;
face forward these centuries with something of a
signed camaraderie of incredulity in look.
Being a Frenchman of the age, he'd not let you see his 'ethnic'.
There was no warm cultura-covering that clothed, you can be sure.
Clearage of the saddened eyes.
Why go author into these and assume much?
To delve depths of anguish that does
confluence with posterity's claim:
the Hours, the miniatures, Charles' red nose.
"Take you aftercomers' this autoportrait of my
wary being coverer your concealed mostly,
where beasts mixed with men in amebic mobs.
Anyway, your author knows because
that's how the Russian moves were sensed,
portrait with a charcoal hand.
His task: 'you shall know me from these, let it be that.
Je dessine cette pesanteur!'

Notes: 'Near the Loire river.'
'I draw this gravity.'

BEFORE GOING OUT

Cross self
toward the shape of a hill
So demons won't heel
and you and your lovely
are faster to the oak.

Lost source and sight
where some bled energy.
Were offered-up-to.
Show em raw wounds,
where the bones broke,
skin lacerated; how maybe
books rescued, words saved.
Hang shroud from nearest two-inch sapling.
Where are my girls now?   Show em that!
Show mewling wrong
for the wrong it does and right
to overwhelm might that is diamond
in the mind.
It pays for itself you'd. Confess all crimes!
'Cause the grass reads, needs no questions
and answers far from poesy loop transit
round your yard actor. What fathering is this?
....
          ... ...LOG READ! ...Signal in.:
          What....? ..Who? What? What is that?, Where are you?
          . ==...: ... "he's coming in!"
          Wait!......What? What? Five what? .....Senti^N........?
        Silence... with raised brows throughout, covering the room
        in question, hand over mic. But, Nope! No one knows him here
     .....What? Sig-'".: ... Rd-QS-in.: ... "Heavy traffic:*
          By God I am patient with you for your trouble's sake,
          but the rope frays." ....Aren't you in the wrong......?
        Rd-QS-in.: ... "What? ...What are they doing over there?" ..
     .... It's an Earth dance! Devotional!... but I thin....
     —What the hell! Has the writer lost all control ... Sir! Sir! I ask,,,,
     Sir! Rd-QS-in.: ... "Truth calls on avoid to speak.
          In embarrassment's chagrin then
        drive deciding into dinner-rooms, where
        among gentle guests, above patois of world's crunch,
        in fine fare you love a lot."
        .....Oookay!

CIVILETTI YET
L. C. Civiletti

Distracted and in 'Jeopardy'
oft pining that something else
to be seen from a height
it was the vector shoots
sent along tall branch stalk,
caught in standing snuggery,
bottled tooldom, imbibed coverlet
and the way block and cobalt
seem to tumble ancestral equation
toward a slope that
washed em clean in 'Vestigial'
yet familiar 'Dramentia Praecox' of valued
salutations of the word that has filled this 'Vestibule'.

Away from 'Angel revolts'
"...to act we had to know the secret of..."
that 'Altered book' of 'Saints' that
as much as any 'Exuviae'
was stitched together fine.

The 'Glove' is the hand,
'Slips of the Tongue' here as there
curl at edge.
The vie of art for eyes seems
at once its long and short suit,
yet if we have fortune, and we believe we do,
the day wears us well.

Note: A Wonderful Artists' Creations are highlighted!

DEATH MASK

Toward conclusions only he could,
before the house rose started his stare;
shadow contemplate head in hands, so much to know.
Year on, another finds poetry's toll, and in.
Death mask for both, and the words are out.
δε έπεα ένορουώ: De epea enorouo
"and the words leaped out."
(You have to get in your head you've said that!)

Then come in your basket-weaves and broker.
From pall to allele moments,
words engulf the book,
and every breather, every weaver in a wind
wants to live caliber.
Wrenched easier life if not so precious.

Proclivities to humour, bubble,
assume grin in moody's face,
gault, at least, a very bad virus,
badge good-sash ascetic otium as answer
in contemplate—as Philosophers knew.

As for dinner, who remains hopeful?
A species of men misread,
claim humans have finished at zero (even I've!)
But this is not our apocalypse!
Pieces move on the best of boards!
You cannot survive if you cut down the forests!

Protect of way of life lilts under duress, was never just.
Fear and Privilege, selfish, spelling falls—
unto whom, was not done to,
is first to scream foul.
But always who've thought it through are the happiest.
Wrenched easier life if not so precious.

Notes: Dennis Kim 22, supposedly followed his
book-bag of poems into the Hudson River, NY. October 7, 8, 2005.
Pall; to become pale, to lose strength/effectiveness,
Allele: containing two different relata (i.e. smooth & wrinkled);
alternative; reciprocal. Gault: hardpack snow.
Otium: leisure; from otiose: producing no useful result, vain.
De epea enorow: δε έπεα ένορουώ: "and the words leaped out."
"spelling falls," misreading, misunderstanding (!?) per John Milton's Sonnet XI.

'L'

Literature, symbol for corner in mind.
Night: further down totem
but not as close nether as desire,
mud's anchor for the stick.

Lambent smiles conjure fifty.
'Cline ear and music
we want our puts should prosper
and seed the loving earth.
Everyone that shits in a forest preserves it.
Like Lorca's 'hope still a nipping wolf' in upper reaches,
Up too, Lucan's 'poverty
as mother to manhood', "I do!" and lover
they adore if Langston learn and discern float.

Mary the which Longfellow, your persistence
to 'act in living present'. Leucippus
with Democritus following Anaxagoras
and all those Africans already show
'a fortuitous concourse of atoms'—
newly hatched 'minutemen'
are sheets: a new klavern, old klux
to be shed, strand ended.

Over these the keeper of no secrets broad Phoebus
alerts rays our tall symbol,
planets bow and the Love we bore
stayed aegis in our pain.

REFERENCE ONLY (in 4/6)

Strikes badly this iridescent tomfoolery of the accepted
by which to mold output, perhaps speak kindly when cant.
Vision-in-interpretation, surely carry, exceed us our
Iago or "Iagogo!" bumf utopian!

Synonymous with illusory,
the art of imagination will ideal God out,
explain as idea of no place or accurate model,
She of the Greek nous, bitty quanta,
light's ripple and stipple with us.

Come out dull Negative! Suppurate now, Crazy!
Unreliable, its dirty tooth stuck in More's mouth,
may retreat with speech salvific along our little cattle road.
Try every perfect, save none for self as Plato dogs Homer—
his render of the gods with men, to get at absurdity of war
and stealing from, raiding neighbors—saying while Bibling in it,
'no work of poetry has ever been considered sacred.'

Eye Bacon's New Atlantis, some flogging El Dorado,
concept co-sensate, image parallel with obsession?
Things present less filmy, as capricious and accident
with opinion have no good day pointing finger, shouting notion.
And work is the great!
From tight lips escort vague, and stay, give!
Calm, true-to-self, be the choice for ever else.

Notes: Iridescent: lustrous rainbow play of color
caused by differential refraction of light; shine.
Iagogo: p/o Shakespeare's speech (short) in Joyce's 'Ulysses.'
Bumf: toilet paper, paperwork.
Nous: Anaxagoras—divine reason.
Stipple: dot.
Thomas More's 'Utopia' (1516)
Roger Bacon's 'New Atlantis' in the utopian vein (1626).

TIT FOR TAT

Should run best? Despite exhorts,
like Agamemnon's second nervous to the Danaan's,
repair answers: flight is better than fight.
With flight life has chance, then and later!
Still honor/dishonor prod, not a little spur.

Yahweh's Exodus people may lex talionis,
but we: if '... injury ensues you...give right for right,
tie for tie, and bind for bind...' is of skyer merit.

Out Old Testament rank and seize Savior came
(You'll not re-write His tablets!) No!
It must have been Father thought best to re-build
old grillage of half-truths, claims of right,
deliver men bog to truest grace; forgiveness stretch—
agent of destruction usually us.
Still, His lesson, beatific.

The tribes still huffed, hectored.
Planet fragile, collared her,
run ruddle, shoes-on through every temple.
Full of darns, the danger, close, clamors goal,
and no coign of advantage is had
'neath Lagosh arches,
but more buck for brother rock and sister stream,
who long—pants down, skirts up,
no more felix the vorous overcharge of the free their fee
which we monitor, sin.

> Notes: Lex Talionis: curse; the tit for tat law. Exodus 21; 21-23.
> Grillage: to supply w/ grill work; framework of timber or steel for support in
> marshy or treacherous soil; framework for supporting a load (as a column).
> Ruddle: to color with or as if with red ocher; redden.
> Coign; earlier spelling of coin.
> Lagosh: (alt.) of Logos, Portugal—Europe's first enslaved African mkt. (ca. early
> 1400's).
> Vorous (L.): devouring (as Lewis Carroll's "vorpal sword in 'Jabberwocky.'
> Auden's "vorpal sword of the agrarian" in 'New Year Letter' coming later!
> Felix: [L.]—fortunate, happy, lucky, etc.

LUNCH WITH A MYTHMAKER

They bated him and sent him with his tail.
He was a great man, everyone knew that,
but as he smiled at those whose history,
other than his take and dissemination—
were scholar or native—
knew the incredible lies,
mistake and inaccuracies-fostered career,
our reporter sat, calling task
to motive, method, true aspect.

I think she was saying he batted himself.
I think there was ample truth there,
this everyone thought. Table, set for celebration
took instruction this hour from ambush's
certain piercing-eye contact that
spoke for all the left off, out, unlisted. Why?
She did not say, but I see them in the parking lot,
after an uneasy march to coaches, separate long before now
of the clash between one man's actions and myth paraphernalia,
waving/saying goodbye or not, wondering would the great one
accede his own advice; knowing he was but human.

THE GENERAL

Empathe makes way despite weight of shyness
and happier the people by a small band
had alternative sets of buff-ready tools could use,
that like grant of equations: all aphoric, wordy,
source-code pulls brilliant and
Why, if exhausting wrong, then now what Science did get right?

Well name them then general!
Ah! I see I'm to answer question!

Chance anger, we are rescued.

> *Notes: Aphoric: adj. for aphorism: concise statement*
> *of a principle; terse formulation of a truth or sentiment; adage, etc.*

'THE REFINEMENT OF GOOD BROODING'

If could keep it fore,
if knew importance
this spring breeze
allowing each blade and tuft its dance,
should squire through time,
forget in meditative, subtly, all,
un-shade crimped eyes and laugh.

If bells are briefed these connected days
they should send notice
so sot through traces can adapt.

But just secret treasure in surprise.

Note: Title: from a line in Proust's 'A la recherché du temps perdu'
'In Search of Lost Time' or 'Remembrance of Things Past'
'Swanns Way' 'Swann in Love,' Trans. by C.K. Moncrieff and
Terence Kilmartin (Vintage Books, Division of Random House,
New York, 1981, 1982), 219...the refinement of
good breeding..."

IT'S COMPLICATED!?

Against grain of truculent, attention locks
on institutions stilt-much.
Father: a man of book and citizen
survived scorn, groaned through youthful ambulations
to get to lunch,
asks to be alerted even now as realities change.
Movement in memory tones louder, previously quiet.

Eludist: involuntary immigration went conception,
that imposings on oceans get their since fourteen hundreds'
at least! rep and payment for work never included,
treasures filched in signs, gestures, 'prunes and prims'.
Zeal for submission, born of little minds, reach crescendo.

Benefited few. Hard times in Black!
"Accept this as white privilege and whom do we pay?"?
Criteria: same as for hatred and assumptions—color skin!

Gray faces more sought amend with who took part,
when camera leaves Black out, when are written over.

Once rules for uneven-drawn parades
made entirely of none-such hidden in plain site
relinquish and men eat at the heart of matters,
see they come wreathes to camp:
hail and dreidel play at happinesses,
begin then to no some yeses and yes some nos.

> Notes: Truculent: Cruel, savage, belligerent, vitriolic.
> 'Prunes and prims': Ref: James Joyce—a way Irish mothers
> had their children practice making small
> lips in the thicket of his "Ulysseys" I think!

BLACKER THE STALE WITH FRESHET

Sheets stack, line; many, patient,
though daily vanish from. In-press,
example for pursuers colors of impression and
blacker the stale with freshet.

Rise as weed under house,
fondled by grayer shades, un-molest,
evidence pages turned-in and
blacker that stale with freshet.

With prayers, come to sing.
Fault with overdone, its antecedent, pull. Efficacy?
One's wife of him—"the labour was merciless!"
—How does good work get done?

Proust no hack.
Sunk in no one's glare,
you are the fool who fires own line.
Ensures: the farther off a shore-safe harbour.

As depth, then, comes to see your dumb,
insight grabs arm, makes
the father of own church, only ringer one bell,
and blacker that stale with freshet.

Wealth can be a cancer to the wealthiest.
Insight expels arm and mistake is still dead-ender
It always was. How to stagger endlessly, never falling.
And blacker the stale with freshet.

Note: " "—Elizabeth Hardwick (2nd wife) of/on RTSLowell.

THE ADVANCEMENT OF THE PATRIOT

After Lowell

There locks in mire a brace of dotty toughs,
none rise-ward situated, all admired
where the tinny gold of bronze, zero titer,
with all batailous aspire,
like bobble teraphim to trip holy shiver
as grief bursts nurse in their cups.
Otherwise one willow coaches in his ball-tight sun,
the one-part-as-whole thallus low lays
with green wet fingers and with brown hugs stays,
where sole other lichen or algae can come.
And Zeus is at Oceanus with the noble Aethiopians,
all the hosts of heaven have joined Him there.
A cathedral whose view
is sky, water and orus for its nave,
with tens of feet of pine step heather for His shoe.
His panoply of brassard and scarlet coat prove
the way a grove-like forest prays.
Parishioners under that nave easy as tend,
confessions shown and steely mend,
in pleasant moments gay
can wit extinguish, façade crash, extend rays
to a home for Peace against nazi blend
of ignorance at redirect, and empties to their hells send.
Flag aglets no conspirers' chest waves.

Notes: *Teraphim: Semitic household god.*
Thallus: Undifferentiated (no clear leaf stem, etc)
plant life like lichen, algae and fungi.
Orus: mountain. Panoply: full suit of armour.
Brassard: here, shred of rawhide tide round upper arm.
Aglet: pin.

READ THE TERMS!!!!!

Passage must be completed by YOU and must be EXCLUSIVELY for our
gain.
(We don't accept journeys previously taken to romp rush and strike OTHER
sites). Don't send (for) your mistress or your wife; there are enough women
here,
as most men behave well in their tents by themselves at night.
(Film and mag are sold by the dozen at company store.
(Those who would banish porn have no idea what monsters would loose!)).
A son or two of any age will be worked as hard or perhaps a little less than
you.
NO CRYING OR BITCHING NEVER NO HOW.
      NO FUNNY BUSINESS AT ANY HOUR
      NO BARKING UP WRONG TREES
      NO MISTAKING ANOTHERS RIGHTS FOR YOURS,
      NO SYMPATHY WILL BE TOLERATED
      NO DEEP THOUGHTS ENURED
      YOU ARE HERE ALONE.
      DO NOT PLAY THROUGH!

Please keep marked areas safe,
remember to forgive when bigger than you is offender.

Unlike other frontiers you may have known,
we prosecute and bury our own; dispatch equaling no come back.
So fence your yard if you'd have one,
dig a hole deep enough to hide all principles when
privileged-authority signal's, and chance we like
what we see, you'll be allowed to stay!

SOLDIERS HOME

Night, crouch in low figure,
has no need cloak and dagger
when two, enough with death,
play on stage of mind, and down a path silver wind.

Battered, blood and bits.
The First: "Now of other days:
song returns, peace reigns!
My home, my hearth, Come constant chore!
you'll beat carnage!
Sun at southern-most sheens winter!
Come whistling, un-complicated praises,
full, all sit Nature's basket,

cordoned trustingly to men who've learned
to smile with injustice no more!
Fear for favor—it lie and cheat!
Enough with long illegal! For peace!"

Other: "Men, prepare to fight only non-earth alien,
I mean the coming at with death kind!
Nothing else warrants effort toward not life and living.
("You mean like virus, bacteria?")
I do! And more! Despite newly halt,
we seem greed will continue to bulk and feed.
See you and I earlier: for duty, wage fifes in maw.
A name, favors, flag. What were we thinking?

"Finally, so far missing tube and caudle,
spread news we'll! Outside praise for rations,
looking down on the thing, disown it we!"

First: "Agree! Agree! Name some other!"

> Notes: cordon: espalier, etc. decoration; to rope off, designate, etc.
> Caudle: a drink for invalids etc. usu. of warm ale or wine mixed w/
> bread or gruel, eggs, other bits, and spices.
> Fife: a small flute w/ no keys.

TO LATER GENERATIONS

Ally, we favor days of wonder,
in which are convinced God's purpose
can't be seen from there, but don't say,
just flow loving it like the crow,
how an unexpected cool may lift.

Were made men all in that day,
feet still in the old world.
Whether causal or additive, were
many of us too close to out.
Indoctrinal quiet and more obedience than now could:
more white boy, more privilege and 'burden' perhaps;
closer the old mat and fuller the folly.
But you who have no vision our inanities
and we so far unable to prevent distortions,
are all without time's lesson,
where complications continue to circle and
divertissement completes.
Resource-pursuers for profit and the living present
who 'must' over-burden?
We can imagine, when Brazil loses her forests
(and why shouldn't that people reap their highway scar benefit)
end is most near. And wail fair, speak Congo obscenities.
Sadly, there were always too few on Mother protecting Her.
And here with sight-sore Hawking agree
(though it may already be too late)
in the search for extraterrestrials,
"...should keep our heads low."

Notes: inanities—inane—vapid, pointless, empty, insubstantial, silly, etc.
Stephen Hawking—British physicist.

81

TODAY WAS SANTA BARBARA TROPICAL

Today, to you, hovelled miles from,
felt all Santa Barbara tropical scud: cloud on painted azure—
old work location, breeze, breeze,
relax, palm motel evenings.
Leisure, product to comprehend with day's pass.

En-route, growth, and successful crew are rewarded
individual exertions in team effort,
sighted differences, fortunate
where character's seat's been saved.

We, being all self-containers, bait enemies whenever out.
In the guarded day, reality au fait conducts the exercise
and one never knows which way incidents fly.
Rabbit baits hawk.
Ants don't even have to be out for anteaters to.
Life, seductively random answers prepare.
Open mouthed, you thought to live it clean,
sure right decisions camped on same plateau question did;
desire rights list-ship, gets every vote.

Still, if we're thought, what we do
when deer are hoofing the melons,
will tell what was left some winter's hunger.
Encircled by the trees you've let grow,
and they can have you.

Note: *au fait [F.]—to the, in (act, deed, fact, actual) reality.*

GIVEN AND PUT BACK!

Much is hidden; many exposures shin among:
Voltaire held the humanity,
but thought less of.
One lords who does such good.
But in seeking truth,
remember half-truth's battalions. Sneer
status quos' louden: artists? Some scoundrel.

Some defend, "If they'd not have that in those,
for their best, where placed?" Politician, dealer of goods?
"I have a job to do!"—Henchmen? Yes?
'Serpents', 'dogs', the bones thereof
call from brush, but don't hear how Newton visited Locke
at Oates—that's for camaraderie!
That Locke took profit in early bought shares
in the Royal Africa Company—that's for greed! and shares,
Everyman is thunderclap!

To ask: why take port with colleagues, friend,
when sea is awash injustice?
Right to bark and veer,
to passel assumptions with scold, hers?

Closed doors open with smile.
...what's given is always put back!
Several thought: this will come to.
Somehow, someway rathe love must rule!

Note: *rathe: early, quick.*

UN ARBRE SUR LA MONTAGNE

With certain sure, now bewilderment,
assumes the front rear. No!
Opposite while going, Mambo, two or...?
Assemble vixen; this abulia has
lost penumbral edge—
like eyes close on an object,
surface to air distortion; the bordered, mean veil*
that sense works, *that* forest is chief in.

Come, eat our lunch.
They, socially involved mind.
It, proximity—short radius,
infinite outreach,
stands there in half its shadow relevance.

> Notes: One Tree On The Mountain.
> Abulia: abnormal lack or ability to makes decisions.
> * though water is the subject, see Phys.org's Nov. 2021
> Article — H. Tasoff, etc. on 'Boundary Layer Turbulence'.

HEAVEN'S WORK

Future not to worry about.

Sense: defends, protects. Try that!
Truth, Justice, what in own time want,
placed in hunt; so laugh the broken millennia.
      As young as that?

Darwin and the Beagle, first painful twenty,
closing on, found, sought.
      To anguish iconoclast,
to briar painfully? To further umbral goals
cures often the pelage itch,
felid inch on object of leapage.

For some the old mean touch call chaplet in air.
Stumble praxis; that gun dreams of cool dips,
How we integrate with aristos in all,
and those coming after.

> Notes: Umbral: in the shadow, under the umbrella, as if.
> Pelage: of hair. Hairy!?
> Chaplet: wreath for the head, etc.
> Parxis: action, doing, practice.
> Aristos [G.] the best, greatest, etc.

THE B_____ BOARD

Whew! It's was like that slick hill as kids we'd down
in a slight rain, which is not the same
as "falling on a rainy day, chasin' a dog!"
(Brother at his Daughter's, same day).

Further from—me watching you (on TV)—hurried!
I didn't see all; was jumping channels and flipping Saint-Léger
as reporter lost head and let me through.

Where: a kind a' frenzy-fix on things broken was seen
oh! broken board of Bfield!
Which in no wise cottons man's wounds, that: all that time,
—in the 'freest' society man has berated, measures Justice how:
'On the farm,' as Waits' said, 'there's always somethin' awful to do.'

Lady-chairperson by now, in purl and purfle, staff as stem,
serves incredule, 'Let's move on!
"I suppose there'll be a lot of people locked-up
over the next six-months.
We'll need to see a report at budget time!"
—Giving the rubric, the heading, category—
eats whey, un-concerned.
A reporter blinks disbelief; not context.

And what is decided, usually, is truth covered in a lie,
budgeted in a palter.
On advance still noble tender!
Against dangle grandeur of a say, Homer coaxed Alexander,
merry on!

> Notes: Purl and Purfle: both—types of embroidery.
> Whey: a protein derived from milk fat.
> I think this is a repeat, Still—One thing Homer did
> was show the Greek Warrior/Producer class—of that society,
> with their pillage and conquest and just plain robbery—
> for the largely bad guys they were, at the time.
> Another—regarding the gods—Know holy!
> As all Ancients, It Is EveryWhere! (Swirls, that—Hydrogen atom).

QUESTIONING SONG

Every day another heralds between the hosts
to staff contradiction
and cut from cloth what today is born,
imagination, loose of self.

Eliot 'measured out in coffee spoons',
we in a chairless back-on-haunches chariness.

Today, just now, as extort nature had drain a pipe,
on walk there, felt like telling effort to back off, shy!
Then a breath and possibility-of-reward of comment
contrive by watch, to front drive,
match garniture with furniture,
polish floor, new faucet and balmorals in box,
and place the thing in wait.

Sooty, 'round freeman's widdy labour clod!
Contemplate snuff ten disputants know little of,
mock discontent, because no poet, ago,
left trace better then we now here! dream wish.

Later, by a window old,
darkening spot on welcome ground shadow of limb?
or like you, yesterday's over-soak limned.

Back inside: issue new vine and wine ideas, dance!
And from concern, desorb minds' glib, hands down, spin!
Know and clear!
It could happen!

Notes: Garniture: things that sit on furniture. Vases, lights, etc.
Balmorals: laced boots. Chariness: caution, integrity.
*Widdy: H+*man's knot.*
Limn: draw, etc. Desorb: give-up what was absorbed.

NOT A MADRIGAL

On Plain of Indifference—
where passed private indulgences,
which were the metron of lewd success,
close on verdant hills,
weather came off trees in puffs
(mimic of bombardment). Eager to land,
vapor catch—steps placed then, were
carved probables no bigger than an "I, I!"
where superior was better: "I and I!"
saltblock of gallantry.

Once, in mad skate, even little family
saved from the rules suspected of too scuffable parts.
All those woman could not the abrupt disrupt.
And was he in, out far too much.

We know a man needs a woman's word in,
no carrier-pigeon and grunt things loved,
balance his dent with she sensibilities somehow,
to tell stories near the house not of moiling war,
but of Nuthatches and Woodpecker and Sapsucker
scoot trunk and branch, recon nut,
and snicker gravity its fall crown to screed anger.
Down how his once broad swag all worked-out, didn't.
Dad and Mom rescuing all the time.

At least market tree, true Dan sufficient without grovel,
you did not with asmodeus and the like-for-like
enjoin God's anger, but are
with and by Him, Enoch and Tolkien blessed.

Man has been apart and is for sale poach his thievery,
where, of late, it is our awful taste to say, such as
stick-bug and frill-dragon are not prized,
nor longer camouflaged, with these in these warren.

> Notes: Madrigal: from mater, etc. mother. A medieval short lyric poem
> in a strict poetic form. A part-song; esp. Glee.
> Metron: [Gk.] measure, etc.
> Moiling: to work hard, drudge, confusion, turmoil.
> Screed: a lengthy discourse; etc. but also as here—a leveling
> device drawn over freshly poured concrete.
> Asmodeus: one of the devil's names in Tobias 3, 8; 1-3.

RISE

The once distilled say, 'no, not nearly!' So back to starts.

Same splendid glows and caps, salubrious,
to distant hump that for miles, could not reave,
though rough sod, knoll form supply cleave.

Molten and blow dust in soon un-hollow arches
that a woman, child, man
could be named and deserve it.

Wherever one walks on earth, she tender mounds,
softens, and lifts the head of man above the high art,
low philosophy his bombs.

When rise—carry height and imagination
seen by grandmothers and fathers who finger-tip heaven,
where no burdens brace.

Peaks, with permission, see sort along their spines
sunny as birdsong in summer's eve;
peopled by kindnesses, truths un-harness.

Road, once all hazard, no marker, has empathy
that raps void 'round a mouth-full of vile,
off-chance to breathe, which is raw skin hide.

Or has make hell out of there, rehearse shortcomings,
run big-rig memories so the tight blue air, less viable,
but more accommodating for factory-town settings
saddles arcs of well-healed passions
whose smudge permissions embrace unburden and
you ride along a greener patch of highway.

CH. 4
EARTH-FIRST SUN DANCE

FIRST EARTH

In sky boat, mind around bluey green
sacred will cross the penny'd yard
at Learning's signpost I ween.
Roll-up britches on watch, hitch sleeve.
And like believing fellows at market in giving eaves—
birds of a sawed-off November—trek belief,
overfly Bleary's drum-major ambush.

That Dim, once used clever glue that imposed adhese,
knocked Wish's starlight with calamitous crowd belief,
then went to bleed in the next sunset and stoop relief!
Apart! Some told themselves. If not attached, that will fix!
The fairie bangles bounced. Chance Meribu, Juju healers, separate,
hit rasp voices stilt walls against.
And the medicine outside the realms of man too,
quoth Save Earth first! "before the felt melts," as radio saved itself.

From the divine messenger, warren in passages, Felicity
reared in moorings' best—blest the female, emphatic,
eternal artist that sticks and won't be frying in any pan
no matter what gross expect, dross content—says firm for all:
   'Who can defend their rights can keep them.'
   Shoot the stars next, first save Earth!"

Notes: Meribu (spelling!?): Priest, Seer, Spirit-healer—Senegal, Africa.
Juju Healer: uses witchcraft ?!?
L. Garr on KPFK in an interview meant to say
"And the fat melts away" on show btwn 1:00 and 2:00 pm 16, June 2008.

EFFACE

They write him letters ask what he knows.
His dreams are of fish and beer.
There are soldiers in the ground!
The buck stops here!

There are civilians in the ground!
All manner of men have need the drum!
Every soul props a heart!
Time has come!

Fly was not squashed,
Maggots clean the wound,
call telepathic dolphin or whale,
it's on!

Give him fast he goes!
Those elephant smell the blues.
In proper dearth
yours too.

Answers few have liked
except as martyr does.
They'll for themselves per usual,
never self-efface, fool as ever was!

NOW SHINE

Dispute to the heart of matters, to soft understand
required to agree on first principles.
Thus the stock of knowing, when time not borrowed,
brings the no-standing, all dismissals, to end
and assays true mettle, which like young men
who cannot be trust in their so-little skill
hop around arguing some, are yet the hope of debutants.

No height then the glory crowned? Do the good die young?
As sentences whimper on adolescent tongues,
or if a mastiff break and run will hounds accomplish some?
When is a man's mask his face?
When he lingers behind grace and graceless stand,
to halt no anguish when but he can!
The humble bumble has it, with hairy belly and sting,
as the once bold mark of man adds naught his tally,
he pats a lifeless bauble now called bling.
    There the ants and all life vie,
      to sift through heaven and God's love try.

Cast here citizen, that you and I must,
not by new-gated, winked-tapers hie,
as shutter as some who do not, but that
we the Dark Ones, have now call to shine.

NEW PRIESTHOOD

And when they had by stiff elision,
the wisdom to sovereign; the duty, courage,
new brickwork of ages, screen of skin,
did not pass unscreened cores.

Breath no sooner left Aaronic gap
it instantly crossed an hundred seas,
and lords of "sad sincerity"' sealed fates.
Θαλαττα, Θαλαττα the tears draw down.
Grievance-milled harmon fills fate's false jars.
Honesty no sea swallows, no partition seals.

Have it, without tear, you launch for Helen her ship
and save world 'fore all is a death of joy in dying.
And, no toff eternity awaits doctrinal fidelity.
Emotional lies gather on food and water
before reality is taken and locked by out-convenience,
that has everywhence lied.

Forest, mere kernel, is holed.
Little, made of the waste laid fine, like silk
draws into eye, happy-frayed excess.
Equally variant, leisure to proletariat in scrim pays out.

How the hectoring strain entreats. Still, if one must grieve,
make room small vengeance cooking choleric meal
of once-better-than. And companions, leave all weariness with us!
For overdone, I am bigger than the last field river would overrun!

Candor, shun the armour-glow protect by gods.
Holy abduction! Its' agony when goddesses bathe in blood!
This is no intellect!
Skill, you could do us this one: find a high course,
    no murderous intent, greed acquiesced,
    restored body to mind, and family intact.

> Notes: "Sad sincerity": "The hand that rounded Peter's dome and
> groined the aisles of Christian Rome wrought in a sad sincerity;
> Himself from God he could not free..." Emerson. From Roget's
> University Thesaurus, Ed. by C.O.S. Mawson (Thomas Y. Crowell
> Company, 1911-1963), 445; under Religion; 1,000 Temples.
> Θαλαττα, Θαλαττα [Aeolic Gk.] = sea, sea or tears, tears; salt water!?
> Toff: dandy, swell.
> Proletariat: the lowest social or economic class of a society, etc.
> Scrim: a durable, plain-woven usu. cotton fabric...
> Choleric: of getting one's choler up, angry, etc.

VIRIDITY

It was when hurled self freebie scurry
over the long wait expectancy,
combat's obligatory denunciates,
that Jumble no longer caught in raffles some.

Old energy, deplorable face in a smile,
privys with cut and paste and "we're not that!"
rebuffs stump in a mirror vile,
hospitable swill-well no more.

Shaft season refrain parenthesis,
pharmacists' portions, mortar wings with them.
I bruxist, and apostrophic! You acephalous countries
try our clamps, gone awry, and pass your dingy suicide.

Notes: Viridity: green, naïve innocence.
Acephalous: no/without a head.
Bruxism: the habit of unconsciously gritting, grinding the teeth.
Apostrophic: the addressing of/to a usu. absent person
or a usu. personified thing rhetorically. "O Liberty what things are..."

A WATERFALL

Dull and shiny it would have been.
Cronos would have liaised annulment doubly.
Washed, they'd have brooked no slice of parts
generous to billboard that up-turned our little wagon.

And if messages were to have gotten out
over town, another apparent solution afloat the where,
would have in un-private pouches found,
The star, so new, it never was a portal to pictures,

that settled disputes in ignorance,
found words as hammer to let acceptance in,
near erased corners,
redacted pointy prows, to dance darn-ly in great flow how.

Note: liaised, liaise: interrelationship;
communication for establishing and
maintaining mutual understanding, etc.

EARTHSHAKER

In toss and tumble country—rumble...
Come glasses, few book,
pen, notebook, fast to door!
Rolled the earth-shaker in that day,
Tweak, like feet fleet on a creaky floor.
Resigned to falling through floors?
Ground runs, rubble rule? Breath hold.

Quick heart! But ahh! Carpenter away continues...
—How one long hammer-blow with one's sit-up
should motion Indra's Net, have butterfly
miracle, slide cement and float he.

How 'in twinkling of eye' no more reads,
not pleasant atmospheres', not again—woman?
Rout lead, panic choke.
—Minutes later the old carelessness has,
safe forgetful sums.

Easing now into skein with other foul, boast...
"I would have gone back in for
That Homer, Bible, Ekermann Goethe, more!"
And mind has alarums yet used!

WELCOME

Every word, rejoice. Every inch quench
envy and the ascension of berate concepts.
Want to write like them, everyone!
That's personal!

Thought wait too much, being in sorrow's toilet!
Each utensil to purpose; but please Homer, Hesiod,
ancient masks, release us much benefiten
that spans our wagon that sky!

From which at present, a red-tailed hawk
patrols the yard.
At which, a cloud breaks over the rich, raised land,
budding ships at sea our sky!
And that how paying attention
can a good omen yoke.

COPYCATS

Initial favors? Good the music weighed
somber, elegiac. There in Chicago Overcoat was,
the gun, doing dirty work, wet his covers all.
And uncertain barrels out over a wide area;
the sky's hem now cloud?

Then entry, ten shots there were
with no bow for launch.
Wind, companion of day, had things to say.
Get shuttle and hod
you mean-as-mean soldier, here for a while.
Let it clank over at its rise, that tower, cathedral.
They: shield wall, trebuchet de toil!

> Tending we to our (torrid) bacilli,
> did dodge you royal?
> Fetid purple slippers, trim,
> gold the auspicious ought
> like the I to know,
> spark ride write for a rile?

A BAD DAY SOCRATES

Out! No more!
       Words, words! Paper everywhere!
A fear a thought, thought pretty good should vanish,
so pad follows pen in can; office, a fright.
Dining-room table words, envelope scratch; the hodgepodge,
you suckling rant, won't stop; some, the floor!

Man, ago, I would have drunk the stuff,
had I spent first decades thinking too much,
but at all events, may still have done that.
And we know the clean-up bird circles blocks,
acknowledges late-experiences he'd not wing with,
that we save as possibility, where n-fold meanings lie.

Anguish too, we see you try,
having our President be the best among us.
Man, am glad tendencies here don't include boys buggered
which was lenient where you were,
but added to your crimes, did it not?
Still, stray sexuality's broken pot I,
a woman might back… but we sense this too much and.

So, books, yeah, they laugh, cough it, I lap.
Phrase hangs air, not long, fire fed.
Nor a conversation, a drink a bite a read that isn't
set on bench, vised, that the stricting ethic can't dissect,
would away with.

Bowshot, listen! Breath cannot keep shuttlecock life.
Afar the forests are aburn; emergency vehicles berth wide,
and an early snow of ash mimics Hers.
—But Even here, swear us our own battlings might!

FREIGHT IN THE AFTERNOON
(Or Liberty Abandoned)

Each action had complaint.
Girt a sound being, this is irrelevant.
Advocate knows his times, delivers,
because first-in-haste brushes-off
placements on slower moving acquaintances
like petty and waste; comp them flips and rolls
to acquire balance.

And since service is in subsidence,
apt merchant over-confidant purse,
tangent a highway, is which way has evidence gone?!
ridiculous rolls and the lid were not kept,
Liberty there bursts a-nonce!

The people are moving, a body like in the heavens
needs a medium, a nostrum of dependencies, a fresh blank.
Oblique, the crowd is on shiny paths.
New faces pose smiles vacant.
Foul and preposterous land everywhere.

Kindly agent by your simple self-defense,
sheet-thin in a wind, visible variant, cast as fan!
Being ready, back out aware!
Sorry, Scholarship, its vast resources pedant,
sends apologies for not being there.

> Notes: nonce: the one, particular, or present occasion, purpose
> or use, etc. Nostrum: a concoction as a medicine; panacea.

A CASE FOR THE ACTUAL

Chorus:
    "Well, spit in the fire and call the dogs!"

Perhaps here we'll dispute reatsy repute
then rank for bravery, not sadism,
the sane? sadist Marquis de Sade.
Reduced to write with what exits, if true.
Vile even to wrecker Napoleon, who,
considered leaving the Sphinx that African nose,
but Quoodle-troubles were coming soon.

Un-blister hands broke the concrete of acceptance,
kept from worth, seen with time if pedestrian,
or clear sight now.
While admittance—our note is brake Orleans—
men in numbers un-breathable exhaust prefer
of scrapes and bows and verace hoist by accident,
to spirited rolls, to fist-pleads of their world.

Chorus:
    "But why vested interest, is your burgundy coat?"

There's Beyle doing his best Stendahlian,
active in camouflage. Beyond drape or not,
so many work across wish, some line should have drawn,
never crossed, carried, to be worthy the salon,
and introduced of fard, fatuous host,
softening to men things they'd not hear. When
A fright, 'easy to get along with'
—more disgrace than purse, to whom, like the Duchess to Hugo,
'I like a savage's better than a comedian's' work.

Redirects mold, as in cups we bring to mind fear a-ride, a-ride,
stun-eyed Arachne Athena seeing—who pulled Achilles' head
by a handful of hair—angry. 'You are here!'—repents boastful Arachne.
And the mass parries too-patrician thrusts and Goes Post
in its just now immaculate living growth.

> Notes: fard: painted w/ cosmetics. The Duchess d'Orleans
> to Victor Hugo as quoted in his Memoir—"At the Tuileries"; Feb 26, 1844.
> G.K. Chesterton's 'Song of Quoodle': "They haven't got no noses,
> The fallen sons of Eve; Even the smell of roses /Is not what they supposes;
> But more than mind discloses/ And more than men believe..." equals
> Chesterton's add-on to Chapter XII of Charles Dickens' 'Bleak House'?

CONFIDENCE

Pocketing advances, trends southerly
assist derelict constitutions swarf their paid assassin;
and religion, a soothe on distraught's anxious face
nearly ever wants rescue, knows not how to ask.

I am your mild thought partner banished from easy climes
come northern realms of dash and pine, to barter
after hate has done!
And you know my accomplice, time?

Query none the spectators heart!
Mimet, I shade initiative under fear's scurry thirst.
For want, the news forms springs right.
Narrative precariously dips haplos left
and many points vector as hope align.

There temper gauntlet: your waste-my-efforts
through the worst waters of your now shored shy!
Hazardous season file brave with stories of moments,
days' concentration in the make-much of plain, straight currency
of belief's sun-dance, that can touch!

Admit, you barely knew which way the wind would
save out and away. Possibly induce guilt on sable brows,
maybe ambsace 'the soul by means of speech'
and droll a little philosophy out!

Notes: Swarf: to remove parts by cutting or grinding.
Haplos: [Gk.] simple, straightforward, etc.
Ambsace: the lowest throw at dice; something worthless or unlucky.
'Lead the soul by means of speech'—poetry—Plato.

ACHILLES IN THE RIVER

Apologies rinse in the king of favors,
a waters' whole glaze, and raze his bark as bite.
The king and he are in distaste,
and the endless Seeker has not lost, un-caught,
his long-known friend on the life-quick side;
he is here at living edge to meet and greet grievous danger.
See running feet; and battle once far away, there?
All a padding; greave, sandal, blood all mud
as a bronze-tipped pole rests next a tamarisk.

At Bersabee, in like of wrong, song,
there was water and tamarisk, oaths to a rise of man.
Here: anger never un-packs
a friend from shambles with carnage.

On the plain, the river, everywhere that day
fear was free to route.
Entitlement, its boundary broken neither warrant,
but waded in shine Pelean.
To the right, left fell Ilium's.
Fish, eel, happy in nibble — no place not turmoil,
and 'wise too late's' rank caps the hour.

Fearlessness, a strong arm, big and beautiful
could many things 'fore the binding twelve.
Now battled river, out patience, calls help,
and hearing, agree! Water, heave, eject scoundrel,
failing, hide for all time the barrow!

None! Assistance comes form of fire, river must surrender!
Escapes and prophecy; an end with Hector,
death, and build a pyre, reprieves in asphodel?
Pride of place among men the best could manage,
and we're sorry for it all.

Notes: Son of Peleus and Thetis (the head nymph,
"daughter of The Brine")—Poseidon.
Bersabee—means 'The well of the oath' btwn Abraham &
Abimelech, Genesis 21, 22-33 and mentioned after.

ALBERTINE

Never a falling down studio by the sea for tea—
you advise a granddaughter at knee
had you not made 'off by nine with your boxes'
and were literateur; 'cause—had the mind.

But what of heart?
Thoughts and paint redeem.
'Casse le pot'? its furthest, is of the tribe,
and men and women already fallen.

Begged launch from women gave—self for another,
(a request for insight) so he might achieve.
Bind deferential? Deemed not worthy?

Multitudes calculate the art of sufferers,
as men go for schnapps in the library.

Fast, an affection in fine country with
open window as part perfect mystery.

As men polish in agreed self-esteem,
send to the stores for more of everything: soda,
food to throw, self-annihilate to stay.

And oh! Did you know you can get the un-attainable
generally, there now. A limousine, a boat,
well you always could but...
and trails off tasting something in her mind.

Note: Falling down: Whigmaleerie: ('gimcrack'
Proust's choice of words)

FEAR OF GOD

He said, as on the plain below, he writes up here.
Obviously, he has seen
himself vacant in a lot,
time ripe, was not missed trine the arc
to educate self to a mountain top.

No, he and she most often go faith deed pursue,
anti-agent, cross more plain than mount has crevice for,
so wish a fair birth and fairer life unhume for heals.
Tender the mercies that tread soft lies!

Venturing only to name vagile valence of what
holy is more gall, a splendid forgery
a Pan and his hit-populous greedy ones,
who always mate with other than secant,
wrote the death of mystery men and women for laughs.

In turn, how does Ida fit?
Was it The Great Father or Zeus pert on shade green seats
and width?
He, that One of many names, out any Olympus,
non-negotialis!? The best of wisdoms...
Oh gee, here we pause.

Notes: Vagile: free to move about.
Valence: combining power; capacity to unite, react or interact.
Secant: a straight line cutting a curve
at two or more points, etc.
Iliad; Books XIV, XV.

AVIFAUNA

This fury, likened by Cecil's *Two Blue J's*,
mounts virile Brush and topknot Stellar's
who with blae pinion hop
last supportive inch, dead-fall,
then glide one tree to next in feather lark.
Who have a wing, may fly!

Full halts over mountain are for Eagle.
She clean stalls with slight correction,
who showed wild Nimrod, hunter assist—
stay motionless, move effortless, a cloud.

Eye this season then of industry's pitch,
when store is fit preparation
for that clean, banked mantel She's soon to cover with.

Flicker, from vertical hammer climb,
with Sparrow and Phoebe bottleneck the ground.
A minute, and... you see yourself pitch on a branch,
hung by a pole and leather sun dance to help.
Cross dimensions, pierce sound,
the warrant, thrasonic in ghoul-full praise,
eyes a bevy of Quail-crests bob in parade!

Behind adulthood is imp, saved or not,
as childlike or manable a soul gets made.

Notes: *Pianist Cecil Taylor's comp. Spring of Two Blue J's.*
Thrasonically; boastful, braggart.
Thrason, Thraso, a character in 2nd century Latin poet of African
origin Terence's (c. 186-159 B.C.) play Eunuchus (161 B.C.) — (Greek original by
Menander) —Terence, The Comedies, Trans. by
Betty Radice (Penguin Books Ltd, Harmondsworth,
Middlesex, England, New York, etc., 1965-1976), 157-218.

A TEACHABLE MOMENT

I

On the gravel paths, walking one day,
Black Bees bike a pole,
homing on that creosote frequency;
and best looking-out,
I, "Back off that hub adept,
follow not our prized honey out;
adopt not charade that is modern life.
Broken trust, controlled-weather might kill the sun,
and take out more than hives.
Radiation before the mast rues below Good Love's plan.
Forgo the hearsay; have a care Historian!"

II

Every situation's karmic.
There's St. Francis in his brother ass habit,
exchanged by us for our gas bag adage.

They thought of each other, none slept.
Sporks stole and forked ways,
'sun glazed off wing', some wept.
Flesh was fey to de-port
in the minor of every failed passage,
cloak seemed passable play.

You will attend students attentions once wrapped,
handed self when are sheen, and faire nevertheless
as well as the un-fumble tribes of men
and hives in assembly, that listened at ear and talked
their shit in sleeves, to miss the old contagion.

III

Outside the self, perils, evident. Inside, Spirit and *Will*—
Lord of all worlds extravagant, sculpts new ablings!

Notes: 'Sun off wing...' Alan Watts on Life through other creature's eyes.
Fey: doomed. Will—Lord of... Arthur Schopenhauer.

EARTHAL

Toward harken bow
First Lady of Pantheon screens visitors,
at tree-line pushes back,
sends sleet, bent, to cut a face, disgrace inquisitor,
see no more wrists turn out,
but does not say choose one of how many,
as patriot-lean hoists praying crowd,
tatters pelf oh maid of happiness!

By degrees, breakfast in her tower,
foreclose no hand-outs.
Endeavour with crevice and isle maun,
chance her deep ferrous smile.
And since no repeats exist in nature,
pour in our gourd from her sacred mouth.

Rafters for a balm, women: home.
Purple dissolves in the dirt they're after,
narrow cognance not a thing saves,
and signs of life message in a bottle
the seeming always violent man-made way of life.

Hermit has his solitude and bear cave.
Oh happy slice, mentor noble pine,
Larch and Butterfly; settle concave in convex!
Character is filed, trouble sloven,
do! grow statuesque, frozen opposable in your smile!

Notes: Pelf: old English !? = money.
Maun: man, munu, shall will.

MNUTE

gesund, do not ulcerate!
take them not foot
for back I wis how
wasn't nome gave spryly
ain't through e'en't master hook
mate or fabulaiment sis near I
spake rabes a'fore; you wouldn't know
less shown, as did there;
but not circle with mind this adventure;
monument was't wave iota fulmerous
chug charl a sigh hip hop, don't! I'll see ya,
with charming charn that's past "gixy" 'nough
touch!

Notes: mnute: newt—salamander (in fire). Also neuter.
Gesund: [G.] lit. health. Charl: short of charlatan.
Charn: short for charnel (caranlis—of the flesh); chamber or building
where bodies or bones are deposited.
"Gixy" Rabelais's word for a young virile woman.

TRANSPONSE 'PREDATOR' TURN

Matters, he would say, had to go the way went.
He die, you survive; resource relative carry paw hence,
another *nunc dimitis* now release, as 'twere, to sail sure water;
you'll get your chance!

He, a special fan; you, necessary to sip woman's ale.

I am not at truck this animate's antic, *hic et nunc* I'll warn!
Sir! That you are here; even sans *mirabile dictu*, your impress?
Impeccable! is enough!
And that radiant-wounds would mend were not
end-all beaten out front just now, for coverts with a neighbor's wife;
I'd have you save fruit where need and joy are able!
Yes sir! No clips meant, no sleeve in dish here!
That's fine, on!
Yes! Then we were at how The Legion must note ownership
in war's not right. How ordinance makers are bereft!
We agreed 'Totally bereft!' wordage!
'Totally' it is! Then?
Then, 'Predator' turn is the finest found this planet!
We agree! Send!

107

URIAS

With olive in press,
figs soon from pockets of branch;
the year was back and he was asked to go with them,
'spoil and besiege' His enemy!
Loyalty, courage and dedication stood,
but he was not in clover to be whiled.
A report, a thing as ruse against good men;
he should eat meat in his house,
seek and sleep with his wife.

But he would not.
I think the foul was known by stifling air.
Jacob's people he'd served well and faith
abused to keep no soldier's fortune, abide joyful.
His tribe for a time would survive;
they said, He had kings of mind.

She slid water from her back for mothering;
and that other, in full site and dumb
from the end of beauty
she was a thing he must, even as Want,
not sole proprietor in men, would bring him just.

Called to sacrifice, a good servant fell at that wall
so the other could take again his wife.
Nor shall what service may bring be calculate.
For being good in all but this, the usurper was chosen.
Cogs remain a mystery,
one or another will end each day, and he,
like so many, as ar as we could tell, was blameless.

> Notes: Urias: Old Testament Hittite officer, who was killed in battle
> on instruction from David so that he could marry Urias' wife Bathsheba
> (II Samuel 11) Bathsheeba, Bathseeba—Mother of Solomon by David—
> note: (Not "to" as the oldest African would have it, "add to or take away,
> nor deign turns to the right or left" but to near Understand inhabit.)

CHIPPIN' ON THE HARDTACK

Some ease with half life.
"A breath" for Mignon,
you are active a child, forget what owes, owed,
everywhere's the bomb!

Mild prattle and milder bungle
inform the weight of logic.
Evening's insular thrice honed, trips,
what outside I missed.

Ninety for a hundred seems fool's falderal.
Mortmain reissues resolve on the 1420 MHz
birthed to traverse a universe that transits.

Oh mend! The back-swept nurse is helpful, can equip
ballast the un-health. The life of mind, set to exercise
fair-housing and topple bad governments, prays
a good man's holiday to ya if you're of same kidney.

And chippin' on the hard-tack, seeking power and insight,
eat; red rocks ar redder in the hot sun. A vow stays
where you leave it son! Things multiple
appear single in the Insula when is tidy our no-pass filter.

Notes: Mignon: the poor little girl in Goethe's 'Wilhelm Meister's
Apprenticeship' also: [F.] darling. Falderal: bullshit!? Mortmain: past.
1420 MHz = frequency of hydrogen, used by the SETI project
to find ET. Oops! Insula: a small island in the cerebral cortex that is
'the platform for feelings and emotion, and learned behavior'.

LIFE IN A LOOSE-LEAF BINDER

Atmosphere over spiry smiles entire loch.
Forty square miles of a trans-Scotland or near-Alaska,
in cloud, of cloud; far across cloud thought-cliffs low in cloud,
and no paint's off in hand with this one.

Creek-bend's been there under bridge all this time,
and what will top if not intention positive,
has adolescent or senior exhaust as plaque in mind
that ones and twos as fees as crawl like bones on a table?

Remember peddle fiascoes and moneyed filtchings
skein parties will wear in criminal back and forth,
and in subjunct struggle to soften, learned,
leave man some knuckle!

Experience proper cloud's prosperity
on the parapet of revised strides in strife,
so all's not some Jefferson half-tremble
that keeps the machabee near forgiveness,

premonition out any old way;
and by the bye—time tow puzzle,
Old slouch interchangeable twirls vigor,
enjoying life in *his* loose-leaf binder!

> Notes: Subjunctive mood: expresses a thought or wish rather than fact:
> they may _____, let them _____, etc. Machabee [Heb.] hammer.

PEN-TA-URT (PENTAUR), HOMER, HESIOD

Love it is 'wants words, wants meanings':
literature's verace, to pylon even.
Cup bigger is banter of hundreds of years.
Hooded bursars account
as squint toothy lip of "day-sleepers" prevaricate smile.
So much dismembering. Sat est.

Say the happy eyes of a Dohgon thinker though
placed your knowledge among the stars.
Mightn't you: dealated, unwung, sans culotte have romped with gods?
Abraham, Egypt on its sapient continent, even now cannot rise!
A fulmine of sighs; luck of draw, gasp, why?
"When you come to tell your story, you too will take liberties!"
At their best, not these, not those vestured
in Mother and Father Dark, not so early in their ties.

Notes: Pen-ta-urt's epic writings/poem of Ramses II (Sesostris)'s conquests
of the Kheta or Hittites portrayed on pylons at the Great Temple of Luxor and
on the walls at Karnak (El Kab, above Thebes).
Cup; as a cup of hands, held up.
bursars—monastery and college treasuers. Sat est; satis [L.] enough is.
Verbum sap—verbum sapienti (sat est) = a word to the wise (is sufficient);
enough said! Dealated: ala [L.] a wing or wing like part.
Sans culotte—lit. without breeches; extreme radicals during French Revolution !?
Sapient—wise, intelligent.
Fulmine: fulminate-to utter/send denunciation, censures or invective.

MUCH ADO

"...what men do, what men dare do..."
—William Shakespeare

Un-finish half-breed of Sparta O/Re O/Re /aroint!
Our General's "Ability to loiter on station,"
in brave's own territory, was task so ardent,
it half-eats swine, goes to knees and wails excuse-me's;
so nothing so much as worthwhile, Leonidas, lies,
zero to five our starch-street station.

Lexeme, culp with Lemma lean.
'Right' thir at school-boy trough,
at Dad's knee, Mom's bosom every child learned
all he'd ever use about suffers of women,
although Adam's truce oh broken intent,
scabrous revenges someone's foot in sail
and wet, every place could stand, left no standing.

The Prayer—to Lord of pure blue skies! And
like Martin at Johnson's signing table, take at word,
but aerosol lies leave heart's walls like 'Zivago's at last,
like paper,' as 'our dubious poet, hugs his private life.'

Was beef with who restrain several convening
till none, not daster even, survive diss
Its buck and shine.

Notes: 'Much Ado About Nothing' W. Shakespeare; aroint!: begone!
Lexeme: word, speech.
Lemma: auxiliary proposition used in the
demonstration of another proposition.
Thir: these (archaic).
Scabrous: covr'd in scales, hard to deal with, dealing
with scandalous or salacious mat'l.
Daster: doer of dastardly deeds, no good.

FRAGMENTAL

Strain stampado for the million-buck look:
'ain't goin' nowhere' solecism and
be the only bulldog your neighborhood needs,
but let some good ones through!

So watch, you may not! (some are fubsy, some fop)
We are here to assign time and correct pole height!
Unconcern, never a best match for
hunts elephant in the squirrel and bunny grass,
lands savants their hurdies, sing selsyn engine starts.

Exhilic mew, cow who is the last look in fields
conducts charade; corposant weaves the end of things,
and 'if people don't want to come, nothing will stop them!'

Notes: Stampado: hollow gold or silver jewelry.
Solecism: a syntactical inconsistency, mistake or absurdity.
Fubsy: chubby and somewhat squat.
Savant: a person of learning esp. someone gifted in one thing like science or litera-
ture, etc. hurdies: dial Brit: rump.
Selsyn: = synchro.
Corposant: lit. holy fire; an electrical phenomenon that
lights the ends of masts at sea, rods etc. in thunderstorms, etc.
Exhilic: from exhilarate—make cheerful, etc.

NATHAN

"Neither to the left nor right" again.
God's obedience to you: "build His house!"
Vacant in a lot, far from Endor, No sir! you may not!
Names turn men distinct, almost safe from crude, but not.

Take what you will! Yes they're all ripe!
Never but bid God, bidding Him, and crossover
to we cousin german!

Quarrel, do not weave. One that was't is new,
breach is for who need!? Exclaim, pay; decide and end!

Amend and forgive! Shy writ, we find not here—
"God save the King" on canopy nor any blanket.

Note: Nathan, Prophet—of David and Solomon.

CH. 5
THE-UNIVERSE-AT-DAWN
JARABE TAPATIO

THE UNIVERSE AT DAWN

I

Breathe adaptations varying worth.
Folklorico, the universe at dawn sprawls spark,
thick Mother Dark does snare, catch part.

Speed gobbles and asks
the bane of Maker's ics and history's bulk;
how do they trust?

Scramble great Times' embrace,
hide in the saddle up
and groan under atom's explosive.

Generics mask to muster,
wish veil on the gathering Self, lone fit.
Etiolate to arrive in port under that skirt or waiver.

Universe, stand with them saved,
they were the temperature and the whether
love or evil would, on the holodeck of rhyme!

II

At curve, across stretch and clime,
answers treed plastid, emptied and with wind-blows
sold outgrowths' clear cornice (life as humus rot).
Mists drawn, see-cross-dale effect sat in place
and met sky-gawker, worry, the dispute, haste.

In dwellings, flesh with wroughts,
Cold the Outlier and Textus Receptus
fold the universe at dawn in piped pockets
and tap to celebrate with the palid ones
under Driven's hunch.

Hale-flares self-drive. Matter cries to fertilize.
Bizet's Carmen, Martin's Dream,
Beethoven's nth do dry-face damp.

Suspect Love, that Life with Art was doing that.
Laertes and Hamlet at the poor girl's grave.
Dying-all-the-time, Hope rides emperium's ne'er back.

I ask, 'Would ya' be a havin' a bit a' the creature then?'
"I used to! Let's see," he said, clanking sheet wood! "Where
was that? Here it is!"
We toggle inheritance to Shane and Lateshia
come to repair verdure's faucet, name it: A Cleaned-up World.
Because, you don't have to sleep to be unconscious
or "play the youthful parts!"

III

A mother beats her way through thorn and thistle
at daughter's high-thrush scream,
and parting final bush, face lacerate, frenzied,
dance pools love eyed, pleased to see them.

Brother held sister, with arm's slender rope
above blind drop.
Sometimes the last act of an idiot's a fool's.
Someone assists, you survive.

Shimmer croaks on pavement,
they native find road back,
un-met of fashion's harm.

Circling crosswinds
in friction's hyper chamber
toss sin in the grail air! After all, humans these.

Ahead, above, artists—as the un-relent storm,
or swirled universe at dawn, all arm churn and leg squirm,
heedless, spends itself—try to keep man's light on.

Notes:—*ics from [Gk.] ika; ikos—study: knowledge: skill: practice, etc.*
Etiolate; to remove the color, take the green out of plants by depriving of
sunlight; to make pale, etc. Plastid: cytoplasmic organelles of photosynthetic
cells that serve in many cases as centers of special metabolic activities.
"To arrive in port": ancient Egyptian phrase for the going after death;
See The Papyrus Prisse, The Book of Kaqema, in The Oldest Books in the World,
G. Maspero, Paris 1888, etc. — Isaac Meyer, et. al.
(Kessinger.net ISBN 1-56459-486-6), 58.
Textus Receptus: received text. Like the Greek New Testament.
Hale: free from defect, sound, etc.
Ne're: [alter. of ne're a]; = nary—not any.

THE PRAYER THAT TRIED TO GET OUT

Pulled, I had not foreseen caulked knee,
nor could run have known we'd long sit.

Mother, more angel than not,
in galoot of wife's chuff,
cadenced the yardwork I thought to give up,
obedience ceded.

Bible, full of sound thought,
advice, like oscillate warning
about poetry's truth-brought absurd
says it should not have been.
Instead a bye! to the sky,
in a separate homeland reached.

Joy and catch the former child, un-release
haute from promises to be still, quite,
crook with elder to ill-fame among disgrunt
angels for a while.

Later, ill imprint, I cried:
if angels stay their own, I'll keep my spot.
Belief in own press, will,
with That-Will of me, if blessed.

Notes: Galoot: *fellow; esp. one who is strange or foolish.*
Chuff: *noisy exhaust or exhalation.*

CROSSING

Existence in favorable face,
seat glancingly from fabled minds
like Mithridic increase so long inimitable,
into the serene valley from boisterous cliffs comes
to rub a little tincture and show a little herb the tongue.
A tincture and herb of sincere imitation
down from the mountain for the way men were.

Art, philosophy's wagon, you have the innumerable hands,
tried and sometimes scaled bale of offensive weapon
brightening the gray coast of heartless fact,
emotion's gasp, experiencing the sweet in heartful breasts,
twirl about for her!

Noun, even tone—the ingénue and reality are circumspect
and favor whole.
Note the fleshy parts that grip medially,
the knoll that lies, simply is the Back, flat
pinnacle of subsistence that holds Alberti's color's recusant,
Luther's impieties, and do mortise stock of men and women
who for advancement went.

In extraordinary quaints, privilege exceeds navigation
met at the crossing, set to announce again
how those best among the Common, grasping
not fleck and scarious rot, leave no turn to safety.
And how sits and ropes of "fine linen twined"
at the green feet of covenant landfall may go passive turgid.

> Notes: Inimitable: not capable of being imitated; Matchless.
> Recusant: one who refuses to accept or obey established authority.
> Leon Battista Alberti (February 18, 1404—April 20, 1472) Italian author,
> artist, architect, poet, priest, linguist, philosopher, cryptographer
> and general Renaissance humanist polymath.
> Turgid: swollen, bombast.

IN THE COUNTRY OF PLEASE

Pie and Paiute, pig measurement yin and yang.
Soften arrant! snow of Cottonwood and Apple blossoms
send poemander justified notice of laud!

Those not dependent, called to enter,
give back tine, quick answer;
voice what match soon is lack.

Moments without thought of one, one as in just past none,
are downfall unable to slide holy manna;
and art, no past usage: a daily call Leander!

Some tussle to tackle if names fly right.

Very respectful, the coat is not the man,
nor hair, nor hand, except strategies to decide.

Someday literature will have flown this world
then escapes will be as little-vim to full-ala feather,
and everything else lack looking for luster.

Confrere, disbelief is sore the eye, moderate!
You were first among equals before makebate,
when flash blue remediate endearment made.

Now pie and Paiute, yin and yang, raised land gone.
Soften arrant! Snow, high, wells majest. Justified in the
Country of Please, go, come as want, steely feel Poemander!

Notes: Tine: a slender, pointed projecting part—as of a fork, etc.; also to lose, de-
stroy; become lost. "Manna was like coriander seed" Nm 11, 7.
Confrere: colleague, comrade. Paiute American Indian tribe, God Bless!
Arrant: extreme. Makebate: one that excites contention & conflict.
Leander: from Greek myth of young love. He swam the
Hellespont each night to see and make love to Hero.
Poemander justified: a figure in poetics
and: from the Egyptian—justified: true of voice Ma-kheru; The Prisse Papyrus,
The Per-Em-Hru, I. Meyer, "Oldest Books in the World" (Kessinger Publishing's
Rare Mystical Reprints, Kessinger.net, ISBN: 1-56459-486-6), 45, etc.
Advanced (via The Negative Confession) Philosophy, I would say, Rorty!
Covering public and private selves, the 'thing' "as It Is in Itself".

YARN FOR A SEASON

"...and spring was but a season of the year."
P. Ovidius Naso

Writ by every mind that's laid on;
known in the yes of nods, no of mortals, bantling cries
and humus sod ooing; sung from mouths beyond number,
this wheel of fortune, this jeu d'esprit
really forecasts no outcome.
At once frigid, warm, hot and thin from burrow,
sayable of beauty, harmon, corybant, then:
'without mode, dissonant'; waft in durian cheer,
she proves ambivalence in fail of showy,
with no care accounts and a very lot of variables,
as Jack tries budge with the frosty steed,
in this 'chaplet month' after 'winter count';
shearing Shrovetide ala Alcofribas; a hail goes opaque;
trumpet forsythia golden riots near the gate,
and for all her summer pretense, Pert primavera,
Theresa of the Undergrowth—tresses mussed,
clamored by all and April, that patter of verse,
collector of taxes—struggles hygeia.

A temperate primary worms say,
where starry night and stifle day portend fires,
that long before Homer burned.
Clear observations bend in effort,
and round corners even moon's luminaria
seems hunch fortune's bidance.
Bobs of cork! Revoked poise of the once neritic,
in its reason, up-ocean-floors waterous, funnels discontent,
washes, wipes at pace, could not keep, through thorn thresh,
bitten bramble. "There are tears for things."

But by heaven myrmidons, when "world is in its dotage"
and you've long since loped with poodle ilky and dung beetle—
others our story—to pen all poodles, save wastes beetle knew,
for man-friendly gain, treaded not footless your carbon load
'cross the plains of air, where Null-sinister accosts Felicity
to loud her motto, shove hell's piles, and lose that 'winter mind',
they're there still on our behalf, like all self-assigned
having "ropes to pull", nails to toe, wounds to wrap:
Null-sinister warning, blood-weal turning oaths over in her hands.

Notes: "Sunt Lacrimae rerum". Alcofribas — Rabelais "The world is in...",
The Works of (Francois) Rabelais; Bk. IV, Ch. XV, "How the Ancient Custom
At Nuptials Is Renewed By The Catchpole," Line 9.

OUT OF SOLITUDE

Etched formless, plenum number like thief.
Hung, the cheap suit and bad rent, un-caught,
so sing poetry's glimmer.
Sola, same achievement for edge walk
of 'smoke' that casts breathless, and branch as favor.

The ire commentary that came and stopped
noisily bract frith its froth, repaired not riparian,
nor doft stream derives lent west;
water's cold for winter's acquaintance
breathe allows of sail into fearless, so bid retreat out.

Eyes he some isoderm once isogerm
drift eighteen instruction sets on the draft esplanade?
"I need garlic!" the one in chaise,
but knew no clarification 'fore noon.

If sight displeaseth pluck south, quoth ancients,
or leave fed indifferent on starved bodies if,
and stand sore salvage.

If writing, be assured most anything can be said,
but what's that?
Men have trusted to a Carlyle quit,
soft like politician that prove inconsiderate.

Descension, biff cup of appearance and bis,
if time no devil, see how to go with,
even as gargantuan box, botch and bollox
rot populace, good Curate,
to staid decency, conshites flag, un-couples rescue.

Cough, build acicular long since,
it's nuts to invite health in a non-stick frying pan;
plastic never unwraps, lest we
over-privilege for those plenty tire burns,
full difficult, contain a drain and die of thirst.

Doctor, nurse judicious fad the sun in our wish,
forget grape-shot as unwholesome death
crammed with salable hands,
in big pharma's planned caissons.
Timeless Weary, our best, haul, against the fall,
and toe over, what adolescence must climb!
Have argument the heart somewhat;
rare, intrigues, already bastioned,
ignore memory chanced in a sense.

Louvered institutions solitaire, prison of study
librarial to shoot Solemn in God-close foot,
use allowance shake, wag: stasis, Socrat,
but mistake perils for good: nor is inferior
Luck Respect ridden code like.

Old Thales never happened on decay
just change of form and function,
only conservation of a kind.

Outside the One, One knows.
Only we have left to do no harm.
Just societies, emprise wide acceptance!
Tree outside runs wild in its wind-embolden.

Sky, crews blue, conversational with pink Floyd
who've traded not "hot ashes for trees,"
nor "cool air for a hot breeze..." snoods woody parent
quarantined 'fore the fight to haste, to friend, savior
and retrieve ghost spigot
where sad itty carbon, snatched from spot
was in old Egyptian 'second-death';
broken true sure 'nough! Hat aside, saved!

Notes: plenum: the quality or state of being full. Bract: a leaf born on
a floral axis. Frith: archaic: estuary. Isoderm: equal/skin.
Isogerm: equal/rudiment, beginning. Biff: whack, blow. Bis: again; twice.
Curate of Meudon — Francois Rabelais.
Acicular — [L.] acicula, shaped like a needle.
Needles = fall; Caisson: a chest to hold ammunition.
Bastion: something considered a stronghold.
Stasis: balance.
Snood: [Scot.] net or fabric tied back of the head to hold a woman's hair.

MEET US

Darling, let it not be said we hated conversion,
but with plain scales probed babbling balance,
and went tree to accuse Cleomenes his murders.

O Agent, thoughts live!
In these mark refrains no man is in pillage.
Overchargers of dispirit have long since quit,
our fathers' moral ties crest in the dust, are yet us.
We have questioned doom and found it worthless.

Still danger, in scramble underfoot,
romps honeyed on surly song
that names men everywhere selfish and heart short.

We have seen the exalted, given lift to some,
and heard of large hearts that in the herd past did.
Known then and lingering there
impulse good in wayward man
held out of thicket of grosser acts
by his kindly helpmate hand,
in august worth of forgiveness, as can,
sighted the short of worsening man.

There is a periphery to ugly anger,
the border is solvent to unfriend, and look!
Crazy fear, mean deceit and gibe ignorance
are not recoiling from what learning can.

I see a fine reveal to the fine thing
of meeting our greatness right here within
the warm bosom and joyous span
of blue-green Earth and noble man.

> Notes: Cleomenes: a 6th/5th century BC King of Sparta who "invaded and
> defeated Argos at Sepeia killing a large number of Argives, by
> burning them to death in a sacred grove. Argos would remain
> a bitter enemy for decades after this attack." wikipedia.

SIGNAGE

Shocks of wheat—short brooms
in the field of his imaginary garden.
Food is grown, one is swept,
steps gypsy drunken
and another day wears.

Time to naked records hidden,
meanings under quilt.
La verité most its anguish enjoins.
He loosens his tie, she shambles a smile;
a dulcet curiosity is found,
unbound to ingest a cloud
and run some cleansing mud over.

No other subject heightens so hand to quill,
casts such glare in light.
There then and renew,
molting cousin, harbourer of truths
Existence comes, rises to air.

ICARUS ACHIEVED

Stunning upset on which hoist
Left
And neither the mechanics,
The tar
Noel the joy has stayed.
We salute
Our victories
To watch.
Got you by the molotov goat hairs.
A well on stevie Canuck
Barely ending backward waywardness.
'Tween that and the elevator
Which are you riding
Pie in hand wave rider?

CLEAN BURSTY DATA

Retrieve we now our flocks of fancy
and sturdy them on mere pair.
Here too one knows more knowing not.
Perspectives glow miracle as before.
And it's nice to know, at these intersects,
friends don't misunderstand, if they don't.
We train, however camouflaged, a human.

As day star twinkles,
the soft paper face of change dictates to arrange.
Our sequester, light years across, slows this drying rig.
Every effort at clock the place,
brings a sear, singing manuscript fearing its conjecture
under certainty's wave lash.

But Toutefois, a page is turned, and we come in at a door,
show at a gate, entrance where alone must answer.
Conundra, I see you nicely silhouetted there,
no safety net, no casual. Lion and unicorn,
watch and child, proof of purchase,
whole batch pursuable idea.
I send bursty data, you send yours.

A-rail the fosse obsession,
now, here, compeer enter cattle-arena,
each finding traces of the faces once were,
none forgetting generators thus.

And with all this said and passed between,
with the going away parties fresh in ears
and still on coronas; on hidey beast
our polluted thought
in grateful crowd belief sinks,
and are sent more clean bursty data.

Note: fosse—ditch, moat, etc.

ICE IN SUMMER

Relent tug pull,
Sabbath in company won't always mend!
Out of the house,
on knoll that is someone's home,
seeing he too banquets palms to mouth,
has saved patient at his post.

Today, handy the rains,
he is rich in grass and cloud on the march
but not happy.
Mind covers all in its think-shop,
addition stacks the balance,
gardens wince massacre of innocents,
nothing hides under glare sun's grants.

Duff intentions, brunts paid earth
and men carving from the account,
reel handy nomenclature.
Wisdom with its capacity and quality of vim
is tabling desires, all out for dame literature!

And there,
buying at the court of likes
tug for comfort, 'eat before hungry,
want of ice in summer' and every convenience,
Virtue, in the hear of Heracles, chided vice of,
men who have yet to wholly scout indivisible,
remove held grimace from res dominion,
be volant thinkers dancing on pens;
and where once started fires, snuff some.

Notes: Ice in Summer—from Xenophon's 'Memoirs Of Socrates" 2.1.30
In Socrates' discussions of self-discipline and moral goodness Xenophon tells
the Sophist Prodicus' story of Heracles (probably after-Euripides) at the
cusp of manhood when one decides whether one will take the path of goodness
or of wickedness and his (Heracles') confrontation with Virtue and Vice.
And Virtue chides Vice that she 'stuffs herself w/ everything before she wants
it, eating before hungry provides herself w/ expensive wines and rushes about
searching for ice in summer.' The then mark of decadence.
Glair: egg white.
Duff: 2.) partly decayed organic matter on the forest floor.
Volant: loose, flying, moveable.

THE SECRET LIFE OF A HAT

Kept painful sun off head.
Shaped for comfort, fit and cool.
Tipped slightly crooked for a time.
There the cause grows weary at edges.
Chewed on.

Left hung hook near door,
more access and ready.
Stepped on when?
Steady warmth noir.

Bought and set for effect.
A Mercurial attachment.
The Hector brim or Slim,
close 'round the rim of it.
Ear muff's as ear to them.

Wouldn't bother normally with this stuff.
Some say they haven't the face for one.
I say cold, wind, sand, water and hot will sort.
Will lift glass, shout names,
make grab gloves, coat and hat.

Aim to keep it screwed on tight,
your head late, very late at night.
Thoughts undercover and out-right,
Come for a touch of their own
Under one set for thinking.
Cap, base-stealing.

Now ought forces pinned back at the heal,
Bear up secrets not yet revealed.
Here missions tempt us please...
Paint our lives in one of these.
As camouflage waves flags throughout.

MOST INFANTILE

A guard lyric immix a snow-storm?
Withy Caution oaths from accused Dictate's un-used back,
good offices lent to rank mention,
and myths and oral tradition pass 'learn-at-hand;'
while a pint of plain, drunk daily, if that,
tries bites tenebrife, hobble of lost sight.

To lain-in smocks, in priceless streams
beside great-walled canyons of doubt, where we washed
and were washed, Slight droned and dressed
crambo and doggerel, if that, maging the most infantile.
Entire days apprising Fear,
down narrow streets of acceptance to get ahead spent.

Found fed and warm as light wore,
Mixing-Metrical drove against Tiring-Treachery.
Couple Dramatic, who never brushes by Faction of a morning,
that more is bump and ride, nearly had that one!

Badly, his alexandrine cannot be saved, nor wanting to.
Izibingi, argas, pamphleteer, ashik.
Griot are rarely in pleasure as Longing's mask appear;
stay 'living in the world and loving it.'

Soon, cull a bad habit, one sings his métier
to unhinge surprise-loving Discovery.
The smoke of caricature itself grinds
of staving new idiocies,
where lobs are all net at that court of the gods.
Where better Plato's inspired madman, than sane one as poet.

Note: tenebrife: tenebrific—of darkness, gloomy.
Mage—sorcerer, conjurer, etc.
Métier: business, calling, profession, etc.

CITIZEN INQUIRIES

In the halls of trees spider webs glide shimmer.
The careful individual, persistent, colony drawn
and called to supper, counting symbol and inflect
(when they ramble is when we love them best!)
marks waddling Barbie, rotund sharpie,
tightwad governors of all he sees.

Controls humane-subdued, see scratch
for some idea of men in whom
the distasteful stare, conscripted air,
moldered wind and fabled sin slink,
uncalled, disused;
cold nighs on the way with them.

Under agitprop, oil wanders: sleuthed the foil.
Cropped rule, liar treated and dibs-fed the world was told
the marrow that swam in those bones of theirs
was blood and fellow and sinless hour.
But mar, uncivil, boisterous impudent
was not missed ghouling all he thought shee needs!

It was death to science and art; it was the poison of similarity,
a dulcet rue with them, when under soutane, alb and surplice
the Romish church was in its latest fear;
where still men braved their Descartes' and Rabelais',
their Louis', Robeson's, Bonhoeffers and Schindlers
Du Bois' and problematic Von Neumanns to frolic dread
And jest make of false belief,
laying waste the un-warmth, purged.

> Notes: Agitprop: Agitative propaganda. Soutane: priests' cassock.
> Alb and surplice: also worn by priests at Mass.
> Joe Louis, Paul Robeson, Dietrich Bonhoeffer,
> Oskar Schindler, W.E.B. Du Bois, John Von Neumann.

WHISPERS

There in high monumental living goes elemental.
The little-trumped increase of mystery and wonder
exchanges breath with sagace trees;
and falls to praise, Cognance, on its contemplate knee.
The shadow-peppered slopes spree and scoff
originality that only by accident plumbs
uncramped, a few corners,
where quiet evening warns soon it's a goner.
Our dismissed leaf of dismay, at decay on branch,
because the roots by Fancy were watered,
mums headlong through the corp air
for virid floor and its manufactories.

For the curious then to appear and save at minimum
a part of life, counting whispers with king Oberon,
who: were not the quest, but offered as guest,
that dribbled down the gamey side,
Inattention must lay wait in their relaxes,
kept from doing great execution among the mortals.
All this owned by, scrapped up,
frozen for one against the other,
caught oftener in disaster's wound hand,
swore itself root, basileous ponderous,
cream, white not black, don't trouble!
superior treasure, "Ere I am!" of us.

> Notes: Oberon: King of the forest fairies. Virid: vivid green.
> Basileous: [Gk.] king. "Ere I am": from Brazil (1985) film.

TELL YOU HOW I FELL UPON EACH WRITER

I'd tell you how I fell upon each writer
like an anxious, happy child on an innocent, small animal.
How I sometimes mishandled them in my excitement.
How they made me love them.
How I slowed to make them last.
How books decorate best of all,
and how growth comes with the practice.

I'd say how I got the scar,
why now glasses appear hung from this face.
You'd know my given name at the end.
There'd be balances mysteriously met,
and the man that I am would weep
telling you how they saved me from peril after peril.

I'd speak of an easy chair near illumine;
were discovered undiscovered countries continually.
How always in crowds and waiting on cue,
my friends were near at hand.
You'd know all the names I know,
and adjacent an end we'd no end
only more signs pointing above-the-mark way.

Some know what they know and it is plenty,
others what they do not, and it is too much.
Dare to say that life hangs from the tree of knowledge
like each stage of fruit, for pluck.
Brave the high winds of change, gutter with a classic.
Appear to stunt your growth for an hour
with something re-read,
as forgotten jewels lunge for pockets.

With the learned of the ages dance,
embark on travels of several lifetimes
and listen, if with courage, to that choice within;
ancient mariner coursed again and again.
Light watches dans le jugement
and books, roughed by disgrunt masters
foot-caught by other forms, will us on our way.

LEWIS

Maybe bend of light was the first sacrament.
Tenon there our too-tired tour management, Pausanias;
obscure poet condyle dragging now!
Tasks open on a rhetoric-chased alderman
wishing on her two square meters.
They go the "C" horizon for the long post-blast,
hook the banned, burned book as living map,
Halcyon their down-cow.

The rest can or cannot Job
darkling, careless womb of forest as water forebodes.
If viridescent grass, of late, wet jewels her crown,
no more empires their impudence; and launch,
if Natural clears her happiness-chocked throat;
Tv will river down, ignorant at frith of the source now.
And we will soar enjoying Michele enjoying Barack's riant face
as verities in their dovetails mortise round.

Notes: Lewis: Iron dovetail tenon made in sections, fitted to dovetail mortise.
First sacrament: says Einstein.
Pausanias: 2nd century AD Lydian/Greek traveler, author.
Condyle: an articular prominence of bone; esp. of knuckles.
"C" horizon: one of the named layers as one goes below Aerth's surface.
Halcyon: Happy, affluent, etc.
Frith: estuary (final outflow).
Riant: happy.

ENTRY

Smoke a blinding itch that tear or research is
paces like racer on heels.
Birds southerly tend that way in winter, spring brings um back.
Wind; wild, angry incommodious indigent, whistles.

In these watery quarters reciprocal-love treats fast and curious,
and they know the admonition Golden.

May gods flashing bigger eye, toll home
and count puffs at, condemned ever to norm a few.
Here awesome jewelry are horses in branches to boast,
patient-travel in diverse bedding homes into or out nidus,
and repaired, in courteous cohesion enter there our contest.

BENISON

As defining years dusty boots put on,
come waits to un-exalt,
except they that turn from bullets from gun.
Truly course can veer
when at last on some heather lay,
when spark a latter day Thyrsi-walk,
green, un-blue
not releasing siege engine on you.

They can no justify attack
course with Diana her dim track,
till dark ingenuity does pyrrhic use.

It's complicated. There's Endymion,
mad-plate love, her eyes,
and draws him through her intentions,
long youth and sleep, things he cannot use.
Jilt by the potent,
shortcomings explode,
but martyr men one way or another.
If 'youth is a gift of nature, age a gift of art,
Life have, a gift from God!

Notes: Thrysi: Bacchus. Dionysus, Pan's walking staff for the woods—
Pine cone on top; ivy entwined.

132

EVERYTHING OLD

Arms would touch the fence;
still, branches 'fight not much among themselves.'

Years, trees dance as veil and weather
blank and batter. And they dance.
Many-turning life, different does;
heels un-leaden lift inquisitor, bring gray matter
jiggle-of-existence that over longing's wall ever went.

May humus un-obscure putrescent do wisteria climb,
rise leaf-love, inch furlongs and streak-trail to you there.
Earth to some—alien. To we—they!

IN AMSTERDAM

Ten by ten, twice the fives was!
Possessive had brushed the Russian dust
and embarked the Dutch air.
"Dat wil ik zien!" I will do/have that! Like Peter!

It was the Aeneas to Dido admit
that hate born alone is easiest,
no family to bare spear brunt,
ills-falling-solely-on-him drove the courage.

Blues-song braved infalling star,
the quiet man's patience secured itself,
and in the magnam fortunam
of who early bode the ill-mannered Burden;
some basic humanity surplused.
Café's laughed their just-us just as much,
timing blazed to purpose.

With ganja sacrament then, we took our medicine
and submerged in its amazements,
as the mousing paralysis, a bonus,
nailed for mind excuse and retirements.
To the young, at last, we institute:
Live Life Like You've Rented It
before the cautions of age scum.
That way gentle giant, great protector Gratitude comes
shoring head to heels with proofs.
And keep eyes on the simple stuff!

Notes: "Dat wil...": Quote of Peter de Gross—visit to Holland
(But that was both our thens!) in: John Barrow's (Secretary to the Admiralty, etc)
'Memoir of the Life of Peter the Great' (New York,

Published by Harper and Brothers, No. 82 Cliff-Street, 1839), 243.
Virgil, Aeneid, Bk. 2, 728-9. The Lyrist of Latium: Horace (Ode III.27);
magnam (great, large, momentous; fortunam (chance, luck, destiny, etc.);
"vilis Europe" (worthless Europe) he has the Phoenician Agenor say.
Rudyard Kipling's' The White Man's Burden 1899.
Great protector: reminiscent of John Bunyan.

MOTHERLY REALM

Bolingbrook Green, sliced salad teams.
Better on Saint-Pierre with the ill-treated
than several likenesses fashioned
not least of which this and its,
as the unborn pray.

This: Be human.
No wed-less bark the winter trees,
no swain to swale, or Dioscuri to bite.
Loitering mute drop charade,
pretense displays care.

Tears farce not strength.
Eyes well for water made play this.
Soul, hollow mid middle,
full of un-hollow Matters' bigger,
hears truth's tease of wisdom.

At the border lines, small burden 'let live!'
the ordinary wean of mankind,
along, anonymity not ditty-beckoned from maze
is saved! their little Mother Earth realm.
Together they've attacked slack
as if it were the last of their enemies. Honour is.

Notes: Bolingbrook IL. A once mostly Republican bastion;
green—golf Club, etc.
Saint-Pierre: Island in Lake Biel, Berne, Switzerland where
Rousseau said he spent, "The happiest times of my life"—toward the end!
Swain: a rustic peasant, etc.
Swale: a low-lying or depressed and often wet stretch of land;
shallow depression on a golf fairway or green,
Dioscuri: the twins Castor and Pollux reunited as stars
in the sky by Zeus after Castor's death, etc.
Here—Deity stand-in.

LUCKY WITH PENELOPE

In some cases, We take unholy risks to prove
    we are what we cannot be.

In the clement Thursday of her smile,
squall in parade tatters he'll come
and it will not be their fifth sunrise

snake in his house, grope quick eyes
his kitchen, his stair, his son, his wife.
Fair and patience at play, Momus both sides....

After flyboat idea's kiss of fall, current;
eyes, love has seized a throat.
Plenty of time to get to that fragrant bed of mild.
Every safe place was there:
warmth in cold, frost for sun, burned bullock.
They could suck prayer-thumbs and clutch answer-blankets.

Wine evenings in that castle.
Distinct wave-front moved restrains.
He and they rim patterned.
Her's: exactly wiles, to wedge in wild-horse climes
of fast and sit there—first fully realized.
Where music fairs lucky hearts aim! The young too young.

In that, nothing more constituent?
In that, Love's sharp muddle, center to bottom?
Do we only an uncouth Antinous
adamant worn; succumbing angels retrained
to again fall drop; needs pressure to react
sights buoy a buoy-safe harbor,
easy trails, bowless wishes, zeal citizen?

> Notes: Antinous: chief among the dissipates suiting
> Penelope when Odysseus was away.
> Adamant: archaic—diamond; a very hard substance.

ΌΜΕΡΩ HOMER OR OMAR

Soon ἱπποπόλος (busied w/ horses) turns a page.
The book is in the horse-fields of our estrangement.
Lost, truth is all flail, screech, wild arm. Not soft at,
alder-like if men in catch of that—on to δένδροόμοιόω are,
as that king of arms; many and much-to-do match.

Thereon to this Cyclade, a mother, gentic same on
to tree who solicits as rind, loss of cairn—
we are all in our tribes, and there the worst fighting is.
Religion may admit of difference, but Spirituality will not!
Are one! On this: Ios on Ios, a son!—

Note: Δένδροόμοιόω—man of the trees, or man tree-like.

MNEMOSYNE Μνημοσύνη

Or like her over then 'never trod sea,' crouch behind a stone,
fog clears and she's finished fatidic.
Girt young Apollo wolfborn stands;
tender goddess who got from Thoth, drops appendage
and with thoughts confined she's gone as fast from him,
turns 'moderate and sensible' like mortal woman and whets,
"If the old guard of "Who told you that you were naked?"
and "Tie him to a rock!" more wanted—as they seem, its vices—
better-possibility in hearts, apple and lit-narthex betrayals
were serpent's wasted effort, raptor's never land.
And to give without receive for general ethos, far superior to,
so needs no inspection from recognition, is content to founder
before un-suspect who muse: if with the mind of God
men reach impossibility of unknown, and God hourly dodge
Fate and Chance as men do, could not ellipses form only Order call,
and buckle under that weight all but love?

"On the day brings sackly drop in ever-shade,
or with trips and falls Deity fauves mortal or immortal toil,
we know a world gains more than memory, fire and hope."

So she said. But for this goddess, her thoughts sleuthed,
"Faugh!" louden in knap paradise
as by aesthete pursuits, slipping time, was forced to bed.
Compeller's intent to daughter-breed muses by.

Man know the stable face of loss, rocky spine of goodbye.
Generations pass and time that charges all will not charge God,
nor can these much envision when the Infer-Hand,
lamp bright, will admit any but to the outer halls to pray.

Staying they no longer than that, she hugged That knee.
In petition, the cut of That brow, gifts and stick to ground,
were the strow only praise and superior could bring, allow.

> Notes: "Or like her": ἡ οἵη; Hesiod's introduction of the heroines in his
> EOIAE, Catalog of Women and Eoiae. Fatidic: of or relating to prophecy.
> Thoth: ancient Egyptian god. Faugh: expression of contempt, disgust. First few
> lines here echo last few of John Keats' Hyperion. From Ovid's Metamorphoses—
> The story of Calisto, "The virgin did whatever a virgin cou'd (Sure Juno must
> have pardon'd had she view'd). With all her might against his force she strove;
> but how can mortal maids contend with Jove?"
> Narthex: giant fennel with slow-burning pitch; torch.
> Ethos: the distinguishing character of a person, group, etc.
> Fauve: tawny, wild, vivid.
> Strow: what is strewn.

PASTICHE

Range never far
from that prospective home
set aside for you by you.
That place where are now.
Yes!
          Here I am!
Every I and every here
roll to manageable size
to make carry to the other side
not a trial.

And each belongs to you.
To each individually.

So, what must follow
is the admitable prelude
to the throwing away of the self,
escaping that trench of low-eyed feeling.
Breathing in of 'gathered strengths.'
Quoting self.

DO NOT LET PASS UNNOTICED

Terry Nickels approached the court hands swinging—
"in little dixie" stands a dixipublican.
Later, 161 consecutive life sentences
for what condemnation was done.
They paraded, those media tuffs, for my sorrows in my hut,
accused minorities: chains for them and suit of orange.
          Nickles had none, was in civil dress.
See how the-not-admitting fosters terrors? Call it mere hat dance,
which is full of courtesies?
Will you out, slosh?
Believe it, it was a lesson pawning spectacular,
ain't 'tacular though; furrow below is dallying you!
Soon you'll, Ok! For what reason was,
excusing self and never others.
The distrust in our hearing is the larva our imago
that after dispense, never on the ulterior soft land,
comfort-on-hand, will give party to,
by utterance or silent nod rout, foozle injustice, you!

ARTIST AT THE DUMP

I

Land-rider Dawn, who's glassy,
root finger pre-soot blackened amber fires
that in the metal plates middle coal up slow—
recede charcoal, yawn dawn,
the long margin civil.
Society you venerated correct, so there went!
Lever pull, armature raise, switch engage,
discreet components worm on a board,
taupe cylindricals, tails intact. Resistance pots;
and a father with electron tubes fletch immortal air
for televisions' tempest, core's innocent
in an easy look back; a day's hot packed,
drawn to escape as mule hitched, from the worry first,
before as sycophant, man married his machine there.

II

Sight an overworked day, "That cart, bring it close!
"What's under the tarp?" stood answer riddle
Sir, nothing worth attention!
"Then show it, at once, you insolent fat!"
As you say! Sheet grasp, light invade,
"May the gods forgive us this day...what! What is that?"
Oh like I said sir, he's found no place to stay;
there with me retries
but (more assurance) a traitor not I be!
This man of cause curious, shiv charm,
labours minute joy to find.
I like to think the outcasts' found it here
with thee sir in thy kingdom, what say?
"A poem from the fool then
and let the wretch be!"

HARD BY THE SEA

In muddled fud spoke finesse,
simple source, richest,
that 'legs snake and tails fish.'
Among, a common man, poor in antithesis,
reckons how with light film
that tumbled scarp to him there,
from heaves the sea, in his whimpery,
her in her beachfront stays a while,
visits clear space, catches breath
and pollex's through simultaneous.

Lay in wait for evidence and it shall find.
One day you will look, and the clouds,
so perfect in their imperfection,
like her, holy, will make you look away
as move-loving trees wrestle wind,
and wild things scratch and tickle pastures.
There, you'll not sleep *your* guard,
securing her safe in valid azure.

May men always op' doors for you madam,
and may you always welcome it!
May you continue a friend of ours.

Notes: antithesis: contrast, difference.
Pollex: the thumb.
Fud: fuddy-duddy—old fashioned, unimaginative, etc
what? Where?

SEC. II
SUCH A SKY AS THIS

CH. 6
BRING-ME-WORKERS CUMBIA

TRÁIGAME LOS TRABAJADORES

The markets peasant, are half-filled boxes
that light rosy scenarios at gun point
back against the hills, walls well used
apply retreat to problem.
We tell restrained decision not to be of
those who watched—debate a segundo,
a triple dores, the cock crows, Dios provida!
Zapata healing and Che suit of traveled foco:
that Argentine and beyond drift into doctrinal hell.
If you dropped first principles and bent to bullet,
it whipped a lot of us—this: how revolution
tries to spiral from paradise to brimstone
As though the fog itself could deposit perfection...
decisions only making new oppressions
and marching, lassos a river, a
whole working countryside,
love and destruction? millions to maneuver
el norte's solutions, we can fix this!
well meant tries, la causa.
But because worth is to bare any scar,
trust red as much as blue and join freedom watch rightly,
farms are worked, hands in soils
and pantries burdened fall lest more fear
finds to thrash we vulnerable.
Red scowls slough when blue's in acceptance,
As will the blue as red joins.
Wanting to drink your danger, I do.

> Notes: BRING ME WORKERS.
> Segundo: second.
> Dores: you gild.
> Pravida! God provides;
> foco: center, focus; a small band of comrades.

CORMOUS

Said stump, Scoff an Empire!
These hats don't work! Get a civilization!
And stood that place a thousand year
weighing, with the good,
out softer than the pointing feather.
A legacy defense of live-land Helio's
curl leaf, helix wrap that in circle with candle has,
whilst enemy and circles, circle.
Trysts he his predator drone to seal that?

Prayer accomplished, as he understood it,
at Good's petition, having time
from now till noon to amend, un-offend only,
as had with harmers reconcile,
that may have had all or little to do
with the life-loss of love-family
in mild mimicry of true benefit.

As blood-loved son and daughters
through the dangerous season:
"he doesn't love me!" avail were not.
A study of Cain's Able, boned to endure,
as half or more destructs tamed at
hairy cormous of late ravished deciduous,
tuberous, bulbous, leap-frog'd potato-like
in slow reverie, shield to aerate!

And while he did that, revived in new cover,
like the root fastener that lives in air: best ignored,
bathed in experience, with the harmed staying,
left the others to breathe and forget, awhile.

ἜΥΚΈΦΑΛΗΝ

Had they not filched to own line,
nearer destruct,
could have used all inner typhoon
and moved a world to health
a sun stood collateral for.

In the sideling rain of oaf that desensitized,
earth did drench, and down to their demands
rich-toyed fools to their cells bent.
The odd gray of black and gold
was even over lambastes. There was no lament.

Society sneezed, "How could you,
Why should you, Why would you?"
through the high fever
that was pardoning panzers back.

In the Èloges of Perse, Varese who translates says,
"… a poem is a super explanation."
At Bear Pond, she, another said, they ran
worn floor and more worn comfort at big business
and won.

And the 'smart guys', 'the only that could',
who, at Democracy's start,
gave capitalism the crony shrug,
cupped mouths that hands could not shut.

That's what were talking about:
end of history predictions,
how who may-tee-be sat aside, old shoddy,
a-kin that moon leant haphazard from there.

It was a notice to frivolity, bad wish and prayer,
that composition being expository, in its mainstream,
featly rattled by wants, chanced with the peel on,
the way souling, else road signs switched, self-stripped,
markers to misfortune re-educated behind.

None are minority the flop waste,
all belong, and that way seasoning!
Measurable the unconcealedness,
moral solicits Onan dismisses,
but like breast-squeeze health needs that!
Happy out, indecency does walk around on the field or
at the Big Dance, whence life for self gets its conceiving immigration
monitors. And we lounge the fabu air, as Asia's pollution stalks.
Bandanna and wide brim—not enough! Venus for everyone!

Note: ἐγ [Gk.] for ἐν—before consonants = in;
kephalin—head.
In head. Brains

144

REAL HEARTS AFFECT THE PEOPLE
(Part II)

(For Chinua Achebe and all Literature's elders)

That you were found by the light anyway
through dense growth evenly.
That one's industry un-tortured
must fashion life's quality.
That appreciative emotes badly cloak warnings,
Dear fellow Good teacher keep rally us;
new, who need our miracles.

THE FOOL

After Amiri Baraka

There weren't supposed to be
stars this far north.
We were
to have no trouble.
And now, choose? Say
whether you are or are not
        an angry Black Person
murmurs mid-day
out gamey mouth?

There is no choice
        but to be angry.
          —Or not!

LET THEM EAT COLTAN

As the eagle landed, back to chance;
oh volant curtain of so much wing!
Universe likened, crow?! No! Honk and pass.
Side-on, a Black proud! tears madly,
careless any observer her carrion, nose-up out 'a there.
See swerve danger line, yet, would her furtherance,
from the place than sklent, silent, dangler meal by.

Anode close-study halls of knowledge. Days too
fin science discovered not faction's extreme disrespect of Universe,
wouldn't make that contact. The right, Just! Any—
from a-you to me for civilization (mea ad absurdum)
that to a you must!

Philosophy, other bother! Am suitable gift justice?

Relationship, archegetes! triangle here your adjacent,
opposite and hypotenuse asides; less-cumber
the abc of depth, catch of camber; ideas that retch!
citizens! fetch! and a leg over folly'd wall of Cronos get!

Site there a Paris right bank a tileworks; a Louis Philippe,
who plain speech to a still learneager Hugo kingly sups
in a once perceive on conflict, when both were alive and paying
some attention! Oh, somewhere both were born,
Lord Happiness squash with war!

After breathe, bring back to plain and mark the speech:
"intelligent princes are very rare...They won't force me
into committing the great mistake of going to war...
the secret of maintaining peace? To look at everything from the good side
and at nothing from the bad point of view."—But, and that's your collar!
where, quire, is the day's respected Congo!?
Its people, its world's assistance, pressed by you, for you, are dying?

> Note: Anode (anodyne: innocuous; comfortable);
> The electrode where electricity moves into...

NO BOOT

Want it faster—the even hand.
Generations palaver:
"...please don't rock your boat."
Dangerous though the keep be,
surrounded by dollars for those same generations,
under a bale of sweat, to pimp 'em in a shack
with the tears of the clouds sweeping in,
our clothed-less elders, from initial bad meets and greets
through the late Victorian, after Reconstruction,
when every thing that had a name was trying to kill 'em...
Maybe these are the reasons to run, ignored,
staying circuit here in our a merica.

Sure! To fix a thing broken! To dance her.
To fireball anger and form it
a molten peculiarity that meander
to peace not bolstered by war,
but by war un-kitsched by the strangest animal among 'em:
a savior peace that rarely was.

In their dotty round the privileged have, assisted
by other privileged here, stormed the capitol. Insurrection! Thievery!
lying wankers! Treachery!

But the finches will return. I guess what far-off will let them.
Little, return! Deflate bombast! Every thin-limbed bush
unlikely roost amble! And "Guess," as dusk and dark seat,
moon in the middle, "who's coming to dinnerrr—Natty Dreadlocks!"

Note: Kitsch: [Ger.] trash; what appeals to popular
lowbrow taste, and often of poor quality.
"Guess who's..." Black Uhuru/ Boswell Winston George, Rose Michael.

TO THE PAST

Flight being ready we shove to side as the train gets off.
Documents feed from normal bin,
unless we've crook and flail with crossed arms
and that flair in mummy dress: which
top hat, blue-black. To other worlds! We're off!

But staying, come across Comte
saying positivism (one needn't crush oneself
to rise to unselfish, social feeling),
sociology and altruistics newly rear questions'
bean count to eternity's spring—
a murderous regalia.

As a man you might, as a god, must
sing it very where the veritas
collect through wail centuries.
Kraken come, we deal with that!
Pursue it Keatsian in there red shift bluing.

And oh, that wind mightily carried?
        Is that Madeleine excels,
her, I hope still, Darlene welcoming?
Mirage?
'Ideas, at first, absolute, now relative.,'
form back again.

> Note: As John Stuart Mill wrote in his On Liberty:
> "M. Comte, in particular, whose social system, as unfolded
> in his Systeme de Politique Positive, aims at establishing (though by moral
> more than by legal appliances) a despotism of society over the individual,
> surpassing anything contemplated in the political
> ideal of the most rigid disciplinarian among the ancient
> philosophers."
> Keatsian: referring to John Keats' theory of Negative Capability
> – being okay with uncertainty, mystery, doubt;
> (or holding two or more possibilities in mind at once) etc., etc.

JOHN STUART MILL
Re: Social and Political Quotations

Crest queue and
bend supplicant high time.
A tall reconcile of opposites
has claim on life.

Lives in crowds attest its provenance:
the drooling growl, found water, grinch season.
—Not drowned by conformity
nor to recuse selves at liberty's trials.
Now! Stand masters of the revels'
immodest feast.

In argo of den
eccentricity equals health.
Touched on preference,
same concern of others with selves pirouettes—
and scored a just system.
Its opposite, help's schemes,
overrun by wealth's parasitics.

You called the time to it in thought.
Affirmed!
And did remember how effect is hired,
'truths' hands bloodied;'
how each star bornes
new winters evenings?
I think you must!

ALL YOUR GIRL

Once I dangled moonless with night's rabble.
Formed the exiled, in featureless streets known for walkers,
in passage-search of female bodies
to cull untameable burgeon.
It turns in my favor that I was just looking!
Now, under late, no-rush circumstance,
have thought of women raped, removed:
how whole civic troubles outcasts as gospellings go.

No fault hers, 'splored by less than half a man,
even as: because a suckling pig he.
Reived, ravaged by desire in motion,
all they get are selfish men.
On islands, in tossing countries—
less of it woman's doing—
Eaten, set upon forever,
forbidden fruit ringed by rapine faces.

Nunc Dimitis! Men right-pressed to control themselves,
argue fair-excuse and caution their daughters,
sisters, wives, mothers
of the ways, captious, of men,
and after the "left boot sanded sideways,"
even Joyce's oneiric wanderer deceive tries,
seems to blame women.
Male depravity here too?

How deckle mood edge at distaff
set to fade the closing time.
'Thighs seen at a bench' or
where stair uncrossed a leg, leibow!
The whole citadel of bad-spirited maw
Disclaimed. Animal kept, but sane.

Notes: Splore: frolic carousal, etc.
Reive: raid.
Nunc Dimitis: [L.] "Now Release"; now thou dost dismiss the servant, oh lord"
(fulfill your promise; let me go; I am ready to go)—Simeon, Jacob's
son's words on first seeing the infant Jesus in the temple. God had
promised earlier that he would not die until he'd seen 'the Christ of the Lord.'
Captious: an often ill-natured inclination to be critical, etc.
Oneiric: of or relating to dreams.
Deckle: kit; cover; also the rough untrimmed edge
of some material, like paper, etc. left by a deckle.
Distaff: implies woman'swork, female, etc.

150

WHERE TENDER DREAMS HARDEN

Up close, a picture show: chary life in hunch,
suited to policed-rights.
Chalices, blood-filled, pound mind's sense.
Laxity, our aloof cat, fall in our lounge!
Rocks and bullets leave the youngest hands,
hoist on field of rockets, flash atmospheres.

This very evening fleet Distrust
with small advance on discuss comes,
has words and sedition,
and like stout guards or DU bombs that fly and bust,
block exits. We last in peace wud,
where tender dreams harden.

Then smoke filled eternal is non-palliative in this.
I spy my 'one-cent society' hard through a haze,
and before the Seven Seals are loosed,
knowing every cheek turn eases carriages,
call a looking both ways in that.

Colonizations, in canto, chose reconciles!
Jose badge's nation. There is a move to grace.
Treachery, with sulfuric grin,
splashes must in our merriment,
and Decent, in matchless solidarity,
heaves poor heaven and pours no battle.
Prometheus has met Herakles;
men smart their Hope, cachent, mean to, and meet it.

Notes: *Chary: dear, treasured, etc.*
DU: depleted uranium.
Canto: a song, part of a poem.
(Jose: announced as the only name to be given for a new
U.S. international spy agency; roughly—end of summer 2005 !?)
Cachent: from cache—hiding place, etc.

THE SILK TREE

As leaped on, a second century, the year has Brahms
entwhirled in the affair
of living within A Creation,
of mind's thought somewhat out,
or twinkle with the familiar of German,
French or New World philosophies
lied on relaxation's green grass back
when up better your donkey horsin' ass, felt, are suited.
We have found ourselves bunting on a wind,
noised by the silk tree's clink pod;
up royalty, up rascal; they play the clap for us
to penetrate into the heart of matters.

FREDERICK D. HUBBARD

In music's deep mine he dug, this artist;
He skipped about on clouds' thin carpet.
His monumental collaborations
and blown lip vacations
reap what outlasts diamonds, gold
and rack for positioning recognition that holds
aloft crucial effort.

What kept interminable strain on,
that day'd its nights and passed on sun
for hope of rote's wise route, whose interminable strain
stayed the great world for but a while,
is leveling praise about this bronze head
who all soul, spirit and endeavour is saved for better creds,
than strength and mere accident's boons
in memory's usually paper-mache rooms;
for example that must, the mealy halls of America.

Note: Posted to The L.A. Times article (as comment)
December 30, 2008, 01:46 AM.

12/12/12

Mountain, caught drift crown, this morning asked
if I knew the where of wit.
Yep, I! Up and over. Toe line, weigh wages of a kind,
bubble pop lets wind in as tickle root-fancies,
evident the way growth goes, picks fruit the air,
where I Am lives; and eaton lunches do two sides the pond!

As Baited Ecologies, in furtive cumber,
we had not known ourselves as thought,
there with the smoke, other air, metal part,
that sat down now, and attend, skewed to ruin.
Danger from screens all the good in them got,
no more animal, no more self.

Spoiler, that concerned its operations, wanted them
and fell off every wagon, almost sought just-peace afoot.
Lessons learned somethings importantly forgot;
they, of more than through their day, thought,
and saved a world.

That smoke sat consequence in favored straight lines
when shaker and curved were best and was thought
an un-thought, against mischievous selves;
where once apron, now crown.

Oh short-term injustice! Greatness stands apart.
Every out-lie fares it badly, lucky in its spot from God.
Triumph monuments the One,
a mile high and mile wide, we mouth a good, try!

FROM HERE

She took the waters in the evening
and care laid on, the lightest presence.
I fed, we were wed, Eros wore his newest clothes.
Surely that glow, in decline, would take eons to detect.
But resentment is an ease-stealer with an hundred hands.

Falter shoals, navigable now that I know
where the bars and banks are respect,
where this little boat holding in its binnacle
not lamp and compass, but light and season,
shows, as in dream, my small and great treasons,
how I am the very cut of man.

As, in shinnery with the "moving muse"
I will prance when weather is in meet to advance,
and thank she and these ladies hence
that my M. de LaVernaye, newly made,
was never so false to much attack a woman,
though I had shameful foray.

"To excuse is to accuse," the Marquis
said to himself.
All children are false
if raised on the meat of adult nonsense,
less effective for avoid,
less affected in this void,
I've gone from gold and dove to lead and owl,
and that has been the way of it.

AFTER CLASS

If I could but dance you twirl this madcap,
I'd friend a flash and encamp
that straight tender of the possible
we, at behest of capacity would never supplant
with vile rancor of tit-for-tat,
but gladden us our welcome mat
with a million courtesies quite like that.

This, old ages would recognize
as common civic, proven physic,
and wish these having-come times
mates, uncomplication;
wizened, willow respect to oak their grasses,
the montane's other elects,
and in that ragged trade complete our magnet.

And since, for instance, all heady for change,
our loft cognizance proves less-well for gain,
we'd clasp brevity to the clean of wants
and levity would certain grasp
the carving avidity
that yelled fire in our crowded theatre,
when young we were.

Also, as thrice the whiny end of things
advances and is beaten back;
when-as the habitus of empire is eased to simple,
those siring veterans align for dazzle,
forgiven, much like us, and spoiled by new soil:
water its spring-wear zealot,
locate easily their memories, in eyes fresh shut.

ODYSSEUS OF MEMORY

What a train of pities, carking woe;
un-wowed we by The Brine's roil,
hungers have too many un-done.
Limp from trial, another mask is down;
sore of lobe, hunch from travels
witful grow exceeding proud.
The goddess does what she can,
despite, avuncular distrust ups prow
of well-found ships; lost they drown.

'The Old Ones' caprice has tests for
believing's deferent devotion's offers, and
that's a trident-laden hand in the misty reach!
You feel your fifty or so; increasing weight
as each year suitors bold, pushes down;
wives their best; she weaves endurance;
usurpers, every etiquette breach.
Most men captain, are finally the gift of reason
to themselves, not these.

Clearly there are those collecting the demise of men.
Achilles at the hole, remorse makes a fevered friend.
Perhaps if vengeance held its hand
these slackers would be not out in pay,
once-vaunt darings flat with them and day
a chance again to elevate beyond mere child of night.
But memory, more home than this, wants you
to leave a son, a spouse after the bow is strung,
eyes are blot, for somewhere away the distant earth.

BOBCAT

There's a savored, lonely road
where oak and grass hunch about their tricklet,
that one early matin, the coyotes' complement,
at exhaust gait, gave surprised eye to meet.

Lynx rufus mowing on to plate,
neglected appetite; dear God, anything!
had that last chance scruff and bone about,
embarrassed skin thin of emaciation.

And there was the whimper,
before last breath ails gone;
that stretch-heard groan, in less energy come to be,
and present the ear its bell toll.

Led to my empathy and prayerful hands,
I asked the Author if She could grant urchin
better ahead, less trouble behind, more stalks crepuscular;
further felid he, in a safer more satisfying time!?

Note: *Crepuscular: of dusk or dawn.*
Felid: of cats.

UNKNOWN ARTIST

At history's glass—no crying mother said,
but the seminary? could not!
This became good deed
since only bright-cell, scholar-coat velleity.

As if rising over scenes, he knows what it takes.
Thinks, yeah! gained in loss.
After no cloister: book and flute;
boredom—a conceit not worth having.

Careful the many mastodons of un-finish
while too anxious to be of use to be of none,
he creates his twelve American dances
and Saturday never comes.

Note: *After the '...German Dances' by*
Haydn, Mozart, Beethoven, Schubert, etc.

THE U.K. BOAST

In that tall TV noon,
I went on about Homer—half-understood
master of war for Alexander.
It was my ring pull, halt, skip-trace endeavour
a-credit the gonna-do-beyond
boast and heady Americana.
In high-trill, a high held wallet-picture goal it was
of those I'd squire next
when Heaven counts her sons.

Father, mine, who coiled pride briefly by,
and those at responsible-minister in books
are The Wise and key-holders
I'd set the young and myself.
And, in time run,
when fuzz to years of gristle come,
and olding bodies carve meek wrinkle some,
through learnings' feral, will
the un-asked and perilous discoveries meet, still.

ADONAI

Some, like an old bear's unscratched,
at new language, phrasings, let the anger spout,
are mean but cute.
Please, if we are not captured and said to be extinct,
let us confess doing that, and not the scene bruise 'or.

Crank science and derelict art clap the start
cling to shadow that yelps, jumps
and mouth some nit junk
sunk with the overload ships of accolade.
Let men lean together on their troubles
and let's see how often
they then dash toward categories.
Great Imagination, Lord of All
who folds gently within,
if something could be written might please You;
would You staff these woven hands?

Minds could wake, souls release weight.
Go the big help, stumble if must.
Life wears rare episodes You showed.
Love us the good angel's wants, Hallelujah.

CLIMBER IN WINTER

After foliage has won her full season, leaves unravel,
meek sorrows in with the snow.
Of a morning, ridges combed of their dropped white,
spiked Afros attire, commend dug-in,
snowed, and for a while mid balance, happy by sight.

In cold's slow, where only other mover water is,
sadness jumps to contend angry gods,
that all, *the best* do not want.
There was never a time to be neutral,
ice warmed cannot stand in the heart.

Held aloft on the surface of our valour,
wrongs trundle off.
And the same fear of forever loss of good in others,
icy shoulders to our lot, a bathos had not bank with,
finds it cannot stand the so ledge of our knowledge.

BEYOND THE FIELD OF CHANGE

At streak and frozen chapiter, clenches spin
in a busy neighborhood among celestial societies,
where honest growl for circus-apathy stands in.
Every fit this stellar cloth, a comet's right,
voyager frets existence, treats Being in the midnight
with at first its fiery, then ice-cold fist and heart.

Ongoing from a tenth a quadrant on transects
limited by the vast get,
adheres its mass, more test the going gather.

Tendency there is in vaults,
to hear silence toss her sole voice
loudest among the loud and farthest.
Lord so-wise fills every gaseous mouth
so a hissing wish sprawls
with track superiorities.

At shave headlong shrunk to solo
beyond the Field of Change
where Giant Impermeable is said to live,
they keep to the country of rounded tasks. Knowing,
otherwise, Great Dark would hold it against them.

Note: chapiter: lit.—little head; the capital of a column.

159

INTRODUCTION TO A PHOTO GALLERY
(Life's ruggles)

Well, how did you get here poet "friend of the world," if would be that?
From the making self known, better known?! Wrangle?
"Read the work" you with Practical would say, I guess. And yeah!
Pictures may help decide, in a world full of eyes, who buy the work.
When, whereas, also yes! is loved the Instress-harvest Priest !
And fathering furthest Frost, use us the crowded speaking voice.
Discoveries well-used stages mount. And can't kelp thinking,
along y-axis men seem better, barely, maybe aren't.

From lookout, look-in on and Poiema, the making, form,
fabricate, do—"from the fault he does not remove himself,"
and piquant, piceous. Stadios, minomen, laophoros; the tyrant,
his persuasive allgemeine Ermessen, sodalitas and pinax of/by pickthanks precious;
rhusos us! Pintle to sheath and all else ; intentional conscience, rift of ages avoid.
Finding, are of All add in calculations,
with who add but a few and cannot talk bride.
—Wishing still, a safe place to space find, hours when you need one.

CRAZY JOE CLOCKS THE UNIVERSE

"How are you S__, I wish we lived closer it would be nice
to hang out have dinner, meet for drinks etc. Miss you
and crazy Joe.(smile)" —Sister

Constant company, source, like to think.
Hearts in sibling concourse at the hostel years,
detach from perched, steely indifference.
Aroint negative! Squall argot de-toothed,
there were cares offing!
Frightened river needed sendly arbiter
as bad faith pooled churn current,
and neighbor, you, err banister, this fold!

Ce bon la Vie! When we have met such as
unravel and wind at host our company,
ready the "Opt-out," Harmony and Contrast stern by
conceived in Art's middle, circus bread a foyer earns.
Circus and libraries, 'dough and roses,'
Monk's aside piano shuffle dance.

And Water, the breadthiest, looking up at vapor,
three or four rooms in the open vault,
fifty to a hundred miles route and high
in this un-panned sky appear. A diamond ship afflicts a diamond cliff,
and someone bled what it can be to be a man.
Still, CERN's neutrinos had 'beat light to Gran Sasso.'
Special relativity back on heels by a sixty nanoseconds'!?
Einstein a Newton? Can we this our obstinacy?
… Back at chair and rest, Conceit is struck
by the deposable roughshod of being accurate.

Notes: Aroint: begone—Shakespeare.
Argot: a private dialect, etc.—basically unintelligible speech.
CERN scientists 'break the speed of light'—Telegraph.co.uk
article: 22, September 2011.
A total of 15,000 beams of neutrinos—tiny particles that pervade the cosmos—
were fired over a period of three years from CERN towards Gran Sasso
730 (500 miles) km away, where they were picked up by giant detectors.
Light would have covered the distance in around 2.4 thousandths
of a second, but the neutrinos took 60 nanoseconds—or 60 billionths
of a second—less than light beams would have taken.
"It is a tiny difference," said Ereditato, who also works at Berne
in Switzerland, "but conceptually it is incredibly important."

ON PHILOSOPHY—JOHN COLTRANE

"I decided—I mean I started lookin' into, you know, I haven't devoted as much time to it as I want to, I haven't learned or covered as much ground of it as I'd like to. I'd like to cover more ground. I'd like to get my own thoughts together, composed the way I feel like it should be, you know..." *you would like to see something like a universal religion then?* "Yeah, it(there) should be, I think. It should be that way. It's like when you study, you see like what these people say about "good," you know. Philosophers (*laughs*) when they start talking about "good" and "bad" man, they take those two words and go so far with them. It could be a complicated thing. But it's got to be simple, to really get some good out of it. To really realize something you got to make it simple... Yeah, well...I think the majority of musicians are interested in truth, you know—they, well they've got to be because a thing, a *musical* thing *is* a truth. If you play and make a statement, a musical statement, and it's a valid statement, that's a truth right there in itself, you know... all musicians are striving to get as near perfection as they can get. That's truth there, you know... And as far as [being] religious, if a guy is religious, then I think he's searching for good, he wants to live a good life...Yeah, I get wound up in it, man, you know, and I get confused. Then I have to forget about it for a while..."

Part of interview w/ August Blume.
—*Coltrane on Coltrane: The John Coltrane Interviews*
Edited by Chris DeVito

CH. 7
A COMMENTS CAPER

On Art:
"American Artist: Earl Mott: Painting Peaceful Landscapes"

This Texas painter, instructor, and writer creates landscapes filled with soft light, sweeping atmosphere, and peaceful serenity.
Interview by Allison Malafronte
Eternal Spring, 1991, oil, 14 x 23. Collection Mr. J. Val Smith; etc.
"American Artist": "For those readers who are unfamiliar with you/your work, please..."

COMMENT
JUNE 12, 2008 AT 11:48 AM

Art at its best is honest and open. And that is why, knowing this about it, the race of Earth's inhabitants (need we point plant, man and beast) tend to trust and somehow revere it.
—Gratitude to Mr. Mott's revelations.

Nearly every and any achieving what may be read as success has probably arrived, at that temporary rest from travel, way of what Mr. Mott named "determination and tenacity", "I keep at it..." so that one sapling will find footing, another not. One grayling cloud will evaporate this hour, the other may not. One man struggling, a Mr. Einstein for example, could say (banking much help along the way) "It's not that I'm so smart, it's just that I stay with problems longer." And there, it seems, is to be found answer, question and method, with Fortune's hand at caress on all shoulders, somehow.

Posted by: Joseph Duvernay

On The Movie Business:
a series of comments made by a New York
Movie Director regarding hiring African Americans
on his films— all positions...causing, we can now say,
a daughters' Crew List!

CHANSON ON A MINUTES' IMPLORING

Still own advice following. There has been a strain in men that has consistently with separation from we handed to their eager once and future anxieties, paving difference's it's-just-business's shame-fragile hand cupping late out of Northern climes, once via Sudan, then Egypt, Phoenicia to have dispensation special prior from, in the laughs of men walked on with. But these have found comforts lying down on the rights of men, general, (just-us! patients these); and never from there have truths useable tried lots on the useable air that was of old hospitality's special place, civility provided. Some wisdoms are beyond Sophia, and mid the ancients is child and senior. But these know not that for 'twas only the really fast fix asked for back when and the feel full part never given. Ziltch, filch, hid intelligence, and pose these-against-those for upper to lower's dualist maintenance—such prejudices need only the nod, whisper and back-stab angle of we-against-them, head-patted, to rise, for a sorry time, ahead. So first or second or third as a dead party anode, because modeling special interest over overall kind. A snake described Elephant written down twice. Here, far from shore, a-tow out, '(ex)plore a saying said not till perhaps now. Of one against another type—view present day America, everywhere, and would The-true-message-learned TO us all of non-violence; but not! of an Israel and a lot of joy-cashed ground on mound, mold mother earth, that noticing itself might have a bit of ease fostered. Life is not cheat, it is we, I without soft touch initiate, again, on the help-if-might touchstone day and night when we are so special interest as to dangerous the whole BE. Many! the re-think now—quickly!—unstable verities

ON AN EPITHET
One Commentator's 'Joke' about the 'n' word.
Published in a comment section on The World Wide Web
(Web Site forgotten!) 2017

Be aware lovers of Good, Common Sense and Philosophy's musings through the centuries, that Thomas Carlyle is here, as elsewhere, asked to carry a burning cross, that reading 'most' of his works directly, one finds he very mush eschewed. Read here no defense of his 19th century foul-mouth antics among that 'happy few' who lived lives void of a sensible, honest observation in keeping with what they often secretly expressed, both intolerant and (with stretch) otherwise, of The Black Man—and hear the foul-mouth in-human fellow, heading up the affair/'lecture' spout his lie-based venom, un-proud of and/or frightened by possible repercussion (this is the hooded sheet-wearer) of whom, only a portion of his 'proud' back can be seen.
"When we take over..." he starts...

Make no mistake, we who are alive to honesty, moral heroism for the whole of mankind, etc. ARE, as we have been for the last 500 plus years, at WAR with these!

PROSPECT

Assign alleged contorts swivel west for prompts Examinant!
Not only scant rest young titan west where new ideas moniker.
But That sturdy sun penetrates. Where life lays down for a little or a lot.

Now your saw-tooth ridge Guardian leaving. Yet anyway expect,
and here and there get that draft that got there. As through a smoke,
always present, clearing sky tells; tumult, monument,
the dietary and parchment, less-angry Sheen whys belligerence;
and conscious more the who's come clear,
as final on severity in high praise to the holy past pray.

'How, where, when and if at any time I did please 'Great One.
With, of course, the high smoke rise of fated limb, but also
with sear-heart, penitent, that savor, then this victory, O The People, grant
over their self-appointed overseers. What foe his belief and picadilloes impose;
who scripts dance round carried cross. Sacrilege. and the fire of fools;
who would torch-up, burn some flesh, but never light!'
"Cause they're not fighting for the right thing. Tell them we know
what they're hiding. They don't know a thing about the right thing."

Then, transitional, a hologram, the Sunday Times Enchantment section
high screening, your dipped feet in sacred non-stress of couch-like streams
have you barely wandered off killing comforts like the all-comic seated,
heated power mower or a dozen other modern helps
—Man invented his coach, but lost the use of his feet Proust said.—

Or like the absent, ancient scythe—chances at exercise in which we,
oh! Savior ourselves saved! Did! not didn't!' And remember your father,
a carpenter was, if he was, who shouldered work others wouldn't
even in that ready-for-rest labour, and who was,
by those held the beneficence to know him,
known as a man could count on to be strong, conscientious, kind,
and ever-patient with God's creation. Add your tries here sufferent!
Guide certainly, there is lesson in, and the equilibriums teetering.
Those harder than necessary through life's beetle-brow
or large scale cowardlies on Liberty, the illegitimate pressed bigotries,
reptile-brains' un-added sums; in A One for All america could say,
discussing, enjoyment receiving at lecture with the traitorous lecturer
on Thomas Carlyle—his texts—also that of The N*^*^r Quest...
and, "I can't say that..." then you initiating more laughable-in-that-company
umphs and knist! In your nazi vein, let ride, een here
"When we take over there'll be no more of that!" fault arithmetics of every sot
climb, with their poisonous brill, the ugly, selfish, unfair incident bespeak you
        You tube!
And like cops on the white bad guys' side then and now—are the biggest of
        cowards.
And I too pay that cops' salary!

Sued soma then, distended agonies encountered less dragon, more rat
from a shoulder from the rear; a cower, and the east may have!
if hiding your 'kind' among; that guilty capture, close-held untruths
to hold that, the wicked story of you wicked one, tell.
Easily loosened, your strum und drang to mankind alter.

Yet here stand. Just here! Duel of death in,
with 'who would destroy now Earth"
and insist in no remembered polite, that s/he not!
That the small, legitimately occupied, vulnerable, least protected
that columned predators have on wish lists for batters,
are by servant hand, dear Dios, made to ease, be happy and able if like,
to watch double dealers, cheats, and pouncers Prud'hon! corrected.
No also easily twisted Ayn Randism, or other serious Thinkers, again,
lassoed and forced to corral for their evil human stain; that no Reason,
nor good objectivism, can bring to credit under any heaven.

Who like bewildered fox mid screech, dust and feather-fly of chickens
scattered up in a barnyard; who now bested, confused, mortified (he fox)
all foul perched too high, at last made to turn-away if can, skulk:
limbs and breath failing, stomach emptier, destined never to come back,
enlists self—an embarrassment in every way.

Or, of friend wind may remind, who by mere blows, huddleleaf phalanx
    disperses
on tracks various, predicted there, never to come back.
Not for ease of attack, but for success not lack.

So. Pallets-of-courage prodigious in ark will not by you be stacked,
put up? Unbundled, spread wide, acquired then entire world that
with Will, Intention and Right Thought helps a little on a side? Okay!

And still, by man's callous shocked, Cybil's and maenad,
Nymph delicate for the most, on every part of realm,
forth for the historic revel, mysticism denier, of man conscious,
through great discomfort and distrust, come, finally, to himself.

> Notes: "Cause they're not..."—Jamaican song. Heard on KPFK.
> Pierre-Paul Prud'hon (who was the kin of victim of Love (her tragedies),
> that many were, including the Danish prince of the bard before him, and ...
> bid apologies for men dear women!) 1808, Canvas (244 cm x 295 cm) Louvre.

ON A PERCEIVED SLIGHT:
OF THE POETRY OF LADY PHILLIS WHEATLY

Striking C. ____ on your going in, onto the property, then way off, away and out past the last lights or edge of forest out back, which haps like detract in a background from ever friendly, one hopes, lungings into one or another piece of art. As is the work done. And no cheap with that.

I find for simple ( ) self, the jetting past One for most that we moderns have these last few decades given over to fears' feed on greed and the like (not accusing you. Your efforts are appreciated.) the miscalculation we must sight away from. Back to one, start again.
(It was the metric breakdown and other scientifics that got me with spear and shield out of tent, I now ascent.) But surely do I degrade.

Yet the start here (I admit—for me. And sharing am.), from my past's with present's view is as you know, your felt point-and-pass mention of the feel of the work by Lady Phillis Wheatly, (by) which as course, of course even the failing less educated, jump, her ship aboard.

ON A POET'S OBIT:
THE POET DEREK WALCOTT

Of Life and Love! Of master workers!—All things go to rest!—Sure the breath is Life, its bond is Love! His contretemps, his peripeteia with the decidedly tricky, non-poetic pis aller against the celebrated, that good literature in its adopt of voracious market behaviors tried on him toward the end, will, like the late petal in earth's change of seasons, sputter, fall and dehisce with the worst of em, as the flora he sparked, begot, in full write and paint, that has never done anything but bloom, does so renewed for discoverers again and again, if we are fortunate! The Maker is thanked for you Sir! now further above.

CH. 8
A TRANSLATIONS HOP

HOMER'S ILIAD
FROM: BK. I, ALPHA

Achilles to Agamemnon and the assembly—

"...Son of Atreus, now that we have been beaten back again, I think
again we shall return home if perhaps from death we escape;

A61. if truly the battle and the plague at the same time we Achaeans
   overcome.
But come! Surely of some seer or priest we may ask,
who is also a dream interpreter, what the idea from Zeus is,
who perhaps will say what so much keeps here Apollo;
and if, of course, he our prayers is reproaching, and if our sacrifice,
whether of the fat of lambs or goats, he might accept
willingly and partake, and us bring back and protect from destruction."
Truly, in this way he spoke, and when he had finished and sat down,
Calchas, the son of Thestor, of the bird-interpreters, by far the best,

who knows that that is, and that that shall be, and what before was,

71. and who guided the ships of the Achaeans into Ilium (Troy)
through his gift of prophecy, which he was granted by Phoebus Apollo;
this was his own well considered address. And he spoke,
"O Achilles, you have bid me, beloved of Zeus, to speak
of the rage of Apollo, the free-shooter lord.
Therefore I will say; and do you heed my words
exactly, as I with eager words and hands assist.
For truly I alone of men am about to anger, he who greatly all
the Argives (Greeks) rule and whom they, the Achaeans obey,

for mightier is the king, when angered than a lesser man.

81. For even if his anger today he may repress,
and alas also later, afterwards he may hold the grudge, until he gets his
   revenge,
there in his breast, but I will interpret if you protect me."
And replying, spoke swift-footed Achilles,
"Take heart, by all means, and tell what the oracle says,
for surely Apollo, the beloved of Zeus, whatever you Calchas
may pray, the oracle will make manifest to the Danaans.
Not anyone, while I live and look upon the earth,
shall bear heavy hands against you, beside these hollow ships,
even if all the Danaans together with Agamemnon say it of me

91. who is exulted much the bravest of the Achaeans, will I abandon you."
And then indeed the blameless prophet took courage and spoke,
"Of course, I hope neither this prayer nor sacrifice is found fault with;
moreover, on account of the priest, whom Agamemnon has dishonoured,
not freeing the daughter and not even accepting the ransom,
naturally the Free-shooter grief gave and will continue giving it.

And not before this the Danaans grievous ruin will he push-off
until indeed, back to the beloved father we give his bright-eyed girl
un-bought, without a ransom paid, and bear holy sacrifice
into Chyrsa. Then perhaps him we might appease and win over."
A101. Having spoken in this way he sat down, and among them stood-up
the protector, son of Atreus, the great ruler Agamemnon,
enraged; and the great anger, very dark, his heart
filled, and his eyes seemed to blaze with fire.
Calchas first, he wickedly eyed, accosting.
"Prophet of evil, not ever, at any time, for me the good have you spoken.
Always with you evils are dear to your heart to prophesy,
and not yet, any helpful word have you spoken nor accomplished,
and now, among the Danaans your prophecy is telling
how indeed because of the Free-shooters griefs, made

111. because I, the maiden Chryseis's splendid ransoms
was not willing to accept—since much I am planning her
at home to keep, and in fact mark! I do prefer her to Clytaemenstra
my lawfully wedded wife, since she is not inferior to her,
not in build, nor beauty, nor as you know in disposition nor yet in
accomplishments.
And moreover thus, I am willing to give her back if that indeed is better.
I prefer the soldiery to be safe, rather than to be killed.
On the other hand, for me a prize immediately prepare, in order that not
     alone
among the Argives without a prize I go; for it is not seemly
you see, that for all this my prize has gone elsewhere."

121. To this then answered the swift-footed divine Achilles,
"Son of Atreus, most glorious, most greedy for gain of all,
how in fact, to you, shall the great-souled Achaeans give a prize?
Not from what perhaps we know much in the common stores lies,
but what we from the pillaged cities have divided,
the soldiery have not reassembled, these to gather together.
Moreover you surely now this to the god should give up;
on the other hand the Achaeans,
triply and quadruply shall atone for whether Zeus could ever

grant the well-walled city of Troy to be utterly sacked."
And this being reply, spoke the ruler Agamemnon.

131. "Not truly thus, although being brave, god-like Achilles,
do you deceive my mind, since you do not outwit nor win me over.
Do you wish, in order that you yourself may keep your prize,
that on the other hand, I thus
should be sitting lacking and be urged to pay?
But come! Surely the great-souled Achaeans will give a prize
that suits down to my soul, which is of equal value.
For if they do not give it, I perhaps for myself will take
coming, either thine or Ajax's prize, or Odysseus'

the revered, for. And that will anger when it goes.
If moreover you indeed and these declare this,

141. then go to and launch the black ships into the friendly sea
and therein oarsmen in sufficient numbers gather so in reverence
we may place on, herself, Chryseis of the lovely cheeks,
and cause one who is a commander of men, full of counsel—let it be
Ajax or Idomeneus or the divine Odysseus,
or you son of Peleus, of all the most redoubtable of men,
in order that we the Free-worker may appease by performing the sacrifices."
And, as you might expect, with a scowling look, the great runner Achilles
    spoke.
"Alas, clothed in shamelessness and mindful of gain,
how can you zealously command the trust of the Achaeans

A151. when neither on the expedition you are going, nor with mighty men do
    fight?
For not on account of me they came, the Trojan warriors
here to battle, since not any, to me, are blamable.
For in fact, not at any time, ever, my oxen did they drive-off, nor my horses,
nor once, in Phthia fertile, man-nourishing,
my crop did they ruin, as surely very many between us,
are the shadowy mountains and loud-roaring seas.
But you, oh great shameless one, we joined together with to please;
the honour of Menelaus and you to save, dog-eyed
before the Trojans. Of these, not any are you concerned or care for;

161. and now my prize, you yourself, to take away threaten,
which upon much did I toil, and that was given me by the sons of the
    Achaeans.
Not truly, to you ever, did I hold an equal prize, when the Achaeans
sacked a well-thriving city of the Trojans.
Moreover, in the greater onrushing of war
my hands accomplish, but whatever division of spoils comes,
for you the prize is much greater, and I, though it be of slight value, but dear
    also,
go holding it to the ships, since perhaps I may suffer in the battles.
And now I go to Phitia, since it is more profitable
to go home with my beaked ships, nor you, I think

171. here dishonoured are, as wealth and riches are heaped up."
And he answered then did the king of men Agamemnon,
"Run away, by all means, if your spirit has been urged, nor you I indeed
entreat because I remain; beside, by me indeed are also others
and they will honour me, and most of all the prudent advisor Zeus.
For most odious to me, you are, of all the god-nourished kings;
always for you, strife is dear, and fights and battle.
If you are very stern in this, God perhaps to you indeed will grant
your going homeward with your ships and your followers
the Myrmidons you rule over; and, of you, I do not reck

181. nor consider your anger; but I will threaten you thus:
Since me, he, Phoebus Apollo is depriving of Chryseis,
she, on the one hand, I, with my ships and my followers
shall escort; on the other, I shall but lead Briseis of the lovely cheek
myself, from your tent, in order that, with your prize, well may they know
how much mightier I am than you; and that they may fear also, the others,
to say they are equal to me, and be comparing themselves openly."
So he spoke. And in the son of Peleus anger arose, and in his heart,
in his hairy chest, he considered two ways:
If indeed, the sharp sword he should draw from his thigh,

A191. they, counselors all, surely would stand up, but he, the son of Atreus
    would slay;
or, his anger hold-off, and desire check.
While he these turned over in his mind and in his heart, according to his
    spirit,
and was drawing from its scabbard the large sword, so came Athena
from Heaven. Sent forth by the white-armed goddess Hera
who both alike in her heart was loving, but also grieving for.
She stood behind, and pulled the tawny hair of the son of Peleus,
to him only appearing, and she, not by any of the others was seen.
And Achilles was stunned; and after he turned around, immediately he knew
Pallas Athene; and terribly her eyes shown..."

ARCHILOCUS (680-630 BC) Trans.

(Loeb; Archilochus, Elegiacs, fr. 19)

49 [Ed. 48A]

> The life of the impractical, they, the elderly join with;
> and especially if may they be fated to turn simple.
> Either stupid may they be going,
> or to desire trumpery, foolery, nonsense generally—
> this is the way aging is.

(Loeb. Archilochus, Trochaic Tetrameters, fr. 130)

61 [Ed. 56]

> With the gods may you place all!
> Often indeed evil men
> standing upright on the earth
> altogether fall supine and quite well going
> where their backs they turned.
> Then, much born into the harms
> of the possessions of life,
> he runs all over the course;
> his judgment dangling loosely.

HYMNOI

229 [Ed. 201]

> Come down, Muses, you good-beside. Consume one and the same.
> Be present here, bring the universe.

236 [Δα. 172]

> And with the coming yellow-red shedding
> stood hibernation.
> Truly life in a hole;
> that had taken up the unmanly imposition
> of wet by continual drops of it.
>
> It is said its distinguishing marks concern
> the return of the nourishment of pine nuts plucked,
> cornmead's brilliantly-lozenged flesh;
> inner things in their enclosed spaces.

NOTES By ARCHILOCHUS (A Translation)
(ARCHILOCUS INTRODUCES)

Aside: In Translation, if allowed, I Imagine, the soul of discovery, and would on sillily, a Chapman, and tell advert, both sides evident. Then to derail from earlier savagery fathers, mothers tribling left, another's soldiery. There to a do in cloud—Poetry, vary your win round that has grip taken!

Note further: At the end Archilochus (probably of the first to say it) says, 'Slay your fully-satisfied/ing offspring (poet), and lovely philosophic creations if they came like final propositions, none are oracle.' I agree. If you think they are that. And are un-needed.—One reads the wind as, with information, one sees it.

Example:
(Οἱ ἀκόλουθες σημειώσεις ἔχουν ἀμιγῶς ἐγκυκλοπαιδικὸ χαρακτήρα.
Σκοπεύουν στὴ
These scraps indicate, show, tell note the hold difficult of/from the circle of favor.
On the height you stood
διαλεύκανση ὅλων ἐκείνων τῶν ἀποριῶν ποὺ ἐνδέχεται νὰ διατυπώσει ὁ μέσος
in the bright light of integration of they who set forth happily under a good omen, sign
verily, you through a beating that in the midst of
ἀναγνώστης....)

NOTES ΣΗΜΕΙΩΣΕΙΣ
A Poem by Archilochus

These scraps show/tell
the difficult hold
of the circle of favor.

On the height you stood
in the bright light of integration
of they who set forth happily
under a good sign.

Verily you,
through a pummeling,
in the midst of that,
are known, recognized.

Limiting-sight and interpretation,
put away where as might smite a sty.
Mighty who, without disgust,
knows well of what to lay by.

Practical knowledge, formative knowledge
and instinctual discernment make the way,
are learned; alone to fanaticize what-ifs
and say of these in the midst of writing.

While down another round-about
are sped, off-selfing,
glissading the inspiration that spreads out.

Slay those, your fully-satisfying offspring.
Away the broad out-rivaling competition
from writers happily;
well-made, verily then, your arrangements.

I defend myself,
stand and rise off these works,
happily birthing future works.
Significance pours from me connecting these marvels
of places from which unable-to-be-free educate.

It was first I with clear fearlessness who,
awaying from the favor of those in storied myth,
before me, but also following—
encounter workers ancient-knowledging
happily you, through your arrangements.

Over another dictum
you bring current laws;

I count it any who pour forth
from prototypical positioning,
having given up whatever opposed.

These pieces [came through the net...]
and [are still present...]
of pointing out how those you select
are sections preceding. Happily;
something having escaped complete.

Moreover, tokens philosophic!
None are oracle;
needed because it starts
storing up the battle cry which surrenders none,
being your labours' circle of prior establishment.

Slay those you like.
Away any ready to bleat,
if you determining with your experience,
something came
like a final proposition of philosophy.

> Note: The Greek text I translated from was in/on a Poet's (I recall...)
> Greek language web site then—http://www.mikrosapoplous.gr/
> 2011-2013ish etc....So, I say I could be wrong about all this.
> But it's fun thinking ancient Archilochus wrote here. It sounds like him.

PLATO TRANS.
From The Apology.
Shanz text (!?) 37E-38; Loeb: 28:

"...Perhaps now might someone say, 'In silence and also
in peace with the assembly, O Socrates, such like will you be
for us going from to live?' This now, is of all, the most difficult to convince
some of you. For if I say that this, to God, is not to be obeying,
and that in this way with these there is no ability, in quiet to be carrying on,
you will not be convinced by me nodding with my words.
And if again I say, that it strikes as the highest good a man might do, being
this:
that very much each day, from excellence, his words to come forward
as well as of the other things about which, you, from me, hear dialoguing
on myself and with others well-examining. And who has not an examined
life,
has not the life of a man. And with these, still, little are you convinced by my
saying..."

Poemata 76 P.L.M.:

"... both the prayer and the sinner who has sold the world,
now, of their own, each, a god greedily struggles to invent."

P. 82 P.L.M.:

"...Go then! And life's flying hours sell
for rich banquets..."

"...That about goodness: that its middle lies covered in mud;
And that the unrighteous carry sails of white."

P. 87 P.L.M.:

There, by turns, fight sea and air;
    here the weakly stream penetrates laughing ground.
There, sunken, loudly laments the sailor his ship;
    here, mild, shepherd bathes in the river his flock.
There, savage, death confronts the unbound fissure;
    here, glad, the curved sickle prunes wheat.
There, among the waters, it burns thirsty, the dry throat;
    here, given falsely, are many kisses of poison.
And navigating the billows, he tires, beleaguered Ulysses;
    while on land survives spotless Penelope.

SATYRICON

Ch. 119:

"The globe now, whole, the conquering Roman held.
On sea, on land, and with the hastening of the two stars (Sun and Moon),
he was not satisfied. Laden, the sea, beating with his ships, he now disturbs.
If beyond any hidden bay, the yellow gold was released,
enemy it was, and doom in sorrowful battle was prepared
in obtaining that power. Not the people with familiar joys were satisfied,
nor of use to the common man were well-established pleasures.
The riches of Corinth were extolled by the sailor on his wave,
searching out the land for the brightness that would vie with purple.
Hence, from Numidia, see! Plenty! From the people of the silk (China), new
    fleece;
and the Arabian populous are despoiled of their arable land.
Behold! Another wound slaughtering and damaging peace.
He searches in the forests for the savage riches, and the ultimate reaches of
    Ammon
of Africa lest he might miss the beast of the Ivory tusks, approaching
costly annihilation.
Hunger possesses the migrant classes, and the gilded tiger, pacing,
is transported to the royal palace, so he may drink of human blood
as the populous applauds.

Alas! It is a shame to speak in words of the dying and the doom to be produced...

..."Not less in the squares madness is,
and the citizen changes his acquired suffrage for the confused racket of spoil and gain.
The corrupt populous, the for-hire state of their fathers;
its goodwill is of a price. Of the seniors, everyone; independent courage
was destroyed, and scattered power changed their rule
and their dignity gold suborned to ruin..."

S. Ch. 120:
"...See, luxury of spoils and wealth among them damns them maddening...

P/O HYMN 4
by 2nd/3rd Century Bishop/Philosopher Synesius

Found in a note (page 288 my copy Complete Works)
in S. T. Coleridge's *Biographia Literaria*.
Translated from the Greek

The closing eye and mind,
These and also those it selects,
Depth unspeakable
near dancing.
You the sire of truth
You the begetter;
You the teacher/illuminator,
You the shedder of light
You the make-knower
You the concealer/protector from harm
Private/personal light.
In all,
Through all,
By all.

THE ACADEMY AND THE CELLAR

(Song Received On Cellar In Modern)
1813

Sing: All along the river. The vault I dared strike; the wicked had known me wrong.
It's almost an academic circle, told me many a caustic wit. But what do I see good friends?

What a covered well mis-put together. Sit down said the company. No, no, it's not like the academy.

It's not like the academy! I saw myself for month.

Power to compete in the voice of the people with impertinence. A zeal on a nobleman or a beauty.

But by half-way, you welcome me glass in hand. By intrique am forever banished. No! It's not like the Academy. no! It's not like the Academy!

Toussaint coughing, spitting. Fuck it then! In a superb long speech saying: What an honour you do me!

Gentleman, you are too honest; or something as strong. But as I appallingly wrong. Here we can show less genius. No! It's not like the Academy. No! It's not like the Academy!
I thought I saw the President make yawn responding, Thy just lost a greater man than I'm worth. God knows how.

CH. 9
BOOK REVIEW SQUARE DANCE

RE: White Egrets—Derek Walcott

Perhaps, because I looked so hard through the slapping growth
(for like and kind). Maybe it's caused by any growth made while
the slaps were sent, received, that a sense of the sort
beyond greatness in the work of this very fallible is met.
Mind these not. From your sitting stand, read and decide.
But for me, reading Mr. Walcott here in his humble (however got)
honest, has set revelation lengths ahead of ego its foe,
and caused what is post below.

DRIVING VESSEL

Be a man of projects.—Scribe Ani

In double harness, wonder a plague,
he crossed the threshold of eighty and asked,
three years back in his Sea-Change,
whether he (and at himself he laughed)
would become Superman at seventy-seven.
Body, ship of state to rend and break;
closed for repair, rest, nutrition,
and the ancient's second medicine, exercise
award greatness the wreath and dodge of attack.
Each hand captains their driving vessel,
Nestor in the cart with Diomedes at a hundred.
All who on this eye, mouth planet, walked, stooped,
hewed, and drove from before Abram through
to a fighter in New York or a diver in Japan,
'must do more than when they were young,'

I think of those two Athenians, in (their) Politeias
who quote another:
"When a man no longer has to work for a living,
he should practice excellence."
"Eat less and leap more," Rabelais has
the peasant ass say to the dandy, court horse.
And my own tall sire only gave in when stranded,
garage-less in his Purgatory at eighty,
final sleep coming six to seven years on,
and still more man than many.
A superman at eighty? Life puts legs to it!

Note: From the Papyrus Of The Scribe Ani also known as the Bulak.
No. 4, XXI "Against Idleness," first published by M. Mariette, 1870, '71, '72.
Papyrus Egyptiens du Musee de Bulaq.
See note above, "The Universe At Dawn"
Oldest Books, Meyer, et. al., ibid.

RE: Transbluesency: The Selected Poetry of
Amiri Baraka/LeRoi Jones
(1961-1995)
FOR SPECULATIVE TRUTHERS

I bought the book, New, here on this Site, in June of 2004
and must surely be of the most debilitant of débutus,
or following closely the not-knowing, in prayer,
to have just now in 2012-ish, as the heralds from Baraka,
have, with such gifts come back, heard them finally crush brush,
twig-click. Then, soft at the door and welcome!
A master worker in our gradatim!

I know these, my enthusiasms, may be a show too late,
or the extension of too point an inclusive
for a less widish few, who are there to critique through.
But I'll only this grateful praise and safety
in the days' Sandy storms beg you.

And could bore further, saying, "One could come to
that spring, virgin in its sat-there-as-that, new,
all the back years as child one tromped green elsewhere,
or like silt was coming to, and be reserved in appreciation."
But now viewed, quench thirst!
As ministered to, as relieve of want
on the strictly splendid knows of the writer Amiri Baraka
we have accrued by buys, such accomplishment,
that here too, like other compiles I may have commented on
by greats—This is a Great and Beautiful work!

So if, on the slope-fields of Parnasse, overlook our Delphi,
writers have 'Starters' that place them in the race, as they see it;
if they're lucky in hard work: he, name him with this his
TRANSBLUESENCY: Selected Poems 1961-1995 and others, one for me!

RE: The Complete Poems Of Emily Dickinson
THE SHOELESS

Hand to hand like a tool her volume went, in this to prepare
I could get to saying so little that would honour this woman,
even with her – unseen – letter dishonouring me.
Come another think much of, scratch purr in turf
cannot come in, called by some obliquity;
oh now we are prepared!
...that I could have seen those Graces of Socrates!
That; Yeah! that one, son of Sophroniscus
who aired at Hellenica. His work of hands, they said,
that stood at the Acropolis as Pausanias tells us.
Why do some think so, talk so to extent
about this "Barefoot" one?
Because it appears his said, and did too,
were the sofarbeyond, inreach all men see,
but they nightwatch on the boneless ladder harrow to pick.
Then to say this is a work of Art is to never reach
enough, even with the capitalization.
I cry when I feel spirit usually. This Lady for me
in my reads, Lady Emily Elizabeth Dickinson, (more
Dickinsdóttir, and again despite the untimely racism) makes
the choke-hollow midpoint in breast that brings the eye wash
at her craft, eye and heart, and is nearly my kind of hero.
What she knew, she nearly knew from
the deep incrementlessness of what animates form.
Titled, clothed ever to accept the recognition
let fly by a stumbler she believed in,
who may have been right about that day's audience,
as today's will experience the far reach of her craft,
but they should have had the choice.
She knew from her reads that her probity was good, real good.
How could she not! For there is some sense that
if effort and not settle rod, one may acquire and believe in
as meal at an inn against the open roads' fires
a boon to contend with, the dry sweat in book form.
She wrote early 'she'd never seen a Moor, or the sea,'
(here again!) this with her un-publishment was, harken,
a Calvinism Calvin to please.
Anyone who loves the wind, flora, bees
and never-cowed butterfly as did this Emily,
has to take rank as friend of mine,
and teacher-less evidence.

RE: Satyricon; (Seneca: Apocolocyntosis)
(Loeb Class. Library No. 15)
GAIUS PETRONIUS ARBITER

There is something we would say to ourselves
had we time and patience, but neither congregation here hold this morning.
Yet would a signal fire send up to readers to notice this poor old Roman
who like many of his contemporaries and those of other times, places,
were lost/found afloat the terrors and inhumanity of Their time.

With squint intrepid then, having taken him up—Gaius Petronius Arbiter—
(Seneca perhaps later) with his, I think, unfortunate secondary position
in the Latin cannon (whatever the reason(s), perhaps including his sharing
of more than time, locale and circumstance with Lucan), with some overlook
of the sexual mores of the time, I have found his full-story prosaic
novel part-inventing poetic sense and strain of the highest order.
Content, what one has to say as writer, Is King!
And sorry the shocks of sexuality above alluded to,
this is a superb read and gather of intelligence,
which many, at least, in fact read for.

I found him (to repeat) intelligent, forward looking
in his helps of mankind, and as honest as history and the scholia
have been able to hand down to us. And so, Highly Recommended is
the writer/poet Gaius Petronius Arbiter, who even now, is
as many a great worker, enlightening, relevant and visionary.
The lessons, sorry to say, are the same. Will man ever
pay his so little attention and learn?

RE: Lucan: The Civil War
(Loeb Classical Library No. 220)
ON DE BELLO CIVILI

Now of the late love possess for record left
by he also of the overburden, openhopeful,
the effort-writers' fee, Marcus Annaeus Lucanus and not least
his hire interpreter/translator A. E. Housman speak.

Seeing the arbitration for modern minds all in this partook
was/is expedient; an easier lift lifted on Lucan's, I feel too,
epigrammatic first century pages; from love and hope
and bosomed humanity I trust, for man's civil, was judicious;
I scuttle head-foremost nevertheless, out swing door,
modern readers' convenience.

Superior to convenience one might find the how of the ancients.
More accurately—how they actually, literally said what was said
to one another, as close as might approximate, hoping to hear
the old language, not just gist of argumenta,
or another's phrasal flourish.

Here in part is the autodidacts' beef with academy.
And not to be tendentious, or drone too much on,
"...will he have the grace to shear off?"
I loved Lucan's pointed-out antiquity impractical
and apostrophe excessive, where meet myth, history, chance
and fact in a man with a pen taking chance.

Now this positions one snob; but let that phone ring!
Why should one not attempt to speak to all that occurs
to one's mind, in one's time?
So his work for the twos and threes of accounts and dissemina
had my fast attentions. And he drew as many specifics (cure),
it seemed to me, from the expanse (environment)
as any I've encountered, only Rabelais (and now the Bible) coming
quick to mind.

Neither the later poet's (Housman) translation
nor the original poet's (Lucan) work is anything but appreciated.
Still, a fine point would apply to the why, again, of the importance
of Loeb Library series, that offers 'manuscripts' and their interpretations.
And while I praise the Library and Harvard U. Publishing for this,
it is impossible to see a vital bud on a rotten stem—
the way they and other Western and Eastern institutions
have laboured to keep the darker of men among them down.

The catholic lack of remorse, the continued drawing of
the dis-eased ideology of whiteness out,
that in its blindness now claims a whole world: Wreck, is evidence
the horrors of this lysis, non-integration, (even as
are peppered some throughout, and even as the facile complaint
of the arts patron, "Don't make me feel bad about myself. I think
we need to insert some humor here or we'll/you'll never get
the receptivity of people, "must re-evaluate where we—the world are,"
in an integrated world, that life itself is piece and parcel soon undone.

But back to the book. There are so many glimpses of inner sanctums
of antiquity in this work, that if I were smart, I should find myself
re-reading it year on year and thanking all who in the face of some,
'I-can't-figure-out-why-they're-there! criticisms' almost initiate from me:
'Oh I get it, you've some kind of bias!' read on, read out and read it.
And still. I don't think all should, read it. Or, to clarify, "not till after fifty"
as once was said of Proust.
Not till one is ready. Ready to do no harm. Unabashedly for good.
Not near, not "I thought..." but gnothi seauton.
So I let its over analysis skid off.

But aloft. Hear what Lucan, Housman, Duff and Henderson give
for what Cato says of God, to his urging generals and thus
quickly fading men, desert-lost, hungry, and thirsting in Africa,
hoping he will test the Oracle of Jupiter Ammon about their futures,
but who respectfully leaves untried that oracle though caught out in
the withering African wastes fleeing Caesar during that civil war:
"Inspired by the god whom he bore hidden in his heart, Cato poured forth
from his breast an answer worthy of the oracle itself:
"What question do you bid me ask, Labienus?
Whether I would rather fall in battle, a free man, than witness a tyranny?
Whether it makes no difference if life be long or short?
Whether violence can ever hurt the good,
or Fortune threatens in vain when Virtue is her antagonist?
Whether the noble purpose is enough, and virtue
becomes no more virtuous by success? I can answer these questions,
and the oracle will never fix the truth deeper in my heart.
We men are all inseparable from the gods, and, even if the oracle be dumb,
all our actions are predetermined by Heaven.
The gods have no need to speak; for the Creator told us once for all
at our birth whatever we are permitted to know. Did he choose
these barren sands, that a few might hear his voice? did he bury truth
in this desert? Has he any dwelling place save earth and sea,
the air of heaven and virtuous hearts? Why seek we further for deities?
All that we see is God; every motion we make is God also.""

A man died here today! Crossing the bridge athwart.
I did not see nor hear the accident, at least I don't recall hearing it.

On rising at about I think seven-thirty, I dumped a load, and got
right on the bedroom. That is: with the vacuum, from top to bottom,
one room a day my strategy.
And, just sitting from that, looking out saw the Fire Dept. truck and later,
the poor guy crushed by the top of his truck. An old chevi that probably
rolled on black ice or just a wet-by-light-snow road. But my God!
why can they not build and sell to us, all would be corporations,
not high salaries for their robbers at the top, within, but safe virtuous prod-
uct?
What virtue? That of quality, service and environment protected.
'I'm through! Can you chime a bell for me who?'

Life is dangerous! This, everything knows.
Let men learn where everything goes.
Down through sieve. Again who. Though beware,
this circuit in the wrong hands may short.
Then keep your weathers back!
One may in traverse any number static upset,
though, through, The On! Speak to us times gone!

In civil contract, aside itself, despite meanness of even otherwise
Enlightened men and women are.
Mark who have no hesitation, or a little in touch,
are big-man-or-woman-vicious praying off.

As might. A strong, here again, lurch and learning work I see!
—That's why they call them classics! re-emphasize.
(And never mind how the author died (How will we, each, when
light will no longer transfix?)
Or one gains hearing his story, larger portions of respect—
as opposed to Lucan's, I fear superbias, as he should have been
in the case of the republic vs. one man, one faction thinking it his/theirs
(which, even today, many go through)—for Julius Caesar. Comparing him,
as he did, to the troublesome emperor (Nero) of his own (Lucan's) time.

A work this, Of man from man for man's, some would say,
own benefit sacrilegious.
—For these and other centuries to come, Travel well! our wish is.

Notes: "Date:11/10/2015: A man died..."
Lucan: De Bello Civili
(ix, 564-580).

188

RE: Journal Of (Eugene) Delacroix
Trans.—H. Wellington
PETITS SOUVENIRS

To say it variably is of the prime tasks of the poet. And I'm almost certain
it's hyperbole, but I don't believe, at this hour, I've ever been
more delighted and informed by a work of literature before.
Such Learning! "Get me a hammerhead Corvette!"

Valuable lessons collect in the journals of many who keep them,
and this, I call upper middle-class, even wealthy, painter, writer, colourist
Eugene Delacroix is example of such.

On the hook to J. A. M. Whistler and the circuitous ways of happenstance
for guiding me to Delacroix; increment, I should be very much too friendly
with inaction; add awry, deliberate loll and loaf egregious
were his name not mentioned here and early,
despite his contemptable stand on turmoils of his day like the American
Civil war and that of the boers Downunder,
whence in future he may get more consideration and treatment than he has
to date, because his views and battles For Art are legendary
and should be! as hinted in another place—J. A. M. W. I mean.

—Early in his tome Delacroix writes to himself,
"L'habitude de l'order dans les idées est pour toi le seule route au bonheur;
et pour y arriver, l'order dans tout le reste, même dans les choses
les plus indifferentes, est necessaire." "Cultivate a well-ordered mind,
it's your only road to happiness, and to reach it,
be orderly in everything, even in the smallest details."
Thus, and with more in great number, both specific to life in general and
painting, drawing, representations of nature in particular,
Delacroix teaches one of the ideals true art finds it must come to,
to do good, large work, found in this work.

Separation of Art and Science—to say that in art there is no science,
or that in science there is no, or little art, is, in Delacroix and others,
shown Rousseau! standing in the shifty slush of life-denying haunts
of falsehood deliberate or otherwise, they thought to make land.
And it baffles now, and brings crier call, how any artist,
of what stripe may, even a scientist! shall there do without
Delacroix's thoughts and observations,
even though this is my 'late' go 'round to.
—And then what difference does anything anyway make!?
The impossible to answer question. Perhaps the only one.

So painters wanting a bolster or lesson in colour, contour, method,
off-tram here!

Musicians inviting both notation, intoxicated point, counterpoint
(that Mozart once flicked to the dust in advice against)
and improvisation, you too should get off here! Watch out Baudelaire!
Well then, the poet? You, I assume, are alike all the rest of that breed,
ready, at full search and rescue of every aspect, sign-totem, inflection
and possibility of art, ideas and language, so add if you have yet to,
this mind to cache.

This wordy (review)...I designate in my conceived negative brackets of
mathematics, or Yeah right! antonym (ready irony) of language,
because often more embarrassed by the loss of good-taste civic
than informed in any real way by art criticism,
I desire to, in the anecdote of antiquity and my dear Mother, say
primarily what is good and little opposite (That's a joke!)
within flow-capture, within which the professional critic will find
no bit of criticism nor much being able to keep up, as probably haven't,
instead, in fact, hagiologies enter.
—And I don't apologize, since, as against much biting criticism
(again, Ha ha!) roused is energy and enthusiasms, so that at these intervals,
unless otherwise stated: these reviews are of of paean, kudo, praise, I pray.

In this, among primary sources, I used—The Librairie Plon, French text
par Andre Joubin with its gifty quires, signatures; the La Palantine, Geneve;
and the handy red Phaidon translation of Lucy Norton
chin-up on that splendid missal India paper.

Across citizens! in keeping with Delacroix's useful on brevity in writing,
which may correspond to that reserve noticeable in the best of art,
I will in brief, attempt the readers' patience and detentions more.

Diversion (journal inspired!?!)
To this dimension: Consider an agreement of terms!
Like in the good old U.N. | The tendency toward disorder in any system
has to add its increment, i.e. number, in the numberless. | Then, with number,
material may be present; i.e. a list, measurement, an article, a thing; or
    perhaps
to form independent power is added, i.e. The Animated!
Man manufactures. God Designs!
End Diversion

Early in the Journal too, Delacroix tells us that... ?
"'Corot goes deeply into a subject; his ideas come to him
and he develops them as he goes along;' this is the right way to work."
Work along. Take what comes; and yet he too planned!
And I greet with laurel his friendship with those lights of his time,
even though, he was as stubborn for solitude as the best of 'em.
There was M.M. Beyle & Dumas, Mme Sand, M. Chopin, Horace Vernet,
M. Rossini. His troubles with his senior, M. Ingres, that I'm not sure

190

we know enough about; and oh! to shutter his untiring Jenny
would be unspeakable; constance! You are loved!

—This man who loved Daphne-turned, touched judicious
on the geometry of wave mechanics, if I'm not mistaken, or
at least he went three-layer or so for their (waves)
dependent-upon-locale on the globe and sand make-up etc.
explanation for the distinct-place patterns he found in different locales;
that there was something un-studied there.

—He mentioned the regular features of beauty, which
recent surveys of faces, using the term symmetry, suggest.
An effort could even be made, to imply he may have anticipated,
fallen upon, put letters to Whistler's so-called 'secret of drawing'
twenty-two years before in his, Delacroix's, 11 January entry
of 1857, in which, in his notes for a Dictionary of Fine Arts,
under the heading "Drawing. (we find) From the center
or from the contour." And although said to be and indeed
never completed by him, he puts such a good start on his Dictionary
in the January and February entries that year, and right through 1860,
that it actually startles and even better makes his book.

But again, as he and others have said, such comes/came from
the study and practice of a lifetime.
His attentions to the details of everything light hits, and shadow,
i.e. "younger subjects have lighter shadows,"
and that "the edge of every shadow contains violet,"
very much intrigue.

—His admonishments against impatient handling,
one of the challengers of finish, will lesson every artist.
—The translations of the eye that, in arts that need same may bring
the very fugitive finish the artist was concerned with.
—And while we've all read others of his era,
and those immediately following and before,
oring mournful predictions for the future of man,
his June 1856 thoughts seem extraordinarily prescient.
—Nor did architecture, sculpture or music find themselves without;
and writing again, gets an informed, airy, often stern place,
as in turns it is buoyed and embarrassed, though
I was fed poetry I thought, and rapture. But that I suspect,
was because a tremendously striving artist was at work.

Now, none of this a reader may find sticks out for them
in the plenty of this work.
Still, like Life itself one must stand for her—Nature, which is art,
and the Melancholy after-awe she too brings.
And I end by pointing to what he said one-day mid-life,

"Spent the whole day by myself; Jenny and Julie went to Paris
to fetch the wine. Worked all the morning and arranged
my papers in great good spirits. About two o'clock
I began to feel tired and walked across the fields towards Soisy.

"I went farther than usual, but still not as far as the great avenue;
like Robinson Crusoe, I am busy exploring the interior,
and shall end by knowing all the country within reach of my legs...
that night I was enraptured by the stars. How quiet it was!
How much nature accomplishes in this majestic silence!

What a racket we make, who are doomed to cease and leave no trace
       behind!"
—I get your meaning! Long term. But Dude! What you Delacroix have left,
does so far remain!

> Note: "Petits souvenirs"—Delacroix; entry 31 August 1855.
> "Brief memoranda"—L. Norton.

SEC. III
MURMURACIONS

CH. 10
THE-LIGHT-OF-PROMISE GHOST DANCE

THE LIGHT OF PROMISE

The light part thinks
shadow of life is recompense in reward,
and as pleasing as She ever was,
laughs her great immense,
surges in the gasp of life.

Rush testimony of flight to simplest got,
winged from chills and callous hand—
unhappiness for the sleeping price—
masterpiece framed stands full height.

That's when you bank in flight,
fling your news along the chore complimenting it
and smile. For more, voracious cheat, failed.
And seeing a bird at flutter, regal on its branch,
Cried you, glad for it.

Innocence shied across the glint expanse
the size, frenzy, and severity of night
retired on the hours, professing
E might not resolve to D,
you might not come out,
Consciousness with other cores to scout.
But, you were just being human.

SEIGNIORY

For Leopold Sedar Senghor

What pooled and lighted occultation
now drawn
has shielded you from my eyes.
The call of Europe, Asia.
The response of new continents
till Neruda interviewed
drew me your high rank, shine nimbus.
And if I much,
call it discovery come finally
with scruff and bent instrument,
under the house of heaven,
to prove.
Where toil in the shop of license
is enough when fair.

DAVE

"Brother from another mother,"
common greet at the time, having stretched like gospel
its fifteen into many more,
used to break me up, inside, at first.
Smokin' Joe! his other.

I had met men and women of service before,
and always, at their care,
rose skepticisms, or simple, wondrous Marvel
given another gaped-mouth to conduct.

What skate upon; what was always collect
with a familiar of,
if not her majesty Cheer herself
came Dave with, where he went,
so all paths crossing grew in kindness.

His wife will know our loss is sincere,
and hears from our hearts anguish,
the cries of never again this blessed aura?
In the near term our pain is nearer.

There is a covert, by the goodness of earth kept,
that will his old, late corpus
in a rush of breeze to other realms,
briefest rest on his way, accept,
and assure the happiness of Happiness.

Then You-Of-All-Things be raised in bows,
and candles lit, and wreaths set,
and the tear that is rare,
each man's cheek wet
for Dave the Handyman, friend.

THE WAY

Akin to a certain beg of suffering
through long meme acquaintance thickly on,
our hero tills the many stone field
of acceptance of circumstance,
wanting buyers yield the over-caust view
that leaves balance out,
and despite odds and numbered hoofs on stipple grass,
all realizations, dim for halt believers,
are churning creamer in the eyes of winners
who won't let detractors stay their way.

And if our shero, kindly, emoting lass is,
cheers her happy slice, on display,
never held as excuse, older,
is conducting useful memories, bearing forth fulfillment,
to forewall significance,
and raves in her tuck sleeve house of it,
it's okay with her I assure you, and we here too.

Becoming belongs in a search for meaning,
and good books, philosophers, and authoress
stopping for a visit
are in time to see selves break into own homes,
speak repentance; and sweet the earned heartfelt.

Reproach and repristinate are hard-by steno repro
in dictionary, and stand between print learning
like a pillar of Luxor, that may or may not
purchase song on the hailing hour.

Note: Repristinate: make like new.

TRAILS

Trodden by step, brave swift
shift-artifice that recasts issues,
plies trip fresh distance.
I geld in phantom heart,
electronics cannot keep up
as drummed world wriggles under foot.

Not forgetting how liquid and solid death come,
like the Oceans out, I ebb, flow, circle
and swear shear sweep to employ.

But has Mr. Superlative the alligator's lasting forgot?
Organization measures intellect,
but response and adjust just as much!
Think we blasphemous?
Shoe you the hip-high grass of good news
that signs which way the crisscrosses
without sly cullies of, say, an Odysseus
that travel buys in storied parts?
Are the elephant in this or coxcomb?

Line breaks into song,
on ebon page Moon glares into wrong,
crepe's cresses haul for greens' smart ruffles,
and domed capitals' plow flying hours
that come and go in redact of morals,
junk ethics' taint, retrieved,
executive spoils, that bonus.

End-frame with the banquet of conscience denial.
There, fair side air roots, rooting in air,
oh aerial, pleased like young wires passim who
want to familiarize stun eyes with hands on
parabola in blouse, hyperbola under skirt, grow!
The best and worse, alike in varied houses,
helped in form of genetics are.

Notes: *Geld²: to pay, yield, etc. Passim: throughout*

BACK TO BASICS

Warning is contact excuse sent and mooring
many battered mornings.
Footrace with life, blatant, presents
words to proof vanity praying in time,
where chore at feet the murdered planet,
without charade and helmeted
in the virile meadowlands of the mind
are sailing vestal yard in high regard,
and rescind the form timidity took,
to tight sentence to burn like skin on contact
with a star.

Thus ferruling sheer net, so perfect in overlap,
bequeath of elements, acting at the long distance,
field centric, of feels; particles, planets aware of each other (net)
again—*apo, at a distance**, spooky, correlating magnetic spins,
where William & Catherine Blake's "the eye altering alters all" is.
The observer effect, and their Spirit of Poetry, me,
quantum entangled (net) without debilitating dissonance,
that arrives at a single scientific (observation, measurement,
repeatability) description of man's truths—being far cries from
thrown papal bulls—that nature's near-imponderable, yet adore!

So now aboard and embark,
cold stands in man's heart,
and plays and moves him bereft those
barren warren-lands of beware and emboldened
where simple abandon is still the mend: yauld, beholden.

Notes: *Bodies things phenomena affected, acting and aware of each other,
ἀπὸ—[Gk.] *away from, *at a distance—etc, etc. See, as to our Early 'moderns':*
Florian Cajori's Historical And Explanatory Appendix (Notes 5-8), and
Roger Cotes' Preface To The Second Edition of Isaac Newton's Philosophiae
Naturalis Mathematica, Andrew Motte's 1729 Translation, Revised
by Florian Cajori (University of California Press, Berkeley, California, 1960)
for 'early' comments on the phrase at-a-distance, that left Descartes' vortices
theory of the ether/space mechanics explanation for his, Newton's, gravity
theory (still Indra's net) of force(s) 'knowing/aware of each other'
at a distance. Wherein of course its old noble, gaseous Hydrogen I again say!
that touches, Is everything. And that is the important point—is <u>everything</u>...
... ... QS-in.: ... But add this: Be aware, Men knowing depletion, of the
destruction of The All itself, as, and if you go about pulling/separating this
elemental from the more complicated molecules, because you might!
R-d-t.t.p-in.: ... "What?"
Yauld: vigorous, energetic.

VARIATIONS OF BLUE
(NOSTRUM'S DILEMNA)

Variations of blue, gray and white, sky?
      Involve in externalities of
dust-ridden populace, more?
      War or, are they human mother?
There, Peter de Grosse was, redeeming his people with farce
      and exaggeration; call to arms
on beard, long coat, rude ceremony and custom.
But it was all bar bar bar as a Hellene might have heard it.

Ridicule do trade alone!
      Will raillery succeed where severity fail?
There, set of beliefs we'd not hear cater:
      the difference.
Anthos, oraches saltbush, goosefoot,
      sprig of sage to brush dishy air, crash full-feet
personification and lift for the rugose Plain her plain dirt skirt,
as jump to from fine-meld basket.

Bow, gold-notched, woe-shoots missal swifts.
      Her's, the season mountibus ornum
where wings release, young children adrift—
sojourn with poor Quagga
as just bad shoe-leather.
Marauders everywhere! Trireme to innocent Holy Ghost,
seven-foot bench to Peaceful float.
Oars that the full boats' full hosts pope; Virtue a kind apparition.

At home alas was a treasured Shangri-La gone minus,
pis aller of vestal forests won't prop.
Perched, verdant had to lump high!
      Every road call: for bear, lion, buffalo, elk, deer!
Then how will the animating principle get on?
Probably, with soupçon-Hope in light-foot Maybe.
With separate bedrooms and the dogs' bark!

EVE OF THE WATERBEARER

In a state like worry,
few sent to calculate the radius
of ownership and legacy, at fault on its pyre.
Bravery thought to unseat the spoilers.
Fed and directed on love-starved language,
the color-nourished house,
on monotint of gray feasted now,
as the blinkered vowed their excess and took stock
by numbers, bad habits for better went round.
Blood-spill hands raised the palisade
"God and my right" on bodies of the commons.
But it was not porphyr in the bleed of night,
nor thirst-quenched in busy waters,
as sword and sentinel kept flank the tree of life.

Questions without borders hid in feral frontiers,
and if native tools could not, rented had no right,
fatted on the *fair* price
we had seen Adam cleaning his ears,
Eve make use the new skirt,
and Reached Rule-by-right halt, best by heaven,
drown, answers swelling over time.
The marred, great jest of get and keep of equivalence
sent the trophy of climb-reason a wound behind its shield.
Sober, displaying the muscularity,
fine, shine pelt sallied for,
gazed longingly to graze near the house.

Privy-counselors to a dry field,
proud pets of the mean—
who wanted their separate-but-equal, privatized,
robber-baron world back—
did not know that shoot would not yield,
that praise for them was not meant.
And in a sky like reason, where bells and lanterns do mix,
The Benefit in all weathers leapt in their lives,
and hearts fair of kind, if not dominion,
shared and mined the great state of benediction.

MOURNING GATEIST

Tovarichs wonder if each entry needs their sentries.
Rabid dog(s) of Hades; why the adamance?
Should Lent be cut?
To pyrrhics such hedonist tricks go.
Nothing keeps but essentials. Who is relative, seems!

Then mistakes want a knowledge modest
to offer equanimity, scuttle excess,
deem naiveté not one of Loves' defects—
the naïve heart being the mightiest.
Chance wears that mask!
He, she is weld of circumstance at roost forlorn,
that catches glean on up-turned faces,
and at oil, tries slack and slow to mend life that's meant
to meet difficulty on its broken branch
and drub indifference its indifferent stance.

Ockham's simple answers startle
in that way they have; and even then,
someone ill-got their quick underserved and troubled,
who, grant: having dug so far and promised, lying, so much,
could not, would not, about-face—
there, turn in their tom-fool apologies in a tommy-rot noon
to glance clean-wins in sacred roles.

We speak of the doctor that is not one.
The scholar that has herself so thin,
she cannot be found even by find-everything wind.
Gun and maze-suited servants hating their public,
who let, in skirt authority only color, money
and the partnered blusters of fear pass unharmed.
The cake? Men slice it! And maybe these, to no avail,
will skulk in their hands, hide in towers of skulls
split their pants and shake, when heaven's gates wide open, come.

Note: Tovarich [Rus.]– comrade.

BEAST

She or he at entrance to bath step in to meet.
Every leg a taut anticipation
for judgment at the house of him, who's killer then.
I did, I toweled squash that arachnid (forgive me Heaven?)
lured by a crack, window or open doors' receipt
he, she might have sought relief.
But I think it
another negative for my consequence.

Here the slope,
here trip always fall,
in wild redrawn of like:
a camp, a moment in tent,
spread on the living mat of the living land at that,
I should not have beaten back Created like that.

So in white walls, clean floors,
in-doors withal to sanitized, take and regret,
have known the beast that is beastliest yet.
       Him,
       Me, j' accuse!
       I am that!

OLD FOURTH

Send one to attain sure sane of many
as adder in the pile of "action at a distance"
convinced de quelque chose of some importance
will lenit scale till catches back
and with buzz at ear, attach,
too faint the health of nations, Feynman.

Was mirroring Gethsemane-like despair,
no call for prophets
or homes' accorded comforts.
None seeing, heart leapt.
Hug of entanglement!

Oh dapple, twisted burst
more certain of brief quench
than laboured wisdoms' welcomed thirsts,
see where our ready slams went,
to cover, to bury in his chamber Jim!
Shut tender, leaden trap?

Here too is where through the thicket we roam,
Invention glad its favorable tome.
False ex animo laggards oppose
resolutions with embrasures deft at their toes.

Oh, let's say we awe eternity in commission enters
with reverence unto the dark, brood mother,
coming and gone, further offering of which,
blows out shady, lit candle and wish.

Yet welkin cups in heart-felt hands,
rests minds' joyous ignorance of Time.
That un-remarked, un-remembered once master of which,
may have thought its place to the loss of it.

Notes: Time: the fourth dimension. de quelque chose [F.]—of some,
Anything, importance. R. Feynman—physicist.
Ex animo: [L.] from the heart, sincerely.
Welkin: the heavens.

THE CEASE LUMINECSENSE

In angry fighter-heat Chiron, noble hoof,
borrow us your yarrow to staunch social bleed.
Will it do that?

I imagine fathers slouch or quick, castellans all,
forgive and are forgiven their downs
as composition pitches plug-ins fallow,
while others lie about six ways screens' screens,
right and wrong relieved,
being music a sight and silence a sound.

And the Dark Ma, crowd in foibles,
ranges over dreams, passes in ease feasting proud.

Sail your telling stones, release the pretty-pleases
that players of this size assent selves non-wise.
Boil not in the cauldron our teases,
kindle us our success in ceases?

LOVE AND REASON

Each time the one approached,
the other remembered its mission:
to nose Unbending in its vacancy,
and ransack Thoughtless for a better way.
Terror and Panic, Strife are at hand in man,
but he can,
like the two giants Dione says trapped war,
jar them for war no more.

Rudiment, in rationales, takes lives
and basks for a while in the old lie.
'Here' is Aeschylus's 'two sides
and only half the argument.'
Crop collect, there are perishes in the reproof.

Far shore of Love,
Reason emblazoned your headland,
prove the blind poet right.
Men need not walk with Fury in the dark.
And the bravest, the honoured, the peacemaker—
though Profit yell false charge of cowardice-
the same as he always was, the best among,
strives, cause high.

We knew, Anguish, would say that,
yet sat the evangelize,
hoping wit or profound wisdom would find
and pluck from the fire this time.

WOO AND COAX

If, in the hour of madness,
we discern savage goes ahead,
will ignorance god the consequence?
The So-well, content on dominance
and beasts lying in mountain lairs,
open out oh poet and warn earthly hire.

Iglight us from that cranky bard.
Comprehend the hour of gladness,
memoir lands a star at poesy's feet,
all will be remembered.

On weighty floor
Faith abides higgle dodder of now flying feet.
No reject of the-admonition-of-the-prophet-gone,
woo-and-coax clean-aims oh yeah!

And in that human morning
neighbor Defeat with housed Mastery collide.
Out of it winged Victory, and lion-led Merit
with man's greatest up to heaven go, good Tiepolo!

Good Thanks, always near,
covers the mealy miles before four,
any afternoon, any day, so often,
time tears its chocolate sleeve
that every beady choice at foot the mugged planet
listens and learns better green growing there.

Note: *Ig: approx=in; il, non, none, not, etc.*

PLANET OF THIRSTS

In hoped eternal,
with landings at your port before,
engines at hazard, we lift brave safe hatch,
and with vincible heat surface.

Our courtyard was—constance do not move.
Planet of thirsts, land of prayer-less folded hands
days' silent marker makes round,
busy-to-survive moisture meet in the far and foreground,
and now we tell why we light.

Numerous once, acquaints dear to heart,
chase the hours delicious our sport,
to win untiring cost.
Dragged care-worn escapes
that in red-flags kept security a bleed,
about ears have brought the place.
Entreat, and beg condition—
Of all that has visited toil upon,
among that book our kisses! with
the treasury of forgiveness!

ONCE-RELATIVIST

Stay long this with sun.
Fumble rumbly among
smile courted in held-morose
at unlighted source who would destroy well Earth.

Tallies lump,
jugglers rise,
belief and dance vary
as just bodied patterns on the unified fabric
as tumble into vortex now.

What church would not deify?
Think, skeptically breathe,
attend no joyous funeral of survival
where Krishna brow beats Arjuna.

Allowable body too matters.
Who can escape Lord Consequence?
Soon, constructed, worse for write,
read not perverse mass gripture,

sweep Her course of relativist manner—
that scheme that glazed salvation over
minds the crossing and is out of solitude.
Eight cycles per second, open the door.
weigh balance, hold hands go out,
then back. The dust may not melt you.

THE OLD AMBITION

He drank several draughts before,
'The answering years have pinned questions I could not.
Me under poesy, you under techne,
mustered now in rows and wed,
good-earth rude, crude wear.

And how did the spring grass get so tall, so fast?
How shall children un-approve madness,
Clamors and ladders,
under same bounty with Orioles out laughing,
Flickers back and forth, and good-alarm Jays
nest-mapping, in sharps and flats,
all accent where mastercraft bees were at,
swoon in sky-blue air's teal.'
Every tool and tribute under arm,
away treasured charms.
Gather mud-swirl of scuffed elation
in clear action, ashen, happy,
cleared-for-best-not-quench-of-thirsts, speak,
and ask the cunning year, how far lonely might carry.

YOUR GIMP SUM AT

Laid out were the sample augers that mince,
that wood adrift, and lying thrift know,
by which priest is rich and oracle gift.

Opposed bligh bleats for reposes...
as you draw near,
still nearer, question poses.

'In the shadow of every crime: a woman'?
is not enough! Only the precise, oh poetissmo,
have blamed the guilty. Self, same, auto. Who else?

In the darkness then, only faith and feel.
Out in lux, wither discontent and situation need no sops
that intend the shallow invent of rhyme,

Level the bumpy road and hillock as troubled mirror.
Flatty tunes, flatly rent escape,
sad trains their fair gusts, yet to station.

Life, worthy opponent,
like a play in two parts,
sleep awake on ladle.

And being the fittest app,
be safe to aim our gimp sum at,
that crosses, light, in the theatre.

THE MEDIUM AND CONTROL

In her late Metropolis
Mother meets and greet
who display veris on their shield.
'Heart is indeed the Mediator' and these the fair!

Arizona and Texas, Louissi their mates, looked the plenty
and seeing nothing could recognize began again.
The conserving sleight had bad luck
in what their 1776 lacked and the rest lent slack.

Fear, the medium and control it measured for,
could not history defeat with falls to ignorance.
Eons would wake another titan
to treat tried tendist effects of pain.

The oily descent, 'bursting storm in them,'
and everything else that said,
'this is man dying,' would draw again.
And in that, tremble but act.

At last, clamped the suffering rock,
guessed the worst enemy, still them,
Anthropic, through the Just and Fair gates even-weighed,
under Heaven's mighty masthead may they pass a word.

ALONE

*"he was alone, as lonely
as a vessel abandoned mid-ocean."*

Crouched light douses on round hill.
As holiday truant, quiet was a spoiled,
caustic relation,
boon, and tactless abhorrent.

I have seen you in raptures at *the sticking place*
seem the company men keep.
You, weaning on the bliss and soft slap
of that kind of solitude
that loaned contemplation its mace
to slaughter the news
—Social heart smashes brief confidence
on stone's stormy solus!—
That unsteady impose finds your callous out,
and like the sudden horror of the long proud,
extracts the hours' penance of it's due.

Note: Quote—from C.K.S. Moncrieff's translation of Stendhal
describing Julien Sorel's loneliness, because he was a "free Thinker"
and not accepted by the other seminarians in the novel
by Stendhal (Marie-Henri Beyle) The Red and The Black
(W.W. Norton and Company, 1954), 272.

SOME POETS II

Some Poets romp the Lady Bug's circ,
feats microscopic. But I wander early and it's late!
Some poets' depth gauges don't work.
By the silty pond was spurt our take.
On the fine measure, rot and worth of man
dead in pursuit, on arrival and accept,
they've tied and slapped their shallow hand
that across billowy chests won't transect.
But if my sonnet with a care invent,
and I shy Erin's advice of let it ride,
won't my spurts too land aside intent,
make reservations travel can't provide?
Won't wild beasts large and minute see me then
red in my green and hostile den?

Or like some, will I risk shy-legislative,
smile up from strapping rock
call all men cousin, native
to whatever was/is their landed spot?
Dear thinker, after proof-wrought fashion,
throw not Feel from homebound ship,
emotion is reason for learning's passion.
In this quoth Rousseau, at his knell I listen,
as Plato's and another who
to throw off cheer, account selves serious,
have despite, left their art and poetics too
intact, un or bent by nature's mysterious.
And their mortal work having few fellow,
could do no less than to knit up sorrow.

Note: Erin: (ancient) name of Ireland—for W.B. Yeats' advice.

213

FROM IRELAND TO SWEDEN

I

In green civil up-vent, two talents:
one, for oaths offered, history of;
other, help-choice and literature was.
Not like burrowing bees invited,
but unto quick house of stare requite.

Soft pad to podium in dream,
a year from where may land when,
stare toward an unknown something,
not great murmur and simple starling.
Whose new coat, rich-gleans in every eye jig.
And though, who writes in one blow flies,
who cannot spontaneity seem dances,
I lay me on my sheet to sigh,
roamed in backward glances.

Not all wrong, that mouth did read,
Yeats, climbs he to his theme
of stitch, unstitch, plan, scheme,
that Byron facing Horace before beamed.
Oh lovely! simplest team
of words and grateful meaning,
while not a few stretch, stress
upon what little Good Deemer has lent,
with butterflies in the gut for spent,

Fly there, on tower then shine
that search and certain shifting why.
Myths, ruins built of sweat called heave,
Synge and the Lady a part of the team.

Of all the restless years thought made match,
Here was a Titan to straddle his craft!

II

In same green, a current mature scout
who bends such general lists,
Heaney model's resilience querying with the best
doffs cap of the Everyman and takes the spinning field!

Their wives, steady as watching world, and family,
are masters of men lucky enough to have them!
The first of these fairly considered was,
for the present, only a year's wean,
to shrink under gold-knit
and petition end's beginnings in.

This second: after-thought not, quick of constitution,
livens masters take.
Both, sent from the house,
to needle at proving spots of love and politic;
brotherly need of brotherly... and sent.

Same labour with ideal intent
conditions sturdy hearts
and swings strong to knit tells
among seats earned of given self.

III

Still more. Here green Eireann
lift for men and women, the laugh-filled,
for whom words traveled far,
hallowed heavens to hear,
to stall volumes all, tangle
speak ready tales while still embarrassing Sweden.

For there is Joyce of choice,
first in name and last in reckoning,
Villon, Langland and Rabelais bowed to at turnstile;
high and viewed among saints of Word,
that next amused Apollo and ladies-nine
in the thrice or seven craftwork heavens must.

So, we may call him wordsmith. User, tamer-of-words,
the lightsome, non-serious one. Even if many megas
'tickle catastrophes,' and intelligence, from rampart
accolade and paean, token blank page with high recognize,
known sense and logic of Live, living Life—come, met—
where (smiling) he is lift and installed
pretense master the masters call master yet.

Notes: *first in... Plutarch. Villon, Longland ... If looking, one may find many
instances in the life of the mind: literature, philosophy, of Stream of
Consciousness writing. Pretense—p/o W.B. Yates' retort.*

"PILGRIM'S PROGRESS"*
OR
THE SOCRATIC DIALOGUES
OF THE MAN, CHRISTIAN

The charged square bulged. Buckled, unbowable pavers
seared searchers loath to empty home.
Cornered at blares, draft to wear,
were towned their country spirits to the global flip,
toni split from crease of care plow and seed once knew.

Stone-worn repetition towed apprehension.
They were all in cities now!
In the abort someone said,
"Oh, that abolition moved!"
Out on the sea, "Oh!" kelp said,
"Looks like the show is over and Otter's dead.
At coil and anchor—
the friendless spoils and plastic shapes instead,
I pray you live on!"
And this was the reek of them.

Rue-the-idyll-of-their-schemes,
rally no remainder salient,
stained on acceptance full-grasp would never allow:
the holy breach crossed.
And distill, they were off
to a mill-hole to fall and rot,
new slights in *happy clothes* to holler and call hell on.

Plain, in cant seam of liberal knowledge,
good guide, 'fore all cancels,
laugh the worry and wreck the scrum,
that all not so much flesh on tables, walls,
streets and chairs become.
But forward last barrier,
ahead every mean to cancel joy,
rayed, heartening send good sums ahoy!

*Note: John Bunyan's "The Pilgrim's Progress" — I. Walton's "The Lives
of J. Dunn and G. Herbert" (The Harvard Classics, P.F. Collier & Son,
New York, 1909, 1937, 1969).*

STORY

Let it be about Jim, a regularly guy
who agrees with who said,
"In all things that add and furnish tomorrows' needs,
clamp teeth."
But he had better eat his nettles Dürer and sue his allergies.
Following distant peaks won't decide;
barrier for just these points the gathered warlike
whose jingle-keys molt in assembly.
And the plight of drought, let's say again, might drop,
when rain flows and they capture it!

A couple drogues rue at this moor,
tanker and platform span oily reach,
fishlands take Jim on his rite—
sorry anabasis, hobble horse of flight—
while the collared victor at the whip-post of history is tied,
and rabid dogs bubble in their beards.

The sea at shore wants to be, he said, and is, well.
But not with burked Mother tortured,
her power surge from rock, smoking the oxygen.
A valiant, left alone in these her evening years,
even he doubles and waits, furthering her dying with tears.
Tall-misnomer now blows the augment.
Combed awns and cashed axils
eat across eating-contest North's yard,
that by a steady course, as someone said:
'hears, but doesn't want to see,
while the Southern one sees, but doesn't want to hear.'
And the shady price-is-right is saved i' the sear sun.

Just then, intent on seeing future generations accept
Early Egypt's Beatitudes, the ancient paths of the East,
Jim feeds first-prophet Earth, and weans acceptance-of-less
as the way, a shade too.
Not whimpering like a mal-practiced pet,
but like imp's feral jumps in Her best invents.

Notes: drogue: Sea Anchor, etc.
Awn: slender, bristle part of grasses, etc.
Axil: angle btwn a branch or leaf and the axis from which it arises

SPRING'S EXAMPLE

In her dawn,
snows roll-up in their lockers.
In her hair there will be jungles of possibility.
She says,' You tell a truth or lose it.
Star's middle-paces foster beds,
by now grow and youth and grin
with spleen abound.

'Story being king,
not all his tracts bob calmer waters.
But like the thirsty convert Sprout
who must rush the pool, close to ruin pipe—
from the edge is value known.

'There dianoia gleams fleshy with hate to disarm,
and with its pen traps allegory to hold fast,
bridges winter's barring aspect,
and forgives the old gloat,
for he only came after long summer
and autumn's dust-blown gibe.

'Follows the portraying Edenist.
The vanity fairs of the mind SHe'll mind.
And glad with the bloom and shirt-sleeves to connive,
manufactures precise, in that way embrace-dominion has,
that joy-dances to express, consort
how glad he is to see her.'

Note: Dianoia: [Gk.] reason, etc.

MOUNTAIN HOME

Pine bough tassels sparkle with their sun-lit wishes,
convey the sense of a certain hour
or yours without my study.
Hulking arks dock on the mountain.
Timber in its wood creaks wideawake.
Breezes bear away if let,
and as I count, contemplation has all its furniture,
and study two quiets to bask in.

In a forest everyone's reservation is on,
but fake by wild is sorted.
The carried laughter, believed seraphs,
ported gloom in rooms of fog
where plaqued brown men stand on their green,
these are all shall see and all shall wish for.
And in that wellspring no admission seeks,
love that eyes no reward,
peace-harvest abundant in glow hours
is universes' welcome charm.

I own, cures are ready in this.
Weather a deep ocean seen from bottom
will do illness, and uncourteous death smiths there too.
But drunk with the power of Earth, lost in her patience
you'll account and buckle at her form,
as all her pretty partners do
when the old selfishness, last seen in a scream un-arms,
and you ink and breathe there too.

NOVEMBER SUITE

Burst seed of trusting, parched, to thirst bows,
as some sisters of mercy
or that Sabbath-collar great religion spout.
Do you not trouble!
High-end, reward-as-rest speaks of Can't,
the horrible, shed effort, bent gasp in a wind,
that marks Jupiter and Venus do moon shot,
their twenty-degree separation
in the gray Descartean west. That was then.

Warm sun in frigid nightmare,
or cool in scorching fare, shuffles modern,
where trotting certainty once stood.
Why ran fortunes backward,
where one dark Friday in November
someone was trampled at the large mart?
Torn, were, in shopping's homage.
Ran wild, the willing rot,
to bury wheelie in his cart, Jim.
They were their saviors want.

Ecce! Back in the fair mountains, heads high,
trees undress, leaders shift in history's bruce hands.
But none are the Styrofoam president,
with Terra cored, Nereus fouled,
and that breathing sylvan sliding out back,
that just hers to our breath wants;
Arbor says we are slaves her master.

And by that, Godly, the king and I, at maintenance,
finally unlearn dissolution, chasten turned hearts,
because you know poets have worrying to do,
and petitions and amendment may halt social bleed.
The house will come to order soon.
Braving garden-to-kitchen fare, destiny's child,
that once thick-waists on sofas earned,
legs and democracy to paradise return.

Note: Ecce: [L.] behold, look!

WERE MEN

The weather some days just sat down and stayed.
Hat'll in indifference head could not peer cloud from fog,
and all the fairy bangles glistened snows chance,
scheme of consequence.

May the day from clay take you when it breaks
into portions for Heaven and some for end-all,
preventing a foul fair-play in that spiteful ardence that tricks
the tricked hearing-of-two-sides.

As taxes skim low over dollars' moors
may your time in grade and Socratic nature
gain but not eagle over the highroad
others believe belongs to them.

All those Americans
cornered in resolves to unslave Americans
can absolve their fight-back against the unwillingness to admit
complicity of contempt for mule and acre as start in it.

They had in their poetics' goofy-foot and Van de Graff hair,
all those enslaved Americans, not stumbled,
every fifth part a tangle, but a bite,
could de-wind generational, institution'd racism.

Then, to what interior do sly answers go?
Was there support or destruction for barriers?
To the shear edge for adult concepts
to the masses floating in bad conduct!

Tule nook, quiet as kept,
these soft, ratty, goldless books of desert
matching wits with their Hamptons and Forest of Dennis
ponder forward he, the common man, guileless.

WOOD HUNTER

Under grief canopy as only man, smile.
Mother needs that shoulder for lean.
Content-in-comfort will not last,
nor cede bane if
like the too-much lumber that built these halls,
meals and warmth
still ravage her once full body.

Scribblers drench in tear, stoke phrase,
lash a few proofs to air,
but those murmurs too break toward fall.
'Yells on paper' point the wrenched wealth,
high-roofed happiness, a couple merchants eulogize,
missing hemp and old world sedge confide
an exchange of air, foul for fare,
that would on behalf-entire, confront paper in its mill
and there, but for bestowal of rights,
recap missal madness, lay snare bare-care.

Neglected-studies herald ages' royster,
and down eras when inertia slept with men,
when squeezed soil ate drowning crowds,
where one thing trailed another,
and rains, oh yeah! absent the philosophy of grass,
ran unchecked denuded miles,
Great-hearts, Safe and Save left Heaven
carrying bolsters as sure, as stout as aegis
for wrestles with demon in the pit.
And Field-of-Justice exempt wring-of-hands bad advice,
crested to verify the carmel of their dreams,
that none again had to climb
the sandy insult of so much desert.

Note: royster = roister; carouse, etc.

EARTH TO EARTH

A Godly mercy is
who lays soft hands on the world.
Eyes charge not his "I"s
with shame of rights withheld.
Of course, that ire that staked Bruno and Joan
'chastised, blessed' in de-flowering fire
or failed sequences with the peace anywhen,
forgot Feel of Reason as best temper of Ideas,
the proper calculation of which
faults not equality at the clean bench of justice.

For any practicing unjust,
born at last to the deathless threshold,
will they ever hear yes! of entry,
ever know proven end of fear?

Superior when disasters' evident,
the wind has evidence
wither the endist reflects of pain
are spread over them and continent.

In this *his* holy Ilium, sons victor lusts;
disgrunt of False, that from course of greed
cedes spirit-moments
is not at the saving-place dressed, but aghast,
glances veris a-tide tumult, tumbles trouble
and wrecks soon-abandoned recalcitrant,
pointing high, thither for the sound.
A seat for entrants, a nimbus for crown,
ambrosia cup, full-plate for all.

WHITE HOUSE

"The voice of Jonathan was heard to express,
"Our president is going to war, I guess.""

Before hurl that vagile white way,
let how, upon waking,
leaf and window ran light-river
upon wooded bed our brown room.
How foot in faint dreams, night fabled visage
of her and her and *that* woman sent.

Innuendo had been that!
Not the long-eyed ppp's of broach with them,
but this now gynid without.
Proper police Procedure remoras remediating process,
slows the spousy part, now cried.
Oriflamme of St. Dennis or Ralph in comeuppance nearby.

Temptations' travails empty joy out,
rule Discipline to tight circumference,
though he puts his jump on radical use
who suits chance not lurch at impasse.
Palamedes and Twain self-identify in this,
and present nameless who many names have
adjust, provide civility for manse.

In the Chronicles, leaf-clothed trees and stoop hedge,
plan of fountains counted: wan accomplishments
the shoulders, back, arms and hands of man put up.
But, the strident part, POTUS, now start,
no longer wag ratio of Rousseau, adopts survival as ready art.
But "We did not authorize!"*
'Men sharpen men like iron sharpens iron,' Nader said.
And 'the shadow of an ass can be taken for a horse,' was also…
—Still, don't mortgage your charms on swells like that!'

Bodies and lands ransom the centuries
whose denies screech still on paper. Do what good you do!
Stamp the mules and sacred acres on lagging bench.
The rearward unpaid whittle embarrass! Pay your due!
You stole from you! Attend, and, men again!

Notes: Quote from a Lord Byron poem.
*Dennis Kucinich, Ralph Nader.
Palamedes & Twain: pseudonyms.

THE POOR

There will be a million townings
in your users blouse of red fitted for ouch,
where shrines scratch the eyes of yester-winning noons,
cries settle on tithe saddest parts,
and any shiny day Brine's trysty bottle
is okay with that blanket gloom.

In the straight seam of a young ones' garment
made line by a caring Mom, I and her being the houses' help,
trek from our shredded half-way houses as home,
shabby by theft in its fine clothes
and misery, her shatters.

Blank tune,
certain of lives cared for by the not any—
those not any in belief-laugh of effort and boot strap,
but more in great designs that hoarse benefit by price—
we have met advantage under tottering table.
And boughten braw and bricked braintrust
saw nor could say trés triple expletive
laid wait in fleck yellow, shear white,
brash bouile of bravura cabinetry.

Only the westering peace by death was saved,
and left clatter, pressed shard the bond
in all occult books of guessing life.
Angelic symbolic, lightly packed
equip gain and trail of sight.
The permanent denial of which,
hobbles ballad Good.

Notes: braw: good, fine.
Bouile—after 18th century Fr. Cabinetmaker
known for inlays of yellow, and white metal, and tortoiseshell.
Bravura: ornate, showy, showing a daring or brilliance.

CH. 11
KING-FOR-A-DAY MOONWALK

KING FOR A DAY

Life in unprop, a kind of surly beast doomed to rot,
a certain entertainment to play still-evenings' stars with
and Earth, call donation despite single loss,
it's a μῆτις maetis world afterall!
Lay-by Roving stench, syllogists' evidence,
worm-filled apples lie the house!

Truths seed in the towns and penetrate hearts!
Oh clowns of justice, do not oppress with
clammy bitters of doubt, known by
your standard inquisition dried and stinking south!

Have fly trusty syntax and slay pully scout,
that led on un-even plain,
upon a sheriff'd badge that profited the people tamed.

Moved airt by this excess fired routine,
so the reaping down that all but closed hands
the treasure burying, bid out.

Now, who resend happy actuals copered by privilege,
who horded the commons,
find Rousseau, my walking backwards or not,
and any scathing-think direction stout.
The once sure access, batailous private interests
and the bad king still purring there,
through bewildered panes, see natural famulii heading out.

> Note: μῆτις: [Gk.] skill, address, shrewdness, course of action, etc.
> Coper—a horse dealer, esp. a dishonest one. From cope—to trade.
> Airt: compass point, direction.
> Famulii [pl.] of famulus: assistant to a professor; private secretary, etc.

INDULGENCE

Anywhere in the postal, dullards reign care,
and rains lather,
entreat one-side justice to on them gather.
Their talk, the all-time blab,
addressed of citizens holding their horses,
wants convince by crook and lash tongue
that grass will not save,
clover is no trifoliate,
and mountains? Let 'em sink!
Optimum would, in this wilding, haloes wear,
and the thready foils of distaste of love not bear.
So pull-up! The lusterware of kindness shines
in the longview lustihood of lightness.
There exists searches that entertain piggly beast.
There are soufflés and lizards loose these breasts.
Are deft at the high notes!

Divine, their once and future perhaps,
called for Nonsense in, to keep minds sharp.
—Is fortune in her evening gown?
Are Appeals' bosky challenge, red-carpet whines
tracing spall, the gold-ring tugged?
This lynch, pulled from scaffold,
teaches brooding-in-diapers, to cry child,
instruction meet, and comparison,
when none pertinent, let it only to the hole!
Men being their own purchase document!

Note: Bosky—of trees and shrubs; of a wood.

BATHED IN AGED LIGHT

On daub path embark!
Like Infallible, countless fill ark
with least and most and every kind,
that grudge, that slime take the terror hind.

Here, kin up faith,
scene it at the pillar place
that radiance sets about the race
and harvest no more pallet harms

that slink bio-slush and surface,
conjure less goodly alarms,
where breath in the great house is feign
to flutter gutless as on a joyless plain

of so much nothing at table,
and reign fan queen over storied fable
of anxiety let at the ballot box,
of paroles high jinxed on the likes of us.

So disorder, have the offal cuts!
Degenerate 'gross-virtues' before sane is up!
Bathed in aged light on the dark and such,
uproariously reflect, slip, weave, dip, dive, just as much.

NUCLEAR MARCH

Loose on martial wind
all the dirty, contraire pieces
of that quickened scheme
are bounding wide Earth.
They are the numbered,
murder-horsemen on baleful steed,
at ride hippomalice that is laying death
for the two of us.
And from that pocked zephyr
the genus blood,
bantered by oh so foolish saunter
of iron eyes
reaches evaporation and dies
a billion deaths
a billion times.

USEFUL

Once, a balmist:
start by doing what in hard sanity would not.
Deft, clip powers with one lone digit,
go where are warned of going, sow seeds of growth,
be Atlas, under sinking mass.

Passenger on disastrous journey,
plan the years' return,
land where short of snores
ports were hazard to your court of knows.

Now, not unpowered,
land weight off the foot and iamb, if
The fest. Pray at last in rest,
and pour a bare-foot poets' late repast.

Send on his way gap shaky bird
that from enclosure tight had learned,
to eye moments of flight earned,
and have a life-sentence overturned.

At risk, health-met stores in turn,
think, speak, write, discern
after classes you have set,
savvy, against designing government.

Ribald, if hypnotic,
grasphold earth flowers
in dark nights' bon office,
receiving light frays.
Point. Rail. Steadfast, aim.

Note: Atlas, punished to hold up the sky his father after the Titans
fought the gods in <u>myth</u>. Atlas, son of Uranus—Sky, and Gaea—Earth.

THE COMPLAINT

Were fear, the years efforts.
A palace for staid, crown for ignorance.
Theory of recollects and blanket of opposites,
grow chaos-of-the-many to quiet heads.
As hunch cloud-ships arch the up-expanse,
I ask Great Questioner in nights' chance,
to listen my sensibilities to late belittles, smiles' attacks.
How some demon plastic-prongs the cake,
the way our safe-being has been his sales pitch.
And how, bid by barely men of better parts,
sail to bother his foist help
for bucks not as spend as thought,
and try our craft past his ill-word shoals of anger.

Justice had never a clear field in this.
Leering landscape, never a trifle,
She held our reverence of the church it was and is
in her glove hand, and said it was not there.
Seeing only commodity's buy/sell,
With teeth bared she foiled,
banked un-fair advantaged, and to take with, where?

Out of that fill-less empty
he packs his thieves' grip and stands station
so convenience-beast can ride down.
Home to no happy Hades of the Greek,
or Valhalla for rough-necks, but writhefull's bare snare.

And when new-nazi neighbors never argued with
were complained of, those terrors were sent
his 'you-make-too-much' ridiculi piled.
Known for the first time, good scattered.
In young days of happiness, when drawn ways of age were off,
steeples climbed to redirect insults were as Mother's kitchen ladder,
and took only the energy shifting in a chair to concert.

Years-in-grade list good delays,
and consideration's turned sour its tin.
Things that can not be let to hold up—
his intentions to do me good and spruce me—
are dirty hands meeting dirty water, wringing a dirty mop,
passing a sordid cup. So that the insult finds
it can not stand the oh so method of our survival.

THANATOS

Tolstoi seemed a Moses at his station.
Keats derailed, exchanged at his Steps.
For Lorca they were still digging.
Yes! Some fall at these walls of caution
to change the hearts of men.

This is not the stomach I'd fend with,
eyes would not relent.
A horse and clear-land are held in chest,
tears go the way gallops went.

How much so for federations in liberation?
Numberless formula test the stations;
John Does read in ink of separation
hearts schooled in passions' desperation.

A chorus shall reject plain text,
such knowledge as rooks and kings get
will measure we are in anticipation met.
Kheperi-re-atum, morning, evening, noon
Megas shifts his bud-right room.

And in Valhalla they gather,
in Lethe's erasure womb
Thanatos moves the legislation,
Strapping on violence, Ares larks all benediction,
Heaven has approved denomination,
Wisdom departs with the warp of breathes' cessation!

BEHIND THE SCENES

Christmas trees bloom in June,
are born south during Yule.
On a street up from church stones
Leopold coverage's been a Bloomsday jaunt
or late 'Deep Throat' pieces.

Shore to Dedalus reconfigures;
the editor on Sunday was spoken to,
he's retired now. What other taps? Will we
cross street, cross selves in soothe to save?
Stopped on a puddle, retained whole day by a book
whose good intentions swept other ambitions
to under-rug positions;
we flowered, broke with mere men who
hurl R.O.V. or rocket with their insane.
The cover, the mask, avert the very smoke!
Conscious too late, does a little money, test-will,
stream to solve under stupefied?
Does it warn all nationals' crimes done in their names,
like glass broken by the unsupervised,
will have to be paid for?

'Farewell, we hardly know you still'—
one newsman's 'Deep Throat' reportage.

And fear, massing rot eating center-out,
you'll friction other partner
and scrape hides, if, to save men's records,
names and dates their place.

IN ART'S TROUBLES

Those unattended beacons could have shined,
if earlier involved in art's troubles, one has no bandage for.
Crane's damp 'jump', Plath's down-heart intake,
Malcolm and Martin's artless abandoning.

Seeing Celan's last despondences
was blocked the Seine and Brodsky's smoke/encyclopedic
inferior to him here.

Through doubt, drought and 'deathfuge'
is a press to rescue one's self;
light steps on arts' pains
and remembrance of cotton-candy clouds
may be all potions need;
and those would have known before their disappearance
were as plenty as amounts of shadow incident a forest.

If then simply: 'everything for best',
'everything for some reason'—
lose faithful strain could save a safe space.

So trouble, old contrarian, seethe as
restaged solus proves intent with process,
and were tours into heavy traffic.

ENDYMION WAS NOT HAPPY

Whether the sight madness trained on him,
or the one he trained on her, whether asleep or clever,
he had many nights a cuckold's savor.
Sordid, she hid her face from view
so he, only he, could not see her.
These, his constructions, she had little of,
preferring to twirl and forget sophic;
her endeavors were the becoming's gayest.
At length he thought, alabaster reveals
the best and worst a man can face.
Best and worst for placard failure.

It was all too Pushkin, too Iago,
far too Madge, Maud, Odette or Fumette worrying,
he knew,
how she'd at once lounge an hour,
then shower with a friend and neighbor
who seemed sure to arrive her favor,
while loath to understand,
he would sulk away and let her.
But why should she be tether in mind?
What need he Diana chimera?
a fear adroit, popping up when languor?
His mistake, hastily pitched,
to break away and leave her.

Notes: <u>Their loves:</u> *Maud refers to W.B. Yeats, Odette to M. Proust.*
Fumette to J.M. Whistler.

ΛΙΘΟΣ Ὁ ΟΥ ΛΙΘΟΣ
THE STONE THAT IS NOT A STONE

Him down the road saw.
Same sweat, worry load, phytonymous.
It was he, Heart, splayer of blood,
trod-troop black to outglow red
back-straight, chin up, pointing from the *stone of outrage;*
leaving curves' panted abattoirs.

Friendships' true—that bite that caress.
Yet! Having bother in nose – deep cold is in deepest cold's slosh.
That fire opposite, at length to explode, sowndrive to mountebank
thrust, out, is upon us. And yes! I here, would Pound, your certainty,
with a non-mind. Such that is Keats' 'at least two things held
in that chamber, jellyfat, living with *uncertainties, mystery,* and *doubt*
as said, at once. 'Perpendicular verities' another set of tappers had it,
ἔνθα καί ἔνθα,' here and there, this way and that,
that short in books for appraisal might.

Oh then a knuckle bath, teeth for snows' sleet debraid, appraisals bunche!
Though now about Selma not uncertain: abed *Dark Horse*—God be mind of!
Square vulnerable Fem fila, this *came first, early,* fire vista to look and protect
all cost, that matter, that foundered ships sheet for wavefall; a once ...arlene,
before green adhese un-cheered her; volunteered best.
Helen! Self-assess your terrors!

Or that, this latest add—'Selma' of my 5 Star because it was the most could
       give
for a blessed child's joined work. Add: Greek σέλμα (Selma), ατος, τό
to upper planking of a ship; deck; timbers; seat that thrown sat; row bench.
As Bench.net might! that matter these foundered ships sheet for wavefall; and
obtain, as said, your green adhese un-cheered, to cheer her.

Blooming dale! Affrit frights!?   No more regard! Wait! Ascend.
Time unbaize! Moon, transcend as Sun for us that on a set of hill, bottomland
'these soul to make' cloud our sheet set for savefall in the at-float night.

Hello Sierra-heavy, limb-taker! Our now-wish: cover us!?
and the crystal trees of winter. Attend! 'Chain rule; differential
of a function of a function as $\int[you(x)]$.' By which Hera and Athene for
       examp
assigned tumble with Hermes, an Iris disturb of untrue Democracy from
above was't settling share troth which, 'under suitable conditions of continuity
and differentiability, one function is differentiated with respect to the second
—considered as an independent variable (x)—and then
the second function is differentiated with respect to the independent variable
(x)(x)'. What? Yes!

Or how, oh how, idea govern thought. Solid mass of people shock.
Like 'professional' saying you can't do it yourself? But! Aren't that they?

Can *ever,* like Auden's Love, *not* from yes to no go?'!
Isn't anything Demos, even alter perspect, anything but fuller definitions'
the thing; that thing that in practice for self, of self, civil was't? Ist!? Isn't it?

Shall we crunch systems more welcome discerning public,
and discerning government? Not? It's now allwise: to restrict bad ones;
show world shortcomings understood, Of all of us (that) for good measure',
thrill of join among cultured classes, largess largest FROM thrust
un-trust outrage!?"

And cache! As come to with fears, that you not "like the sun"
a Trojan Alexander, puppet in armour, back, showy to war through Ilia go,
with the bow that would-be-god-smitter Diomedes taunts:
"...*Arrow shooter, foul-mouth fellow with plumed-hair, fine-maiden oogler;*
if indeed your arrow has done real damage) surely now killing,
soon, my armour may you be attempting..." but he did not.
And that chamber of the people, that clays old mud, enters from feels
where smarter decides, only to regress earth-born, counting coin
equivalent a forest; alien blue superior that life in a πολύκμητος world eyes.

And by all Scamanders, stir in sight astonishment of bounty,
and rise in Cali-tries; not doubtful, not de-watered.
Remake drained faultless fissures' slurs
that She overtook! and wail scared waters. This,
the shimmery of mad men.

Soon, myriad mad fizzle-as-dance, young winter grass
crew's at eye level. And wry Rosemary if did, had frizzle,
mapping mad brand river dance.
I notice because with shadows, at run, we are familiar:
Jackson's backing up. All-ways in dare
a Diomedes. File: a Meriones!

Thank God that hill, quiver of web atop chaparral, love's fence's assists!
There, separation thin as illustrious light rally sheer on sheer
dresses mold for night. All out who's Troyan!

Then, that well-shades have for us drawn a-fray The St. Lucian
a little more, and more, till lived comes wound back, splay.
He never and I in own, someways seems, immerse be the we'er-blood,
shudder-staunch, plot sayer who arrays rebuffs, defaults,
for gruff conservatives and seasoned friends, whose
I live in the world winnings we're just about to sort.

> Notes: ΛΙΘΟΣ ... Lit.: *The stone that (is) not a stone. The philosopher's stone.*
> Phytonymous: ΦΥΤΝΥΜΟΣ—*name(d) from a plant or tree.* Stone of Outrage:
> Pausanias I. Homer: Diomedes...Iliad: Λ385 *also 'The river god called by the gods*
> *Xanthus, Scamander by men.'* Abattoir: *slaughterhouse; a bloody affair.* 'Vale
> 'soul-making'': John Keats!? Πολύκμητος: *of many schemes, used of Odysseus,*
> *Homer again.* The St Lucian: *Derek Walcott.*

THEA

Her conic was the startle point;
intensity, helpless in effluents,
knew not of ways or go, or why or how.
Like roads and hours that did in ethics attire
a fresh-rest glow to cheeks,
it would do to point arrivals and stops entire;
and Fanny, her attempts, lounge
in his waystead ideas from that fixing head,
draughts behind conceiving heart,
near the dear nudge all aspire.

She became the pictured society
whose thwart was gift and disquiet,
whose lift also mired,
and whose bright, Beatrice or Cordelia, was dark
even in color and estimation,
profound in the midst of joy.

Leaden sorrows mark for picturing
betray the body down,
and in turner-fashion reveal cracked vessels'
spill oh vanities! on holy soil!

Ducks and succumbs together tricked,
not like bounce quandaries of swallow
or butterfly's vectors souse,
but such akin and heightened sleights
as intoxicants borrowed to treacle, beauty and a spy,
dispatched by sobriety, madness and love's lust,
lilting lightly on high.

Notes: Thea [Gk.] ΘΕΑ: Goddess. John Keat's muse, all-time love,
goddess—Fanny. Dante Alighieri's muse, all-time love, goddess—
Beatrice. We could go to Yeat's Maude G, and others again, but we'll not.
Good daughter Cordelia, Lear's brightest.

239

TWIST

Little Greek, Little Latin;
at begin and amend now how Swahili
a subscript must enduring matter,
when both inner and outer ballast social,
shave in its heavy mirror,
returns that are the transports of love,
with pity at the tender trap, to foster care.

Service 'the once happiness of Socrates'*
there in that wooding, that tattered cloak
begs kingdom of enlightenment just fine!
And lean importance, sentenced holy and certain,
to active environs for life and living I!'s.

"Only an hour after you die," the quote,
"does your real face appear."
It has yet to entrance the great emptiness,
but grands, a tear salting cheek,
so abandon can weep the hero ancient.

On another side, that chichi wallydraigle of time
banishes impose deeper for protection,
proffers none but the meet'd, the ambush snare.

This then was device. Grown, all a-buck trend,
in non-plus attain, they had lain twister by.
And agreed! Were better for the knowing.

Notes: *Jean Jacques Rousseau in his Discours sur
L'Origine et les Fondements de L'ineqalite parmi
les Hommes or Discourse on the Origin and Foundation of the
Inequality Among Mankind, Edited by L.G. Crocker
(Washington Square Press Edition, Pocket Books,
New York, 1967 by Simon & Schuster, New York, NY), 204.
says: "the happiness of Socrates and other geniuses of his stamp" was
"to reason themselves, into virtue (if not) the human species would
long ago have ceased to exist," 'but the common run can not...'
"...real face..": from the (2001) movie "Dust".
chichi: frilly, elaborate, showy, chic, etc.
Wallydraigle: a feeble, imperfectly developed; sloven creature.

TO CRITO

To the wringless hands of Justice, with the most answered call,
shrive out-garment, be firm and on injustice slather.
Skin can no higher than live and verify
adept at why's answers, hope's attires.

Friends' petition survive,
existence without the light on wastes power;
and clever is a foil, a spoil, a wearing tact
that too much paints, misquotes and smiles,
where frowns are meant.

No! No concurrence, no silence patents
on the threat hours use, statii, to make it so.
In its drag coin it does not low all.
In trials, one of a thousand their devils sight,
and bruised, steeled, ride Justified
clear out of there.

A friend, nothing poor good Crito, life not a lie,
saw you superior vie against type;
and since low knows not how far below it may go—
Having swallow the condiment,
took to length coward-mob's foul act.
And as you know,
made yourself master to cankers like that.

Notes: the most answered call—death.

241

OUR LADY OF THE ROOST

With breath for children smoke-like in gauze gaud air,
Sushi and raw-grind anteing worm count, habit culprit,
they were joking, all cards are on the table!
And don't let's go again on plastics.

'The latest' means we and they will do the tests;
our mass over unseen cliffs.
Some passed on popular instruction
to lessen wholesale suction
of me's in the we of them.

Our Lady of the Roost, some died;
"Be assured," some lied,
"futures could not be seen."
Positive-thought buffed
to stand-in for precaution.

Distract, fast of hand,
would steal for consequence,
and despite uranium's radiant candies,
the burn of trees, however nascent,
let the peoples power elsewhere;
take their given slack back!

Dear Lady, factions slide in quick-tongue,
say un-fail of each reality it was none.
Teach turned to instruct, history fell;
and all could, in modified dinners with the fourth estate,
tell deception held 'a good quarter' of the all-time postulate.

White turned the hated black,
and black took the slippery right back.
Did twilight sink in night's cold lap?
Appeals for reprieve land greeted with
the people's heavy boot and parting wit.

Either! What a tale have spun.
Drink flag from hole, and come,
Dear Lady let a day in-track,
when destructors clear their no-smile eyes,
and golden rule takes the hug-right back.

Note: Gaud: ornament; trinket.

242

SOON THE MALEFACT

Truce frames yell,
sends options' quixot,
opened for deals along the water front.
In yeller, power shoes
gropes bland dark,
abroad healed shade of light.

Next, queries sunny-spark,
zap, and heal governed de-salve,
abreast salty variant
that quips Xerxes folden in latest
arrest of disasters' chaotic:
shrill toward peace and in monument hat'll,
that applauds, gnaws and bites
Entropy in better parts.

Bear it you sit down. Scribe partook the mash,
sudden-swamped, apodict.
To him Virgil and Varius honorif.
Gulled by your bad weathers and error,
Bard-canted naughts in princely mouths,
swab duende's sweet sweat season;
and reflect-sun, gossamer in ascent,
that love may—across a feely continent;
malefacts at waste to train.
As the great bold conducts,
adjusts, again, again.

EVERYMAN TO

Tersid, some angels succumb
in paper-towel shrouds; trash they.
He sullies it a practice of the West,
the good polemic loud to protect,
inferring names of men and insects on cheery stars.

Boughten crest fallen,
once-chic mantle trod
on the sodden soil, if not taken,
the un-shield dress of back-bites has;
being "in the storm so long,"
at no rest beside 'wintering dragon,'
vies beyond sense,
displays slink at glance,
points the skulls and femur.

Add obscurity to the testimony of measure
and affidavit to the light of promise.
Was Ihr Vater Name ist?
Was it he lent the no-compass?
Morgen sehen wir, and that is that!

If vigor is deliberate though,
if Sun portend from portal in rags,
there is madness enough, power will not lag!
This far to unattend effort?

Canopies, umbrellas and roofs
force rain to saving channels.
Heraclites' 'destiny from character,' steers and truth flings,
leaving evils themselves out.

VIRTUE TALKS

Already counter warfare dims above the trench.
Loop and trash of same, led to rim of garden sought
by parts of speech and men
have the awful sights survived never to further.
Mud essential, key natural, has words this classic,
scores bend to sighs, make helpful right;
and selfish that for the worse we struggles,
that paul, that small that rubs nose disaster,
is not gathering peace-like for smile shots.

Hold (together) categories our language got!
Adjust men's lives to thrice soily lock
and sublime rubric of gospel spell,
revered again by they who breathe fine air.

Home is recovered of a dark continent,
and bursting udder of birthing mother,
sits one intent, have you loving it.
Her stand accomplice with the Pelian importance
of severed strand upon the empty scale of riches—*idn 'it!*
to steal every trace of Love's lived evidence.

Clear for acceleration through the high order
of low entropy's destructive mechanist, that I yet
murder complacence while I sort of live, good anchor;
for I have come some acquaintance with
Trussed, a catch, slung invert, a pole,
vices un-caught where the self-inflict toll.
Few right acts move to mass,
till the loss so great, so near, could do nothing less.
Reader, to more of these I apologize!

Clay for wrought, excuse nothing bought
for a few tosses of clack dime silver!
And, as near the unrelenting as are fit, go, young,
without fair looks before and behind,
because to Heaven there will be no sure climb,
if you've never met yourself.

HEADBANG

VORONEZH

What is not true of the two together
is true of each separately.

But the bond, no bloodless corpus debile!

Ferried, sham insistence that would agate
buy consistence of purchased fluff,
enrobed to better order,
as when harpers bent over vanity Fair.
And no mope, in just under a century and a half
Robeson's abolition'd broke, like Peter's great-hewn,
from "quiet desperation" to crowded inspiration,
'all pleasures, precautions' rampant in the terror,
and funneled ongoing, eloigned eluant
to revel divisions just absorbent.

Divested, truths shrank narrow paths,
represses of Einstein en mass...
but I did not come for this,
to gray more "Hey! I've had enough!"
Not by piddle and guff. No!
Had frank eyelids with,
and stood against, in shark mid-day
to resolve sailor his hands down
and affront perhaps alas to center some other
along broad, cuffing back of change. Oh fudder!
Anyway, acquired-finish sat secretaries to lap,
kind from start. Site success limned large expense;
his navy, imagined from a rooftop, remained secure;
allowance first, then order inclined.
Fab'd cellular congruent with efficient, smile-clad favor
Hosannas, the gravid air, burst, bent, anon.

Notes: corpus debile: weak body.
harpers mag: was for abolition of slavery; vanity fair was not.
Eloigned: to take oneself away to a distant place; conceal.
Eluant: a solvent used in cutting.
Gravid: pregnant, etc.

LOVE, NO TRAGEDY

There is a wind on the green allowance.
With rehearsal of sorrows reinvest gone loves
and tell sigil lumen, highlight of signal day,
that it is show-method of madness
means and matter of wind
whether he, center furnace,
be at this or which angle,
that carried spells profane to Godsend,
and acquit strange, grunt powers carrying away.

Brief tears publish memory's attacks
saddle-back and lean on purpose to admit
that if you loved, you maddened as you stayed.
That life's lusts could not fail
to bully cautions thrown winds' decay;
and that on the fingered lapses of the heart,
if she had but lain yellow by
and red, red, red taken up,
bold had adopt of trust,
and play, play, play megas to decide.
Then Malibu and Madeira, lethe and lenit,
name and number, naked, taken up,
as nobble guests were, on that guest-filled planet.

Notes: sigil: a sign, word, device in astrology, magic.
Nobble: (nab) to win over to side; swindle, cheat.

DIURNAL

"All days are holy," wake to it,
have their stimulant at heaven's gate
and start from there. Too easy,
debate and philosophize, watered, fed,
strain answers behind sudden walls.
And lest forget, in the back of countries
they are spending spare men that have none to spare.

In agree then with Emerson all days are holy,
And all things that live, Blake!
Time placates renew.
But so much contraire, the offscouring so high,
who would care for a bilked earth and damaged sky?

In the above white north, sun stove-hot,
Nanuuq pads what ice, no seal to warm stout heart.
Goodwill cashed for rude and short,
like soap-box sighs selling why rest would not come,
lustral machinery a-tuck, said,
it was not that I would not buy,
but that I should name the un-named,
ignite cinder pluck, maybe start again, that angered.

ACROSS THE YEARS

Number resolves beautifully
finger to finger across a mind.
When young: jumped and pounced,
endless challenges in a lemon sun,
but vigor canes who of age won't
reduce stamp and humble in the face of nature.
Worst thing a man can
when all the world wants his full, open chest,
is harden to rock, made pitiful, hateful blench.

On foot with real wealth, lead,
junctioning 'not now' and 'never again'
at the possible houses' radiance.
From ignorance, that jail in the dark
that lours swell breasts,
the couraged—sick of ills' yabber,
scenic in smile arc of reward—
lean the always heavy dark and success guard.

Then, not then the furor sparks,
these, not these are assailed in disjoints,
nor snaky in slippery waters gloating,
but ready with the part of love,
unspent in going.

MATERIAL NONSENSE

Green, the like of sun through leaves
took their tendencies heavy through handling years,
and wetted appetite, and sprang realizations
that laid bare sickly treks to tan and sled in star's gaze.

When great gruff felonies gambled on their names,
states feigned assembly, ate and drink and
made party the mischief.
Fancies broke across ruin, grain bellied in silos,
worry at the fat state's empties winced,
and thirst made such plays at sustenance,
none but the lab-rats stood with disaster to haul-out sophists.

Consciences re-made of scant hills,
described what they'd see on arrival:
yellow sun on, creation standing in blue pain,
and evening, in its great light theatre,
waiting the worlds' blanch o material nonsense.

I saw a green light through the leaves bivouac in their favor,
permanence catch the shameless eye;
and win and loss, tried, at trials of sweet air,
with high gratitude finally fit the oath:
To quit the unraveling of the species,
sign restrictive document, dance and grow;
imbue Love, final piece in the puzzle of sustainment.

Note: Sophist: … a captious or deceitful reasoner.

FIGURAS VERBORUM

I drone! But on the bandwagon,
we in the wan baggin' were tied,
and 'had too, too many pretty toys.'
All the dry and barren lands were pretty toys
when verdant sat a jewel on them.
The business of and war, cause of prosperity
and hell on earth fed blood to profit,
'serpents,' some say, 'push the core,'
garbage adds diametrals in its gyre.
And fay you this.
Not as more tripe at celerity,
that has with the other quick got—
if richer, thus poorer, less full to admit
unspeakable glory of the world
running naked through vile, sore wind
with favor for dollars
loving the unspeakable endurance of poverty,
who am I to stop, the eyes closed foolish say.

Even as water is scorch in travels from the tap.
Hills, like bowels with the gripes, flow and park in town;
and we, by death's minions, are hissed to return to silence.
The state of decay, seen and waved in the richest schools,
dries a sleep his eyes,
until something alive in defense
placed away from the delicate buds that flowers
and blessed children become, gathers strength and intelligence,
and one must stop elsewhere to wonder why
this was duty's way always, fresh on hate to pounce.
Science does but muck, brattle about, that with art
the mails watch for grants' tightening cuffs,
that gas the car and pay for gowns, at best, an off white,
who now, with the crowd, some crowd, must throw unwise,
make relent, — who work(ed) for animals, you predatory beasts!
And knew it. That's happened down here before hasn't it?—
Methane ladness with the brush-stroke clouds!
From old madness untie! if your in practice!

ALL DAY WITH THE HAMMER

If he gives all his spirit to prowess,
Both with expense of money and with toil,
To those who have found it we should pay
A proud song of praise with ungrudging temper.
For this is a light gift to a craftsman to make
In return for troubles of every kind—
To speak a fair word and set up
A fine sight for all to see.
      —Isthmian I, Pindar

Occasionally a blossom would collude!
Something old, of frore north mostly.

Walk smiles all day with the hammer.
Legs more step than brick and mortar.
With dig and lay of form, strongest of strong,
could point back as ideal. But none!
In for the long haul, longest.

Forearms popeyed and doubled in the place,
smash pound, lift, position length at depth:
half-n-times-n-plus-one equaled that good day.
Others, sharp back pains curled like the melt leaves of autumn.
There would match, that strength my hero gait.
But probably not till houses built themselves Dad!
—Yet, did come close later!

Bench to benthic in single glance.
He and the Woman who suffered, bore:
were all learned holy, hold-and-decide by.
Safety for feel of others smart-heartest, pain and
was caution, pluck, that hand-held measure
And Oh Pop! I have your wheelbarrow!
All here are so many fish yet not hooked.
Courtesy death's earthal guidance tracks the boon,
is praise touchist.

And, this morning, as Sun peered in cavilingwindow
under that apple-tree visor of his, I knew
you'd spent years in search of a kind of excellence,
nearly completely unassociated with your children.
Then tap,

And I befriended that few have done more
than one thing at a time to perfection. And even if,
and there's question, and choice was no option;
hope, sacred, for good; there being so little time under skin,
one accepts one's station! Feels Blessed!
And gets back on the train to you.

Notes: *Frore: frosty; frozen. Benthic—of deep ocean. Half-n-times-n...*
-the general formula of a triangular number—Greek Math. Works; III,
Pythagorean Arithmetic, Triangular Numbers, Lucian, Auction of Souls 4,
(Harvard University Press, Loeb Classics 1980 Ed), 91 note a.

IN A FOREST

Came a personal—
that survival or exploiting,
falling rock, turf that tumble,
the rights of others to same—
lots of things are allowed in a forest.
Crawling through cracks,
bounding brown patches,
options on delirium at night lights
and scores of tree limb pugilists,
stealth ambles in the dark (I'm hungry!)
stashes of food, digging holes.

At once, Sink thought to seat
that monsterallreadygivenboot.
Scud clouds operate defense, so budget.
And forgiveness, basting, rolls, so
'no monster no more,' while back on asphalt—
Let the little one's walk from school equal.
Sign it respectful facility as dream-lent expedient,
and the whole world pampered to.
Then, other ways we might achieve
'others want what we want!'
Dear, let's read a book, not dislike him!

Finally, safe place, palace guard; hole, hut, hovel?
Was so easy, when had the why,
which was way,
along child's covered in effluents
and thinker's jumping jack tricks.

FLYING OUT (2)

In the faithless house of fateful irony
small resolve believes little in self, selves
and takes shieldless cover in full-reveal corner,
unaware mute body screams
here I am to pounceable, mostly beast
sharpening answers with bloody teeth.

As answer now in exhale, expanse,
in systole is going out,
soon may it diastole, that slow-beat heart,
crawl to particle of part, breathe in,
collapse, take breath,
so the quickening start start.

From the squeaky cart was said,
"Revere the negative, keeper of the positive.
Know drag dark to apprize bright light;
no storm, no rainbow; yin and yang;
'manure and rose'; both sides."

And in that to self:
the natural is the complete.
How will Possible compete
with smoothing arts?
How, anteposed the merchants' fees
shall pine castles be clearly seen?

Then, with some thinker tried
difficult with hard and found,
'when digging the soil,
we too were turning our mattresses.'
And that has been the right stuff.

THE DADDY ICEFIELDS

His never maddened over these wastes,
a saint at home and abroad, was a plenty presence.
And that one's father too, raised four boys,
and slept at war's end with one or two in salute at bedside.
Neither great-grand nor grand-pères known,
not unsinewed by a weak heredity's example,
but by youth, crushing society and his
peace-sought generation, he failed
and found himself in these Daddy Icefields,
excuse, like cold, bitter comfort.

The uncertain nature of fatherhood is a strain in the male
that fastens avoid and solitude, for specie-good would.
And he, unable to live with the woman rescued,
needing rescue himself, spun-down for a time,
then: to persevere or bust.
A curious kind of fatherhood it was from afar,
brillig, like absence and thin breath solidifying on air.

Even with that, the children he never forgot
as he walked his shameful arctic.
No derisions sting like those self-assigned.
The end of fortitude is the trial's acceptance.
Not wanting to be borrowed at breakfast
by the same shut silence or a lie,
to save a dissident nation try.

So, inside and send the earned home.
Sleep with struggle at the back of Mother's house,
that all, truer lives at the "frabjous day" might,
as he, the world's problems consider.
Seems, in this, he was the scapegoat and escaper,
wielder and the knife.

IN THE STATES OF IGNORANCE

Before fall, in complete obedience to its power,
above the town's oblivion,
a tree-squirrel goes by wire to forage his found.
Climbing, mr. clown is unprepared to drop,
But I've seen him do that.
Then police are predatory!
Startles cross well faces,
but the best lineage homes to gutter crack
in this the 'art of ignorance.'

A tear, a phone call might.
But here too, in folds of the state,
people, after a look at,
the well-healed continue to hide,
in the grind glamour of selfishness.

Moon, I see a scripture nest!
She is handling it here. Too late!
I've never seen Love shrink,
except in own life.
From can't to can't to set it right,
cheek not cash-accomplishment!

To be no embarrassment across the floor of life
is needy trick.
Icon voids pending flight,
giants and sages of the sometimes explicate
race many years in one night
so clear sense in plumage light.
A philosopher when asked where it hurts,
may, "In the mind!" Half-explaining inner eye.
Direction is Dimension in this, too.

Tender beauty of ignorance,
knowing release from interrogate grip,
leave us the old haunts and pleas,
the un-schooled baffle neighbor,
admit 'La belle difference,'
add motto "Be mysterious".

OH! DAYS

See how afoul the honesty of fair-play
slumped forward chin to chest, corporate
all day who had little time before,
now all day in contemplation sat.
A testy prostrate, bad back
the family of old men reweaving youth.
That all the stories heard attention and a home
Once and he is absent no more
Leave gift to that his hungry pack
tearing his best interest in the bowl.

ENVELOPE POSTINGS

One year, after a rain
    when winter's coat was mottle
    and the solid soil softened content,
    so many Robins came for wet Earth's bounty
    we called our home Robin hood.

In any group of any too, there is enough
to allow survival of that group never mind how
with or without the wrist the brace is thrown together
if only fairness rule!

Known neither by name nor number Muse borns,
which is but the wonderment.

FLIGHT

Come! wind-way near; house sits ready
amid tones attent only by tree, bush or window—
I could fly, set on course, careen and veer.
My dips and dives would dimple
and through the soft middle
not a wherefore or with-bow would announce
ego of me or them, fellows unreleased,
tamed by their terra firm,
who have no faith in frivolous, unnecessary flight.

Above, prying down, sweet sonority,
secret and subtle notice
do not entice from this rite.
And yearning moon marries
at the half-way point
I seem a rock perch best,
then not having dived,
bear up the cup of life
and toast these california of mind.

INSPIRATION

I knew from experience a secret once,
I've not since exercised in years.
Hie oneself to an outside to be moved and write.

Now I've spent hells inside, that were quite nice,
to myself I'd confide.
But nature in her salvant is so lone at top,
any pile or list,
I wonder how reason let feel lose sight of it.

Let raining seconds flake on the running ground.
I can't help lessening imprint,
and like that curious laugh in spite
that crowning frown, that loss so deep
no longer to the depths creeps,

I will speak in tones beneficial
even as dread shapes cares I am home with;
and drub damps with the flying spores
loose on a wind or chance by—
enterprise of life gone strata high.

NOTEBOOK

When I form, reform, nulled like a bad suitor,
better fed, better said,
the common confusion of liberty
sets out to do well
and the most good for the most would
find allowance.

Missing the pages, I scream in private life.
Note the rascal thought
moans on dime not caught or kept, better paid
spare mason shoring the houses' behavior.

Here Mercury, for his virtues, supports
somersaults over the wire. But Mystery,
one with uncertainty and doubt — The Keatsian Three
lounging in his negative capability,
having nothing to do with paper,
scoffs and mocks, glue at the gate of presence.

I sandwich between false masters,
fix eyes on accountant stranger.
Then think, to verify edict to write,
flub must scratch page, blight
till symbols link and line, that pure country,
ahoys in sight.

CASTLES OF BOOK

Heart-soft under touch of bodies wasn't.
Succumb view of loft under sheaf-watch was,
that sought, if life bungled apprehension with
better books than attempts and courage,
Holy Numa taking burial with his.

Under clank fear—being bookless, self-seraphed,
file the duldrum 'faithsofarincompanionship lost'
that squishes futurity under the foot when stepped on,
with cry taut dryness of risen independence,
that is a way wonder takes.

A hint, B discrete! Affairs of state scream
for the gentleperson asleep in sham.
And why not Night? Reap lax donations!
The hours sacrificial anguish mornings' disposal.
Crumbling year to keep count the mischief.

Very cross the aloof, Verse!
Drowsy spectre Amour fast from study, secures feel day.
But, do you scoff kithe rescue,
and drown now Lust
in library's shelves and sheets.

Notes: Numa Pompilius.
Kithe: chiefly Scots: to become known.

BOOK

Attempt pastiche; show amalgam
inserts fair and right of dervish—
that left Doubtful, undeserved, nervous,
and scout more churlish, dry-hump purpose
that dashes tender head, still against,
stones of otherwise ill-thought service.

When mind, as a tangle of branch,
interests site and imagination,
put leaves and flowers of feel to them,
as Spring does with convince-her-logics
and perceive flats turn to
bumps that are passions' furnish.
May the universities please.
May Time ancillary watch of clock
order in the breast comparison to stop.
Stumble, doddering past is no reason to believe
in futures that prove her blood-born needs
that are tumble out-voted
gnash on these new firma.
Common Sense, the page turner!

And we would our book, and rage it there—
Life remained on deft, cold brooks
that slept in the eyes of dangers,
whose bold was our tutors' looks
and cries from positioned chairs that point
departments illicit in their Rousseau lair.

CREW OF THE PARALUS

Ἐπί Θουκῦδίδης ὁ Ὀλόρου παιήονων

Here, could be a coming along unscathed
by cheat podia nimbling gadless bromides
to ready winks and choired nods.
Was elixir in the where!
People-rule outstretched the republic of interpretations
and drops of coin and surrogate minds
bent law to tyranny, but were shorted, shroud—
a bow bear—locked, as the demos climbed.

There was the Crew in its time:
confusion, false-hope raked-over better intent,
hid Deviant under Welcome
so miscarriage could ride.

Here, elections sacrosanct meant,
when vowed vote sacrament.
That was not your fathers' uncorked liberal
sealed now from all manner perceived harm,
but an uphill blood and gut took to page,
of The Crew of the Paralus, brave,
who messaged to those well-healed,
in crimson bright who misdirected to un-wit
the commons standing their un-adorned white,
to render wrongs right.

One jumps fence in the years
and has to indict deceivers.
But that like sheet and oar on storm-toss sea
is not a comparison that will please
a strip-searched public, ponderous, doubly upon knee!

The cold of infidelity's night,
as those stout of the Paralus,
may we all know. Watch earns the right,
good sits above selfish curse,
responsibility in individuals
is plight and badge of worth
that allows no more, injustice,
its bold, slippery anchorage.

Note: Thanks _To Thucydides, son of Olorus._

264

BEETHOVEN AT THE BOX-OFFICE

His glance on time and circumstance,
tide watered, was at high tide in his chant.
'Divisions, unities,' might tangle, route
Humanity to strain where un-natural went.
Yet mariner extends from home and family,
not to cool, but to a fairy land to blend and
end-clamp life over constituent and continent.

Oh "smell the whales' breath" shall?
Who sailed further than eternity's context,
who down the offal drift of time thrives in schools
and rests thought in! Earth, make men of them!

Sketch the tenth cod can't;
explore insanity that railed honour,
so Buddha should process Beethoven extremely fast
and cash who fired that caliph hand.
Oh! save us from the cruelest noon,
ill plastics' boon.

Throw, read rules with the riot, stampede,
that shall by share and exploitation be said.
And Usury, you will unfold your godless hands!
Da sho, "No money, no tournedous!" —
who wears triumphalism as tragic mask.

Who is prance and bangle at catchy chance.
Who is you, you, me and you
who sit same key like in his string quartet,
and never with the 'Three Poisons'
greed, anger, ignorance are shut.
Strict pose our bafflings when best of us!
Scratch Bonaparte zero with holes,
and banish selfish away our sus—
in the world that is an art's theatre.

Notes: _Da sho_ (Chinese): _he said_ ?! The Three Poisons of The Buddha.

BRASIDAS

Io paean! Again, it was that Son of Olorus who bore!
And I was, by his report: last run at an enemy, left stunned,
quiet, like an incredulous, open-mouthed child.
Judicious effort flags time well spent,
success needs failure to mark how went.
And men carriage hope between sets
of who won against whom;
select wrongs by guilty guile, stable only for a while.

In the homeland where Eurotas reared that daughter,
battered children and the luckless huddled evening stars.
Stolid faces tried solid carapaces against death's tin bribe;
and that same sun that delights on horizons, burned mark on.
Here too all the serpents' minions appeared as men.

At then that water-walled door to Thrace, near the Nine Ways,
there was stratagem, a speech, bare care, a high trill run,
and oaths in kill air, that failure not eye the start,
that bravery's canker be the on-air in respect like that.
Otherwise, war, a gall in mouths,
like insult rising within,
is not washed by the dapple dictation of waters.

And mothers' milk of round kindness,
droned by adrenaline as much the flood-reason in crowds,
overtakes fame's high name, un-bids good dying,
when lesson's us from that battle book
of the sometimes noble, always sorry, flummox drums up.

Otherwise and out of time, ownership does get things done.
Memory, goddess form intact, can restrain acquisition.
His oratory good as any Athenian's.
And let's say, shall, in anyone's all too serious of the all so serious,
they in their's and savage Ares in his, pray here never again,
to run another downhill at an enemy that's a friend not met.

> Note: Son of Olorus—Thucydides, 5th century BC Greek historian.
> Io Paean! I have here: Yeah Sing Praise! (to you much is due.!)
> The old Ennea Hodoi, the Nine Ways; amphi on both/all sides,
> all around; polis- city—Amphipolis.

ATHANASIUS BY THE GOSPEL

Little dreams track in the blue petals of desire
unaware Unicorns have been chased from the stone folds of statues.
Mindful magnificence cowls with a tenth their annual misses,
to muddle dissonance in wilder muster of beven plank.
Joy fits fine shattered bottle.
Oedipus will tan the sweaty content, Dumas count the pages.

At fuel, distal elegance of say-not runs from cannon
to fade borely in a crook of the carline's arm.
Who was that left un-molest at slightly headdress
and why have Rome so rot her likeness?
Some days pass bounding thin forage,
allowing lid the lidless lickerish
in sight of feckless parallelograms,
and children, to the office tomb to fit bodhi remembrance,
valor importance imbibed in truth.

To contain that hirsute, absence drowned in a droplet.
Frown would train alphabets on retention
so can it raise its rail body, append everywhich,
indecent the fractal a-grip ship to get home.
Nine, inoculate of ten, scarred and barred the shirt,
but in high Penelope, dirt between toes,
needles went wells, undertook duty,
and labored shin at the twice captured dome.

Now, you may hear of Athanasius by the gospel,
but Anthony dulled in the shoe.
Each night home quarreled their lives,
speared by nanny at the board, who lied, remnant of john,
killer acclaim, pitiful, shat in its blue-yellow blade
brought neither light nor warmth.
Some of the past we'd reel back in.
But where we are is where we've been,
and that's near enough for him.

CH. 12
MEETING-WHISTLER BREAKDANCE

MEETING WHISTLER

With pillory and praise excavate something rapido!
Evacuate a storm that chose that shore to batter, as all the many
leagues out were drinking ruin through the always-summit sea
whose self did not suffer! He said, *It was our amusement to convict*
and something shines in that snare, but I dare not; *they thought,*
he continued, *we cared to convince.* Whistler words we think
work well this time, even as was The Mother laced, titled, side-long in her air,
Then: fierce nineteenth century suarez barbarous
carnie-hawker-in-a-booth look, youngling feared that came.
A raw thing, a back full of sores.
So, here too, neither to convict nor acquit alight. But brief practice,
with concern, and overall solicitude, the components of care,
to eye clear the artist and his curious, in survival saving with—
In their creation, Works of Art remain there fashioners,
makers to give, amend—'recent' law precedent!* and good.
Since un-like his, this is not exhaustive.

Empire and commonality, pride and dissipate,
epigram for posterity those at heavy work those days
by use the elsewhere pointing mot after decided effort
"We worked like n...er's!"* Later-day digs at wall street New Yorkers?
Then, fury, steal, and out slight apanage! Out diminishment madness!
"Dash asunder ...set at defiance, even 'to' selves..." UNIA,
under Zeus-dark brows, Father Garvey, and King finishing Cowper,
always and all-where, "The mind is the measure of the man." So again,
Out staid Oh!—it-wasn't-important! bias of same-one-upmanship,
scratched from photo line; there-were-none-there! falsities to highline, or not!
And yeah, still mad perjure prestidigitations that bottom justice,
that immorality plays to faction soothe; vile corporate,
that immediate gain with devoted selfishness held priorities most observed,
worlds of dependence those Days where the very denial,
unravel of which could not sustain. And Wider, Whistler, wider!
Adopt Seeing Homer lent On-Both-Sides-Lame*, our claim,
and reserve handed by Velazquez, which would have better done.
Then, as in velocity constant, with us, at slip retrieve with lead-less moving,
beyond present-worthy Chance, way-wind across a now road
at equilibriums' butterfly slow whap and wing the interspace middle close!

Know, we follow *nota bene* Gide, Claudel, Blanche and what,
juggling, spare, listener would pass as great enthusiasm and art;
soft, trenchant call now, soon aghast; that flowered in grateful minds,
"...on 'imagined' blue and glassy summer nights...like his

[P. 1]

270

'abreast the brown and shinning river,"* God-held prayers for watch
and comfort shielding, 'before reveal-mornings' dégrisé'* of bad ideas
and worse treatment of Black People, his true "soiled and miry ways,"*
seen from this angle. 'Straying about blindly in his brother's garden
and bruising himself'* among round of cutpurse shirkers, flinchers,
runagates, immoralist swells and forgetters of basics.
Where one hand, to embarrassed heaven, holds wine of a dead baby or two;
same risk-diet too long hung in throat, ethical hypocrisies that foster.
Even as on the wholly side ichor, a thing of gleam, fall, very light,
dislodges treacheries of selfishness like disney & rome and governments'
on Black Man whole, in their usual venal against the worlds' peoples,
who now-cleaned wands want. But let Denials form from who—
having not the same inhumanity of greed, vile armament against to wield,
those innocent, opposed with these others, of conquest—
having only their rich Indigenous to defend, ring in no iron-ringing evil.
Does it matter? This, what dare not, locks bounce (I think it does!) skip,
what used to be deride, child-like over?

Mon Dieu! "We don't know how we and dem ar gon work dis out;"*
au bas mot at least to support the self Dasein-with*; without minstrelsy,
to "The end of foolishness"* 'Demoniacal in controversy...'
gone bright when sun danced? Or, how dare it now,
at trough, a-slip in an ocean? 'genius of mischief,'
"The McNeill"* "Dinna ye hear the bagpipes?"*
Who black as base, Gleyre's* early timber, "universal harmoniser,"*
in paint never forgot. But that in the life and civilizing of anxious,
dangerous, verbose man, at last—his 'care of nothing for the dark figure,
only that black was wanted there!' (or what?—media offends
'it may not be good for america but it's damn good for we,' remembered coven,
of the Whole against)—Ok! It's like that!? Pass the badass.—So slide in
The Lange Leizen and Variations in Flesh Colour and Green:
(that's the scientific!) The Balcony—that seem apology rough, slink precious,
un cri du cœur to the enslaved-enslaver system, anger oh! he knew
he gained smirk from. Dégringolé*; is not simple!—His mother,
'we did not fight to preserve slavery, we fought to protect our homes.'*
A thoughtless thought, slightest of slights Then as now,
as she and doctor son, apart, huff to the continent for rest.

And yes! This is after the fact! And comfort all want. But "You know,
You people are not well!"* he said and applies. And that is why The Law,
Just Law is need.) "We are all egoists"* the master once to Fantin,
—and an inclusion one can, with scoff appreciate and credit with—
the Unpopular One stacked about the shadows of the house (ICF's* in the kitch-
en)
an easy education Legros? and 'virtuous idleness'—"unyielding belligerence,
may it make conspicuous, at the entrance of Janus;"* where for-a-fraud-time-
to-exclude-when-inclusion-better-brethren, wordless in laz lair go?

[P. 2]

271

Well, Memory points outside reason's gold-arm norms toward safety of all;
you get my meaning—to what in being, doing, must be stopped;
having rayed-away scoop side-hustles, that Civilizations list, bust;
and among the multitude, as Mencius taught, hands-even message
of defeat and end of sappy impertinences send to universes
of convey-less words at stir 'round cocktail-tables, to tell,
as we our contemporaines, that with this judge and grave smudge—
his love of Poe and Baudelaire drawing Yeah? And? to recall,
the oppressive silence* Bacher described of "Jimmy" at work
hoc opus, hic labor est, and the silence, sunshine of individual creation,
diacritic of clarity when smiled on, so also, effective tool of miscreants
and the cowed, they say he exhibited when near Degas; born same year,
'only Degas and he for paint!'* one of them, that has us—
Do we know our silencers, that is the Befindlichkeit, *Heiddy,**
"state-of-mind" of *our* would-be fire-breathers?

You know, I think I do! Spy from the record, and cognition's fine hills,
Fantin, same road through Holland vous trois homme painted on!*
—Norman Parish, Ben Heine and Moore applying in my day!—Yet suggest,
any, having seen Whistler's work, by gestures words written,
perspective brush, corked needle, feather, (not cephaline hit)
dental explorer or probe, crayon, pencil, chalk or stump, to a picture invested,
"the unlooked-for arrangement;"* (cloud-work good Sherry,
bright, in a glass, shadowy pleasance and relaxed hand.
Rye, single barrel, on average dies, but not often! to keep the taste
and protect the Body, you know! As snow cones' the tops, but also
sky-holding arms of trees these days as with lemon quarter!)
he would have proven himself a near great Master. Loss due lost humanity
that drink on ship brought.

Yet even here, one must find ways to live with oneself; as this
Magnus Defensor, Adeptus Argumens of Art, who among other
accurately affectionate *ad rems...*" wizard of feminine apparitions and
intellectual expression;"* "Bacher, you don't know to whom you are talking
– you are talking to Whistler!"*—And more than "Master of Badinage,
Apostle of Persiflage,"* "'...who fist-aligned a Haytian for tumbles down stairs'
(the loss)—woe till-bettering to they that stand, beasts among, Marmalade!—
scuffed 'for swagger and colour!'"* who had just won a war!
Who indeed, this painter, as in near every instance, pathology's ugh oh!
psychology's lure and bite convict on own swagger, and show—
giving F. R. Leyland naming privileges* (Mantz*) of proximity,
and cause for strong nips at pump heals*), Your Vanderbilt leg!?*
Taffy, the Laird* and Litrebili's mien all ≈ sum of Everyman
(his own "'de trop spread-eagle'" Mr. MacMonnies!*)
That quite un-gears a "choice rowdyism" attained unadmitted,
unfair addvant age, and dark-described self, "He was very Brown..."*

[P. 3]

(elsewhere, 'he was very fair!'* ("If you don't leave me alone,
I will put Boggie-woggie in your bones"* do it my Good Ghost!
and gift him "a little black-looking conceited thing"* recorded another.)
Making his Jeffersonian Fumette, or was it Finette, scholar?
Wherein History, Experience, Governors on Phenomena, record:
the worst haters of any group, those most against same group,
often live within, among, are of that group! So advise Sew of Caution!
among all groupings of them, men!*

Along this strain then, like in a severance, The Islander* everafter he disliked.
Still, into the cause of all, on other occasions—the repoussoir* element—
his last to a stranger or friend would. And in, find we him, John'd
"not by measure does God give the spirit."*
And "'I AM"* sa hamm That is Everything!' less actioned, in lieu
at a doorpost, erect at a house of The EverLiver; with this sullen:
he had, of fault-free Fairness, been more 'born, than made.'

With these els sansloy, sansfoy, sansjoy*, investors jolt from chairs,
shares clutched rot in slack hands; slobbering fairnesses of curt,
court, greatly abhorrent privileges and selfish's never-as-yet-
to-fully-sight-round joyous all in love and art, as in war, is fair,
hawked inaccuracies to falsely convict, much commented on,
and capitalism's pseudos—from market, union, civility, concord, G&Rness,
that on civilization—under soiled rock even now
the hate-breath intracks and thrives on—but more
of that Something at the feet, speak! and "It would have been nice
to have painted that!"* "Ténébreuses ébauches* tentative dashes,
"gloomy sketches, "murky daubs"; fool blanc minds
trained bigot in that doctorate! Redundant, un-maned,
"a species of misunderstanding"* perhap! Where one driven contrives
and heedless, with Ares in delight ons, self and friends against, who
with authorities' quote odious, dulcinea of the duffer; *I will know myself!*
and 'Take the work out!' early and late, good things tout—
At finish were, like the multitude, by the sinews of war, often made blind
to the opaque with crystalline brilliance of the young, piercing eye,
at any age, of the Simple jumped and worked into nature.
That un-ease and ease at work on good work. Quoth Iliad: *wonder-sparks*
putting in and *seeing into the heart of things...** the 'Miss's Jimmies'
in service, Le Faux Pas Watteau? Beatrix's shores; caryatide!
"The ladies you know are the ones to win the world with..."*
'Writers touch feeling (female) territory' William Carlos Williams
Transitional 'while holding the male ground,'
—a Cordelia me! and will not in support, our watch,
slip arrant in mention! Ignorance of The Everyman, still
tragedy of the ages! And a Good story told!*

[P. 4]

But come! A dan must have had greatness beyond or to
The Spry Olympian's. Presentations, half-wayers Phidias, Sesshu,
Michelangelo, Shakespeare broke never chisel, brush or pen on
to contemplate (sans *vita brevis* to scribe! of injustice on!?)—or—
bereft that ready knowledge, free in its place of superhuman endeavor
(see affected reviewer!?) who reads Mr. Whistler's "polished," often prodigal
Ten O'Clock*—(great Ruskin at fade in his time) (before E. Lewis, Eakins,
Wilde, Tanner, Robeson, Garvey. After Dürer, Wheatley, Douglass, David,
Goethe, Carlyle, Ruskin again, Delacroix, Laviron, Murger, Champfleury,
Gautier, Baudelaire and Courbet* ("Où est le temps, mon ami, Où nous étions
heureux et sans autres soucis que ceux de l'art?)
Or was it Du Maurier, and a whole Οὐρανός δῖοιο* of near and far ancients?
Including usual mentions Longinus, Demetrius, Vasari)—
to be unmoved by the slackless Mistresses of Apollo, who "without haste
or pre-occupation... same devoted absorption in art,"* even in his polemic
'that he knows how to conduct,' (Now! Malvolio-Macaire!*)
"rendering with usury to the critics and journalists, the blows wished on him..."*
Have gift slayer, 'plan' and execution-unfail his grand Art outcrop!
Rake with the Dandy met well in "that... most un-English*
(le petite American!*) of painters..."

So then, Chance, whom we have introduced, as all *Art,*
*science of the Beautiful** that comes, as some know, and all find
benefit of gladness in, due to that happy completeness of wish;
and not the philosopher's "All retch and no vomit,"* again,
(Hayden or other noctes ambrosianae* where 'value and intention' brought
the line and dot* catnip, valued vignetting) that! to the free-flight realms of seen,
scene → in This! that way, going as against one's own incredulity;
in full safety, with goodly guide, easy force of breath;
for an hour, a day, list eternity, accomplishment in anticipation,
the bestowal of which men cannot count on has indeed come upon?!
Is fantastical in extremis!

Whereupon, that is not why any of it is done. To act and at completions' bend
if summitted; by choice, be graded, account *ad quid,*
by whom in looking only, have spent a life, in bravura imagery,
with the large group nimieties* of coatless ninnies in once fine parks at nap(p).
There to glance, glare, "ill will never said well,"* quoth Henry,
'...a rabb, mob, naer-do-well...' hits the old verser, flower Mére at the gate*,
against this her prankfull, many times, exemplar foul-tempered,
we've turned back to, up to his high-head charging. Who
the Secret of Drawing knew—which: of once poor, shrinking-in-action
but not writing, good Jean-Jacques remind; who gave and lost much
to conquer men with men—Whose drawn lines (picking up) live:
a revelation! "As realistic as a photograph,"* or "as the light fades..."
where "the shadow is lost but the picture remains,"*—going on—

[P. 5]

274

whom others, often without civil's long lived understand, court.
What understand, in its pass, hails none, but who in receipt are,
for however long, are, by (and make this the twice truant dative,
left off the Goupil notice and later Mr. Eddy;
the Ways shoring the fortunate-mistake way here)*
their individual steadfastness at the trough, from, by, and at
Mnemosyne's mad ladies' buff, prod, as said, there,
randomly among the labourers, scattered as by sortie, fancy
and no clear conscious aqueduct, Art, the "chancer of things;"*
but who had and have through the trials* like Carlyle, the Mother,
The Creature* himself remained—
"Well," he said through best professorship, and it's seminal!
"It's more than I know myself'"*—who (again)
though sore of foot, ill clothed, a little itch and put upon,
have gone on. Which was always Proof purchase of Her hand!

Lengthen, end and draw alike?! A bore at parties too, reined-in,
no Bourgelat softness* by careless women ha! ha! Where one should
be as impenetrable by eye and wisdom in simple earnestness,
intimiste, as that honoured, head down the daylong who munches,
having only dual sore, sour sensoria, in the long and short run for worry on;
manufacture the fault plied, to reecho—having seen Mr. Whistler's sketches,
etchings, and the rest his most certain representations and mood 'impressions,'
—dismiss the period and palleted 'un-finish' Diderot did Robert with*—
as would please water from a stone—A Woman at tide,
Think Madam Finette again, and Mme. Duvernay à dance;
Maud, Standing; Jo's Bent Head; Trilby shoeless; we're off to the graces!
"her sweet wan gaze"* Victoria! Marry me?!—
and not come away with at least one near tear to attend there rally with.

So Maude gone, not Goone, commend further and doubly now
(quotations 'confess less inferiority', I say, and more
reverence for the word and its arrangements) in the duende of conscious,
ragamuffin delight at bound off table, high praiseworthy! call,
his arrest of mind florid in the orchestral write.
Even as, boer atrocities' like american whites',
contain for runs gorecaked Herakles-like through his house.
And comeups composed for that one Haytian,
if Stations "Euston or Waterloo"* didn't, in salt teutonic,
to his low breed step and launch stiff boot and stiffer Right,
"quod autem somnia pondus habent? An habent et somnia pondus?"*
As there, like a paste-on-a-flatfloor land Barkeep!

So, further this ire house; billboard the trouble Jo* had raising
Charles; that son's worthy laments. Daughters Ione and Maud with Maud?
My own few rattles of breathes in space that destiny drew and

[P. 6]

275

with standard scars sketches, traversing the much harm, to them I pray,
did not! Or that Rodin, clipping Camille, assumed being statue
nice to him. How Monet was tableted: little confidence. Ala change,
to end and step the same step, how Holloway was lift to comfit.

Truly there our bell switch, slash stitch, too-wide ricochet,
heedless torrent, that tore soil, critter, root, and rock
like bad poetry from early sympathies has slowed, gone quiet, and
has nothing left—Having taken down the sign, changed channels
in its proviso meet and greet of the wily artist in happy find.
So, 'We too (must) cleanse Menpes*,' As sifted Sickert shift in his piety*,
to an inaccurate, un-flattery to Gainsborough* and back,
that no charge gained, that was treacle and had nothing of eager—
to wake dirt to mud, make for Lotus, and deny your art Mr. Art—
growing on your stem, "turned aside by no indifference or ridicule,"*
'...the diligence required in cultivating... endowments unspeakable,'*
And accede, 'Art seeks the Artist,'* So, "Most independent man of the
century"* Mr. James Abbott McNeill Whistler! Presente!

Our twilight approaches mild night says, whole binary, real Garden,
Verne Utope, Venice madam, and Grail holy, was his Santa Barbara,
and your writer's*. Love of the arts of Japan, China, the Liberty defection.
Sharing of Greaves's and Thames boats rowing,
'whispers-on-glass impressionisms' with J.M.W Turner.*
And such eye-ear as work, the Lover of Mankind, habits,
without noise, press of same, posting in far-off thinks of consequence
watching for good of all, where too are in addition for similarities
his Duveneck and the "Duveneck boys"* cambial through a sog.
A 'Joe Simpson's* barber acquaintance, which gathers
from the-hazard-and-joy gardens of 'California,' to repeat,
and similar St. Petersburg purpose: where unite, all, to push decidedly,
and 'you may lay it in your heart.'* This 'when I am moved,
I am just that!' kudo, in whole rally and the moving air buys
for this Itzpapilotl!* Padre papillon* with-a-sting,
formed and forced full out shout mouth, capitaling it, we toast
and Wreath him, chin up! and everything detail can contain,
who painted night!* Clap! "The most original achievements of modern art."*
In which we federate with his best infrastructure
"Autres gens, autres mœurs!"* Other people, other ways!

'Sun Tzu said, he dreamed he was a butterfly, and waking, said, he didn't
know whether he was a man dreaming he was a butterfly, or a butterfly
dreaming he was a man.' Am I here, or do I just think I am here?
We may all have done that. Art does, Jimmie, happen!
Borges* had your back, now I!
And only from a list of yesterwrongs swear to pick nothing!

[P. 7]

[P. 1]

* "... recent Law Precedent" See Eden vs Whistler in Stanley Weintraub's Whistler A Biography (Da Capo Press, 1974, 2001), 406-420. Hereafter: Stanley Weintraub, ibid.

* "(we) all worked like..." E. R. & J. Pennell, The Whistler Journal, (Philadelphia, J. P. Lippincott Company, 1921), 10. Hereafter: Pennell-Journal, ibid.

* On-both-sides-lame: Hephaestus, Craftsman! Homer's Iliad — Most texts: Sigma 380, etc. Bk. 18.

[P. 2]

* "←" & "... abreast the ..." Pennell-Journal, ibid., 310.

* dégrisé: Pennell-Journal, ibid., 92: soberness, sobering, the morning after!

* "soiled and miry ways ..." in E. R. & J. Pennell's The Life of James MacNeill Whistler (Philadelphia, J. P. Lippincott Co. London: William Heineman, 1911), 66. Hereafter: Pennell-The Life of, ibid.

* "... Stray about blindly ..." Letter to Swinburne, J. McN. Whistler in Stanley Weintraub, ibid., 331.

* "We don't know how..," From a new Song released 2016 (?) posthumously by Bob Marley.

* Dasein-with: Being-with — Passim in Martin Heidegger's Sein und Zeit. J. Macquarrie and E. Robinson Translation (Harper San Francisco, 1962).

* "to The End of ..." Stanley Weintraub, ibid., 306.

* "The McNeill," Pennell-The Life of, ibid., 360.

* "Dinna ye hear the bagpipes?" Theodore Duret's Whistler (Trans. Frank Rutter B.A.) (Philadelphia, J. B. Lippincott Co., London: Grant Richards LTD. 1917 — Cornell University Library), 117. Hereafter: Duret, ibid.

* Charles G. Gleyre: 'early' drawing teacher to Whistler and others, Stanley Weintraub, ibid., 39-40.

* "universal harmoniser" Pennell-The Life of, ibid., 35.

* Dégringolé — Degraded person. And here is meant, how haters degrade and indeed sicken themselves.

* 'we did not fight...' —Stanley Weintraub, ibid., 117.

* "You know, You people are not..." Whistler as President of/ to the irate members of the now Royal Society of British Artists in Mortimer Menpes's Whistler As I Knew Him (London, Adam and Charles Black, 1904) 110. Hereafter: Menpes, ibid.

* "We are all egoists" Stanley Weintraub, ibid., 87.

* ICF: Insulated Concrete Forms: my lightness on Theodore Duret's discussion of concrete form given to Whistler's painting(s). Duret ibid., 273.

* "... entrance of Janus ..." See Marcus Annaeus Lucanus (Lucan): from his De Bello Civili or Pharsalia, A. E. Houseman Trans. (J. D. Duff) (Harvard University Press Cambridge, Mass., London, England, 1928), Bk. 1: L.62.

[P. 3]

* "oppressive silence ..." From: With Whistler in Venice, Otto H. Bacher (New York, The Century Co., 1909), 197. Hereafter: Bacher, ibid., 177.

* "In art, there is only me and Degas!" From Suzanne M. Singletary's James McNeill Whistler and France (Routledge Taylor & Francis Group, London, New York), 123. Hereafter: S. M. Singletary, ibid.

* Heiddy, my 'affectionate' for Martin Heidegger.

* "... road through Holland ..." S. M. Singletary, ibid., 102.

* "unlooked for arrangement" Ch. VII, Success, Duret ibid., 102.

* "Wizard of ..." From: Robert Howard Russell's Eden Versus Whistler, The Baronet & The Butterfly, A Valentine With A Verdict (New York, R. H. Russell, 1899, Now in the Forgotten Books Reprint Series), 65.

* "you are talking to Whistler!": Bacher, ibid., 197.

* "Master of Badinage, Apostle of Persiflage," Pall Mall Gazette article June 11, 1888, in James Abbott McNeill Whistler's The Gentle Art of Making Enemies — finished in Paris, France March 26, 1892 (Vertex Editions, Los Angeles, 2015), 160. Hereafter: The Gentle Art, ibid.

* "... for swagger and colour ..." Pennell-Journal, ibid., 43.

* F. R. Leyland naming privileges; Pennell-The Life of, ibid., 115-116.

* Paul Mantz: French critic of the time, in Pennell-The Life of, ibid., 73-74. And in Stanley Weintraub, ibid., 86. As well, like much here, in many tellings of Whistler's life.

* ... at pump heels: Stanley Weintraub, ibid., 186.

* Your Vanderbilt leg!? See Portrait of George W. Vanderbilt (1897-1903) in The Paintings of James McNeill Whistler, Young, MacDonald, Spencer, Miles (Yale University Press, New Haven, London, 1980), Picture number 310.

* Taffy, the Laird: from: Gentle giant/warrior in G. Du Maurier's, Trilby (New York, Harper & Brothers Publishers, 1895). Hereafter: Trilby, ibid.

* "'de trope spread-eagle'" Mr. MacMonnies: from: Pennell-The Life of, ibid., 384.

* "... very Brown ... from ...', Duret ibid., 99.

[P. 4]

* "... he was very fair ...' from: Whistler: A Life For Art's Sake, Daniel E. Sutherland (Yale University Press, New Haven and London, 2014), 35. Hereafter: Sutherland, ibid.

* "... I will put Boggie-woggie ...": from: Song: Jerry Lewis, Reggae Singer.

* "... a little black looking" Sutherland, ibid., 178; Stanley Weintraub, ibid., 385.

* *...all groupings of them, men — See Charles G. Gleyre's group of students described in Pennell-The Life of, ibid., 35, etc.*

* *The Islander — The British Isles, Pennell-The Life of, ibid., 394, 397.*

* *Repoussoir: set-off, contrast.*

* *"For not by measure ..." Bible, John 3:34.   * "I am ..." Bible, Ex. 3:14.*

* *Els: already; without-law: sansloy; without-fidelity: sansfoy; without spiritual joy: sansjoy: from Edmund Spenser's "The Faery Queen" — I, ii, 25, etc. The Complete Poetical Works of (Edmund) Spencer (Houghton Mifflin Company Boston, The Cambridge Edition, 1908, 1936).*

* *"It would have been nice ...": Whistler quoted by H. Pennington to the Pennells concernant a work by Sir W. Q. Orchardson, Pennell-The Life of, ibid., 230.*

* *"Ténébreuses ..." "... murky daubs" from: Charles Baudelaire, Le Peintre De La Vie Moderne, 7. Online.*

* *"... a species of ..." Pennell-The Life of, ibid., 339.*

* *Homer's Iliad Bk 18; L. 380—"daidalea prosekeito...iduiaisi prapidessi"*

* *"The ladies you know..." — Whistler, concerning distribution and sales of one of his written pieces; from: Sutherland, ibid., 161.*

* *And a Good story... See Josiah Royce, California: A Study of American Character; From The Conquest in 1846 to the Second Vigilance Committee in San Francisco (Originally - Boston, Houghton Mifflin, 1886. Now — Santa Clara University, Santa Clara, Heybay Books, Berkely, 2002).*

[P. 5]

* *Ten O'Clock: an address by Whistler delivered in London, Feb. 20, 1885, etc. The Gentle Art, ibid., 127-140.*

* *(Où est le temps, mon ami ...") P/o Gustave Courbet Lettre to Whistler Feb. 14, 1877. "Where is the time, my friend, when we were happy and with no other cares but those of art? From : The Correspondence of James McNeill Whistler, Letters 1855-1903, The Online edition, University of Glasglow 2003-2010; Edited by Margaret F. Macdonald, Patricia de Montfort and Nigel Thorp.*

* *Οὐρανός δῖοιο—Ouranos dioio; Heaven of the divine, bright, god-like.*

* *"... without haste ..." from: Bacher, ibid., 199-200.*

* *(... Malvolio Macaire) from: Pennell-The Life of, ibid., 282.*

* *"rendering ..." Duret, ibid., 72.*

* *"that ... most un-English ..." Stanley Weintraub, ibid., 309.*

* *"... petit Americain ..." Pennell-The Life of, ibid., 40.*

* *'Art, science of the Beautiful,' Whistler quote; Bacher, ibid., 51.*

* *"All retch ..." Alan Watts.*

* *noctes ambrosianae — Katharine A. Lochnan's The Etchings of James McNeill Whistler (Art Gallery of Ontario and Yale University Press, New Haven and*

London, 1984), 5. Hereafter: Lochnan, ibid.

* "... line and dot ...", Lochnan, ibid., 189.

* Nimieties: Excesses, redundancies.

* "Ill-will never said well." Duke of Orleans to the Constable of France in William Shakespeare's King Henry The Fifth; Act Three, Scene 7.

* ... flower Mere at the gate: from Pennell-The Life of, ibid., 40.

* "As realistic as a photograph," Stanley Weintraub, ibid., 384.

* "As the light fades ... but the picture remains." Stanley Weintraub, ibid., 139.

[P. 6]

* "left off the Goupil notice ..." from: Thomas R. Way's Memories of James McN. Whistler The Artist (London: John Lane, The Bodley Head New York: John Lane Company, 1912), 199-200. Hereafter: T. R. Way, ibid.

* "chancer of things"— "Whistler, he was a subtle chancer of things."– Artist, Patrick Hughes, BBC Fine Art Coll.

* ...through the trials—See French Artists of Our Day; Section: Gustave Courbet by Leonice Benedite. And literally The Eden and Ruskin litigations.

* "The Creature ..." —The philosopher (Carlyle) grew increasingly annoyed at Whistler's painful for-the-sitter painting style, and began to reference Whistler as 'The Creature, an absurd one,' to close associates, Stanley Weintraub, ibid., 158.

* "It's more than I know ..." Stanley Weintraub, ibid., 441.

* Bourgelat softness—Claude Bourgelat, Élemens d'hippiatrique, ou, Nouveax principes sur la connoissance et sur La médecine des chevaux.

* Diderot did Robert with — see Denis Diderot, Hubert Robert.

* "her sweet wan gaze": from: George Du Maurier, Trilby, ibid., 2.

* "Euston or Waterloo": from Pennell-The Life of, ibid., 97.

* "quod autem somnia..." "But what weight have dreams? Or have dreams really weight?" From Metamorphoseon, Bk. IX: Achelous and Hercules; Publius Ovidius Naso.

* Jo—Joanna Heffernan/Hiffernan: long suffering painter, model and mistress to Whistler.

[P. 7]

* 'We too (must) clean Menpes', Menpes, ibid.

* As sifted Sickert shift in his piety, from: Bernard Sickert's (brother to Walter) Whistler (London: Duckworth & Co., New York: E. P. Dutton & Co.), viii. Hereafter: B. Sickert, ibid.

* 'un-flattery to Gainsborough', B. Sickert, ibid., 19.

* "... indifference or ridicule" from: Walter Richard Sickert, (the yellow and white walls could easily have been his idea or any number of forefather(s).) friend and

student to Whistler and Degas; Letter to Alfred Pollard; The Stamp of Whistler, Robert H. Getscher.

* '... the diligence required ... endowments unspeakable' from: Johann Wolfgang von Goethe's Wilhelm Meister's Apprenticeship. Thomas Carlyle Trans. (Collier Books, New York, The Macmillan Company, New York, 1962, 1968), 89, etc.

* "Art seeks the Artist", T. R. Way, ibid., 144.

* "Most independent man of the century" from: G. B. Shaw quoted in Lochnan, ibid., 254.

* Your writer's... — Your author, in his Industry days, helped build several Advanced Telecommunications Computer Systems for the area, employed at the time by AT&T, etc.

* 'whispers-on-glass' — See for instance Turner's Landscape with Distant River and Bay.

* 'Duveneck boys', Stanley Weintraub, ibid., 244.

* "a Joe Simpson's barber" — Joseph Simpson and his Wife; Black barber and confectioner (Wife) at the time at West Point. Sutherland, ibid., 23-24.

* 'you may lay it in your heart' — Homer, Iliad (passim).

* Itzpapilotl — "Mexican Indian goddess ... whose name signifies The Stinging Butterfly." From: Marie Norris in Lotus, the Magazine; Special Holiday Number in Memoriam — James A. McNeill Whistler, December, 1903. 20.

* Padre Papillon: Father Butterfly.

* 'who painted night' The Gentle Art, ibid., 33.

* "The most original achievements ..." B. Sickert, ibid., 52.

* "Autres gens, autres mœurs" — Other men, other ways. The Gentle Art, ibid., 261.

* Jorge Louis Borges.

PHILOSOPHER

HEROS, Agapenor, not bad, first,
who truly to men honour brings.
High sky battue. Variance to analyze.
Bliss insists the moistened air—
a system of gate and lock
that lifts, deflates as times go
and leisure wing—
are holp by fresh sun on herb canvas.
All else a penury.

Thinking long, mast collect; heave hard
you've mentor-mention about imprisoned anguish
that lopes lack, fills herds with:
"From others will help come to our existence,"
which thing barely exists.
Trail loose the battogues of reason, welcome!

Devote smiles and simper,
mass times acceleration equals force,
cold rest acquits singularly.
Excursions notice tumbled from nidus, exhaustion heats.
And in the table of thalamic definitions
slave is rundown by enslaved. Blackmail and blackball
are from under Victorian and earlier sheet come.
Burrowing for references someone must go for meetings
where our love went.
And the best teachers are still student.

Notes: HEROS... ἀγάπενορ agapenor: loving manliness, manly
—of Hero(s); more than mere man,
Shower of kindness to fellow men.
Battue: beating the brush to flush game.
Holp: past of help.
Mast: fruit of forest trees.
Thalamus: p/o the brain—integrates sensory information.

POLLOI

Told timid torn tooth terrible traverses trending trouble tried
To tempt torpid temples toll terror to trip track traces
That the top talents taciturn turned to to trigger tailoring's tone triplelicious.

Backed by bold barely brawny brains batched bright bracts branching being
by briar breasts braced, babe'd bright beams, broke bright bunches;
bowed baby branches bacchant.

Said, so! Soothe sought such sudden sinks south sunder standard stitches
stretched,
Strung straight strophes, strong, sure sent shots strummed, so sunk!
Such savory sabbaths secondarily seditious splayed sordid since Sam sailed.
Sallying sumped sanely south; said sooth same sad sandstorm
Sold some several sending surreptitious, sought.
Barlows barreled by bonhomie burned barns. Bowed Bands Boxed.
Bit buxom betty babes bellying bambi beside bachelors
Bodily botched baffle bright bunks bandied 'bout. Brakes and banks beer'd.

Both bare brows broke beloved, bachelor bottles bunched, bunking braces
billed.
Bane brought backup. Ballyhooing ballyhooers beef-ate, brought bound by
bales,
Beached balls; but, begotten bots burped buff's big balance some.

So how, with all this ma-lark—bold's begs a beggin' bad baths button bails,
bereft before bailed babes aimed arms abaft action's ascending ash,
and abbey aides always by babes' bottoms baring,
turning mere-rumps-of-humanity face forward to heaven,
—can anyone, get anything done?

THE LAST PLACE

Where they were, for them
was dull forgetful,
possessed none of the loop-trajectories
careless childhood in free association
and experimental yard and field,
they were told, learn so much.

Those small accomplishments,
by better than adolescent hygienes threatened never to be forgot,
never loosened, by they "that never grew up, that always need Papa."
Says the philosopher, "the trouble is the boys who always need Papa,
they're the violent ones, they have the guns…" and position throughout,
with never a progression to social helps, adult,
that know the place of protect, instruct, with wholeness found.

Ever surly, big deals smiled in the offing.
They had moons to mine and asteroids to strip and that weight bring in.
Distant outer lights attentions swirl, they admire.
Lies fed themselves, grew sate.
Faux-knowledge and poor math theory,
foundering understanding,
kept the 'innocent' destruction up,
and ease of listen and go-along was in continue.

But I'm told they never did find that last place to stand
in a great grass naked, breathing real air,
having given the gibbons their trees, as few of them went to their needs
to stay the human flood of disaster business related.

DAWN

Miss me when I've come and you're not there.
Let the stale air in some tulle-fog not kill you.
Eyes on the fare, register no complaint,
yet send commonality back down action-chute
with its hazard easy way.

Make a superior try of spinning Imagination
for Art's insipid imitation, which is a good start.
Then, from whatever nosebleed lights your bulb
the long road is the highest,
on the marge, take that one.

Day will mark itself as can.
Hands that had you to interrupt
now have by opposed energies stopped.
And wonder, the whole,
every bit of it added, or naught.

You had served well. I cancelled your card.
But that was one day out of many.
And the living green laughs frolic,
and tomorrow, as lazy vapours rise
and broil sun chides making for his top
will I again have my bronze-armed, mighty son,
sing you a piercing, morning song.

LIVING WITH THE KING

That offensive thing of him.
But she knows best that self,
as the end of mercy had come,
and brats and Mama's boys found their lesson one.
Gathered rights of polite society to learn,
and lad experiments awful wrong to pay the sum.
All phenomena with him do not begin and end he found.
A fright to know you are one of many.
Notice also as do, the large ganglia w/ head-sized palm
and what hours of labour fumed, wanting rest, can, if concerted.
Soon, empty nest with runny nose and scuffed knee
when was the prince. He's out at elbows
and flight, and night in elm's upper arms invite
ease, promise relief, silly sanctuary!

Fatherhood that keeps the safety, corrects the errancy
is the most accepted tyranny when pure.
Nor here shame old Lear who only *slenderly knew himself,*
and *usurped his life,* or 'gray Denmark'. No! Ago,
a man, each in his setting, nay estate! was king.
Each a very Shaka, Great Dane, Otho,
hands heavy in true Gotha going tens of thousands back.
There, a sonny, a junior advanced as father,
his queen, keen to notice children count clouds the air.

But 'Bob's your uncle!' if living course dare:
Roof erect, fished rivulet. Books bright.
Out of the house weather flocks in this dream,
to boot bad chaos, its effluents there.
Oranus, Kronos, fathers killing sons, fathers.
Sons son'd and hating it. What? Usurped, driven low?
This the king will not! So, him killing him, father, son.

Man's mad story havocs defense and razes round.
Defense is an act of war! And *Two things equal to a third,*
are all equal to each other. Which may be our best reared yet sergeant!

Notes: Gotha: Europe's Royal Book of royalty.
Bob's ...! Aussie—right you are!
Euclid's first rule: If two things are equal to a third thing,
then they are all equal to each other.

THE OLD FLASHES

For the grab-ass, a nose for spite.
Tike or adult saw its clear red light.
Later, manic mate tried that closed gate.
Found his pawl, paid-out dragon, couchant
'tentive to abate.

Debase jokes, not permit!
The fence-tight teeth, that flash of red,
haptic armour, against these pit.
Otherwise on excess of love
and un-erred sympathy fed.

Once in a mean time, I lie not, it was maga this, maga that—
true only under moral evidence, ethic and humanist hat.
Now, little minds and smaller hearts with a people charged
to govern of a long grown, nearly proper law, which they themselves
were to be higher above are backward at large.
F*ck 'em! What's you're twenty Sarge?
Cuddle, cuddle keep your trouble,
let your fires learn.
But they weren't all that. And Heaven will hear!

Yet another time, Cynewulf seized Sigebright.
The captured's kingdom, up for a charge.
Till him, his long-accustomed alderman had to discharge—
and thankful and acceptance lessoned freedoms large.

Here, a warranted anger broke across his bow.
Been tossed, E'coutez—moi! many a century beguile.
And the countertop feeds and bleeds far back.
And the taste in mouths lingers ruin and rack.

Here too, the withy pretty in a one-piece nice.
Here, reach, rest, tools housed for the night.
And that wild, old quite flashes, runs the lawn.
His anger invited, put to yawn.

Whence in the morning, say it! Again, he will rasp all the non-delight
into a trash dust to sweep off a table.

A LETTER

Late Sept., early Oct., 2018

Mike,

No staff. Sheriff strip-search halted. Not! Hot days ha ha! Self so. Cottage.
But Guys sending guys pictures of themselves? Seems suspect!
Unheard of by our fathers! Heck! I barely like women, the female sex
for companionship! Men and boys, no chance! Still, for amity, proof of purchase,
where as warriors Good Men had better as you say Stay on top of the physical,
and not having seen each other in years...

—Himself! and some mental excursions! three days into a five-day fast.
One day after receiving your Pic last week. For the flat fun of it!
Not!—the fast,—Cleanse!? And as you can see, Mr. Muffin needed it.

Coincidently. Got caught in Cicero's De Amicitia 'On Friendship' a while back.
Impressive! And still ranking arguments and agreements with,
from the working-artist standpoint, who, in scattered cases, must be alone.
And, these: what seem like thousands of years later, I hardly, until recently,
recall having one, being, it seems, long alone in the work—few complaints!
But I remember we were, there in that life, on that planet, then.

This is your second remind of the tequila (Mescal) so to that—Throw that
detrite out, aeh! Or keep it souvenir on a shelf. Few need eat a worm any time;
and story is O' the trick on the gringo! I don't know what the ruck I was thinking.
More like not thinking—a plucking Chicken following movements on the ground,
no looks up; quotidian, common, everyone's doing it, herd-behavior bull-sit,
false civic, the young go through. That shit'll kill your Humanity! The conformity!

—Talking to myself.

—Good men, with themselves and the-planet-at-heart had better stand
against today's worlds' traitors—right-wing worldwide—who are:
from their survivals' greatly chancing men, with their disgusting nazi,
little-boy behaviors.

—I've recently ordered Sweet's Anglo-Saxon Reader, done pretty good without,
but, better have it... and the whole Bowyer's Bible a few weeks back.
And according to amazon, some new Josephus—his Against Apion
is on slow boat heave here.

Haven't run in a while! But if The Big Guy/Gal lets, that may soon change.
We had rain yesterday, and it was what I was waiting for.
To wash away, down and, I know! to us, but... the long-stand smoke, that
for a soil, solid two-months of fire-burn assailed our once-breathable
and confined to post. Update: Fri. 10/05/2018—rain did not work! Smoke is back.

—Wondering how Maliya, Sydney and Sophia are (perhaps explain some day).

288

—Hey, have you seen The West/Unger Class and Interventions out of Harvard earlier this year

—On you tube?—Magnificent stuff! And I appreciate their attempts to guide correctly.
There are counselors winners would have on their side I think awake in the world!
There is sense and retort!

And I mark, feeling more than a little dirt about it for his un-civic, nazi,
call them authoritarian tendencies, how correct I think Heidegger was about so much
in his Sein Und Zeit, (and his becoming, guardedly, my new Jimi Hendrix, James Brown,
James Joyce, Robert Plant and the band; and what about that new Charles Lloyd
and Kamasi Washington? that's what the Sax I'm finally talking about! hero.)
Men have sped, far too fast, past first ideas and principles,
and have to go back-to-starts to rescue truer sense
of what they mean by so many Dasein interjects on the world.

—Spied an anagram in the sky the other day, cloud you know! that figured a nine,
with the definitive bottom of old exclamation-point the fifth day into that fast,
that, like omen, if I let it—bade me four-more-days-to-the-fast-consider????
Which quickly, ego, a tightening center, with temptation's sixth-day
break-fast meal-ideas-pictured, slapped hedge 'round, and badge stuck out
to stay me the "Boy this is going to be tough!" begin-test original five-day goal.
So, I did that, and made it! Out at five! I'd only done three-dayers before,
so this was bigger trial, and recovery's been interesting.—But here I sim...!—
new skin—just kidding! and all.... Though not about Life's sneaks of consternations
mid-trial, and again the tightening! That was serious.

Yet look, the sun shines. Winter-preparing Grays with their brown ear,
black toes, downy chest and dust-mop tails; and family—all-the-rest—
are out, about ways, means, scurrying. And I'm still eating what I broke the fast with.
Mess of Wild-caught Salmon, Chicken, Turkey, Barley, Beans, Kale and Tomato—
Man did I need the carbs for energy! Thank you God, Mbaba Mwana Waresa,
Ashnan, Osiris, Demeter, Ceres, Hoori and Sara Mama to name but a few of the Ladies,
for the Barley! Forget taste! Eat for Nutrition!

—Alone? Yes! he said. But fortunate in that I can devote all my time—
to study/find; read, write; translate, and try to help man save himself, even if he doesn't!
Because I see nothing if not the brink ahead!
Even as there is wish men could find that perfect soft clench for their—
"The serpent tempted me, and I did eat!" wonderous companion.
Who rightly, all, are eyeing as somehow-truly not-enough, we, male counterpart
these days—while they, deep in the can-do-without deserts slough as wholes,
bizarrely forced under long mis-engagements there to wander.

And well! What fools would kill their own planet? for starters.
And where the heck is man's cosmic base, cure-ist of all, simplest prevent
and life-save invent, long-sought, given from start, that never failed—
their one-plus-one-two-equals Golden Rule?

—Be well, stay with it! Continue to help man, please! Talk soon.

HIE PLACES
(A Morceau, Morsel, A Very Short Play in Four Parts)
(For the Left)

AUTHOR
The author in great Dylans of engagement; his self-proclaimed—by long sustained
word and violent mob action—enemy/protagonists, and their enablers: the "anti-
discussionist," morally ambiguous, "move slower!" who backstage personal, but not
outspoken revulsions of the inhumanity of their daemon-like fellows ogling strange
fruit; draining life shear with Bombs, Banks, Insurances, Home Loans, many bilks
rabid;—how was to fend, steered wrong deliberate?—and continuing from-justice
and the-equality-of-man seized privilege are solely responsible for this work.

Then participant, as trail thick foliage pulls over itself, as bear; as among
remainder, toing and froing, a civilization recounts selves old tale; know, that like
a mother, long suffering, any species, we ferry stubborn hope with teething faith
our backs, glory your suffrage and...But brisk! We're well past emissary noon, and
brumal roars ahead.

PERSONAE
Man (Mr. Angular). Comrade. Woman (Lady Rosaline). Sister. Chorus. Our
Philosopher (Philolaus). Wind (Snapdrag). Tommy Doors.

(Overlook a great lawn).

I. DANCING WITH SHADOWS

Chorus: Without ray moods as we sang these phrases. (Addressing an audience).
Disappointment and vile possibility tied gore philosophies.
Ours would, the loss their hate-filled wages
in word and deed, as cross gaunt reveries

angary about tent thicket, swart snort boar fore
entertaining rabid to thwart.
And stood yet mild flat, mid-hours, gravid with herbage,
over there (points) cow after amble to their oaks sat.

The man sung night as he had seen it
but could not un-cloak clad clown.
Unlettered opulence in an uproot,

Woman: wore draggle their sorrow!

Chorus: staging whelp lowage left town.

Man: Some rather more or less radiant spokes of
latent sun to tired surface sped;
long in faded radiance
before plenty of crop again met.
Sister: It was a ball or was it hole, a heaved grace
grant of old its mighty load, content dragrags of prophete,
to land and life, assistance great, orgone consistent souls.

Comrade: Under noble given, there stiff necks lent,
containers naught of Grateful's scope,
God of mercies even then drops in to compose them hope.

II. SAY METERCOITES![1]

Comrade: Vector well Greek poetic slam then Preakshow
others had too, one form, another; when reduce cry baddest and
wear that m^&f..er like a coat came to survive forced thirst.

Chorus: Imagine! You could not! Being otherworld! Such helpless, as to die if
unsuckled on plop, sprout these poisonous.—We have ever looked around!—
Have nothing'd him! No wrong, less animal urgency. He comes at me!
For this (all point at arms)!

Woman: Having kept same short, stranded (so guard) at tore 99...

Man: Travel with Michael, off on one take-that-back! hunch—
again Jefferson et al—and grow wicket percentage
slung stuck Saul in the bones-shake

Chorus: while monkeying us some monkey do;
whose logical connectives have no receptor sights,
platys of same genus.

Man: 'Don't evil all your white boys! ad captandum vulgus!' ideal father would
wed. Though yclept the issue blamed; more haruspex[2] than harum scarum now
our pursed arrival non ad captandum vulgus![3], under breath breathes.

Chorus: Imagine. Could not, as he (some look on that old Mars) went long in
that! Such helpless, to then not-a care-for, lay-in-waste-everything ill-breathers
become!—Sound the Braved Awareness all ought!

Woman: Something like drawing 'tis! A one third fakefear, if't!
stopping evil's one third across fine globe in every type, salvation is't.
But bid awful trouble Jerusalem! Thus soldier seduce; sleuth, convex.
Woman & Sister: Oh sully dream reaper arrive with something truth;
that sum is too, rein twice then dupe not, sly tax breaks;
...you pee pee'd, Uups! Sinicize nor USA Euro-trashed Africa!

Man: Once say 30 days to platter plein atmospheres
aims ways a-coning, passage of time in clumps
wares revolution; sorry, close escapes Wordsworthian!
(whose early Afric sympathies are appreciate[4])
where smash metal terminus...

Chorus: trackback wouldn't want together-with lest runaway!
sad deceive, liar immaculate, in that sans-human Hungary,
USA, Israel, Greece and feral Italy too...who, all who, in falsity
are named but a few; that wealth forced from whom?
and 'mid lock-step panache hurls loose (You do! "Sold media")
"poor Africa! (while buying her)" "poor Asia, poor old Balance America south".
What does Europe have save what's stolen? ask!
—Who had on entry gift Air as breath for a man,
later mother-skewer tears and misshapen am.

Man (looking at chorus, shaking head with perplexed exasperation;
turns to audience): Youuucall me Mud, whom I only Mother in;
say because of assignment of color you hate me!? And I should what?

Chorus: Elevate my consciousness?
—Understanding your, and this lack of respect for such loud, any color, dumb
un-civil bumbler disturbeth the honoured peace; once again
arm you wrong in your ancestry from me would wash.
Is un-civil! Crime against, instant! And I should what that dismiss out of hand
for genus age, color, manner? Dark Garb of Humanity usurpers wear least,
their worriest, you are innocent! And Be That!! vertebrate mixture roundabout
makes just as many of them in gray's tumble paintment!
who won't afford kindness.

Tommy Doors: And that was the extent of my fence! And I don't give a f*#k!
A muth#@!*kas' coming for me, and I know about it, I'm not waiting, most like!
I'd be "ereon geneaen te tokon te..."asking after his family and offspring[5]!"

Sister: Shoo shend[6]! Age In Preservations—
Legacy, the wright, wedges something sharp the year'd light.

Comrade: Borders that came on humane progeny
that were only, on walls, note! hung as portraiture!
Man: There, Wind, currented notch of poppies gents!
better rent!

Chorus: Orange lupin, benignant in slim share, near outhouse spore,
was plaque for explicit, no or the space with Reason wore!

III. DIME STORE
(time passes.)

Woman (looking toward near cleft of Godly rock): Reverent went
not scrawl hire terrain. Men've a great deal to put to themselves;

Chorus: she said something early in her voice.

Woman: Good-bye color him, rang at a place heard by knock.

Sister: There, Spoiled had grateful what Givers obelsed "Take!"

Chorus: Igneous the magma bone shared as sow.

Comrade (having gone to, and now from, just above them, at hiked seat):
To stillness! Clouds gyre, grope glum mountain;
woody troop move. Round mickey mouse ones poke around.
Sprite throw spear; over sprat seeds sprent.
Other moist, at gallop their un-crop the winds wear,
pudgy dragoon on parade, some. There's a jellyfish!

Man & Wind: Tried tare workouts to survive!

Man: Lux shone on that sixty self portrait of Titian;
and George C. Scott on Carson, "Hey I just turned sixty!"

Our philosopher: At least half way there Scott! Of a great year.
A son of Ariston[7] unions belike, in which, 'What has a man?
Days and nights!' (eves and morns of Daniel)!

Sister: 'Then 364½ x 2 = 729, Philolaus.

Man: The number 729 hallowed for men...

Our Philosopher: and more than pleasantry.
729 Months = 60+ years'; but dim pivot to border,
then set men. At least half way there! Again!
Possibilities' conceived prospect!

Woman: Stretch. These are all that are left; Mothers from
Ios, Wilmecot, Penrith & New Orleans rear, complete phantas—
Beethoven fugues his Boogie-woogie anticipate, you, rest there,
any laurel; away gripe ripe state fear is; glad
e'en Circe's divertissement as glint for a while, in this back then.

Chorus: But clear!
From the lower trough will! And. 'We go by feel!'

(Quiet. Slowly, all from the lawn to the Hall retire. Slaps TheThunderer.)

IV. CARPOOL
(Time passes; runs Dusk away, pulling her skirts,
taller than you remember; later evening.)

Man: Weir-whistler Wind there was a bobbing true purple sliver
out window; strong girder for spider,
life line, what you and Sun do, just then!

Wind: A handful note for cull? clay catchment, happnant?
File. Save As—For 'Xtreme poetic try Virgil!?
A tear courser Gentleman's Agreement?

Man: The out of true in men softs' yesterways' wit on troubled mirrors[8]!
—Who Virgiled my family, Head up! With you always was I there!
It's a huge thing to be simple in the world! "Hail regardant!"

Chorus: To a philosopher too her truth is hurtful.

Philosopher: ¡Mira! Tear where Go went no Stop come by.
Labour's Lost euphoria, scad enjoyment!

(Walking from one room through another to a window far end).

Sister: Yes! They've 'lorn the slim grass and way mislain Lady Rosaline!
Still, news! Gate forward to Africa not totter ledge bade.
And territory? True who Sabbath man to his heart,
no charade shakes. That it surface there'd be
some sumped sense of pain or ist that… 'termin it sane
even in dung beetle months[9] men said something kind to the coming year,

…Chorus: These The Days of Their Lives.

Comrade: Ugh oh!

Our Philosopher: ῬΕΝ ΔΈ ΟΠΙΘΕΝ, ΟΤΟΘΕΝ ΟΎΤΙΔΑΝΟΣ

ΕΓΩ ΒΛΑΣΥΡΩΠΑΝ ΑΥΤΟΣ, ΕΝΕΡΘΕΝ, ΧΘΟΝΩ.'

Author: (Many bemused, find it something like: "In the time to come, man to man cowardly; I, grim-looking, same; below, to ground!")

Wind: What was that, old Greek?

Chorus: Hand scratch ugh oh's! this way and Out!

Our Philosopher: Yes! Another stance just would to south build lock
so's do-up moon overhead was in same isle we were!
Chorus: Said said 'spirant.

Man: "Here, onadvance bush mount, ΩΣ ΕΦΑΤ."
(Coming in from a side, smiling secretively).
Woman: Where, was a stand of tree that had his heart?
I heard you from in there! Got he, reads the wind in them?
And wondrous bend, deadfall perch just past drain pipe,
had he thanked All for?

Wind: By now Outidanos, Ridgement! I shy not!

Man: Snapdrag! End! Lest found ill-magic's table bent!

Chorus: Agreed Mr. Angular!—Tiller of what Old Man was—
See Trees are waving thyrsi, so we're on right track!

Wind: Some have word runners, breed of Thersites! Bigmouth for laughs, at Ilium!

Sister: Add rain ramp reign-meant; save whole animal, sooner must!

Woman: He too sacrament, guy, lie-in!

Comrade: As limb shadow, by you Blower (staring out)! squirrels it up and down a wall, in these our Nine maidens' smile-chased enallments. (turning back). And like a once, and hoped ever poet, through the pain and hired pestilence—we too 'would all to Time except[10]' so many evils dalit; and prate οἴοθεν[11] shall we? under old hell's doused flame; enter new Eden, 'mid fewer walls elected.

// Append to margins of this parchment: R. Frost's—Once By The Pacific. A Couple of lines in Archilochus about Muse to him coming, please, "and bring the universe..." Robinson Jeffers—something on being near the shore; also. S.T.C's Monody On The Death Of Chatterton—from "He hears the widow's prayer" to "... makes Oppression feel." P. Neruda's I Begin by Invoking Walt Whitman, entire. St John of The Cross's Spiritual Canticle 3—"...Seeking my Love/I will head for the mountains and for watersides,/I will not gather flowers,/nor fear wild beasts,/I will go beyond strong men and frontiers. etc., etc. Much of Derek Walcott; Amiri Baraka, William (& Dorothy) Wordsworth. Aristotle to Alexander on the best way through life—in Plutarch ?... Confucius. Certain portions in imaginative power overflowing of Milton's Para. Lost. Amos, etc., etc. Suemonsteroidian, oidoid, doey? Where the take is thief, of life you'd lief.

295

Notes:

[1] Motherfucker. Written earliest perhaps, by poet Hipponax against one Bupalus, sculptor, and his mother Arete; 6th century BC.

[2] Yclept: named. Haruspex: a diviner, basing prediction on the inspection of entrails.

[3] Non ad captandum vulgus: not to captivate, attract, please the common people.

[4] William Wordsworth poems: To Toussaint L'Ouverture, & September 1, 1802 ???!,etc.

[5] Homer: Iliad, H128

[6] Shend: kill, destroy, etc.

[7] Plato

[8] W.B. Yeats; 1919

[9] Dung beetle...: "...translation might be something like "throughout the month
of Bull Shit..." Greek Iambic Poetry: Hipponax; 78 & note, etc. Loeb.

[10] Robert Frost: I Would Give All To Time.

[11] Face to face.

HELPS

At the beginning season remember nothing much.
Years' trough break of deep, dusk dulcet water,
earliest age, mothered as stayed.
Through affection's aperture
world kept handy, sterile, cowed;
showed it possessed love whether/if
only survive forward hour, then as a now,
little else. Respect, feared,
ignore sash beauty of
harsh lessons shut.

Crib-mates and demonstration for pass over,
of autos—Gk., same, self, credo of kinfolk.
Thence to "High Office," playground of Joyce
and many another who mirror-point, 'self-donned,
unafraid and unfellowed' like the monk in write;
and run horns, as luck, as might, on all airs anyway.
Your share—How to abrade hate n'est pas désolé!
nor beg sorrows for labours on the side of man.

Note: n'est...Without apology.

CANTHUS ELEGIES

I

Autumn, and hibernating babes,
In dormant, in bundles, lie for and against timelessness.
Sincere, books-yet, in fantasy jettisoned with
Standards' un-represent in passing age of impoverishment,
That Duty's tired soul reinvent, and mark in tones rapid, meant
To project assination her cerement, who! like Herakles
or Tydeides might slight a god!

II

Round referrals, better to heal brief grappling with,
child of Earth, oriel through thought, claims settle went.
Withless succession of Season's retirement and lode of Pi,
confused... hums hunch in purchase.

Finish for a day, soul is sounding lodger;
Straight, staggered ship rounds Isle of Purpose;
Sad eye sane wits betterment.
Distensible pride must grovel dishevelment
And that through the picket of tight teeth.

III

Soon, to markets' cashed sustenance; the molding month wears:
Pulled, trolley brought bacon to roll consumption down hole as mouth;
Overtook cloud's insistence, and sec,
Outpaced drip-nonchalance, who's hands-up contains sway.
And what a mess was made of touch-type involvement,
Their mud: the other's arrests as currents: his dispersants,
As the trickle-down dammed on the up-side,
As biered whole exercise was damned treacle lie;
Gadarene rush into brusque lawlessness,
That like wink un-mannered men of the ill-stared Ithacus
Grouped fall round blame galling mannerists.
Posturing defense trammels Democracy.

IV

But fear! What if their worse were their urgents;
Were thought more book than cover?
Is not that part false-happy's blandishment?
chancement that makes Disbelief,
then in rescuing turnaround Up-fingers new tyrant?
If you are but pushed by unseen hands, felt,
Loaded to fire by once shelled behooves,

Are not still bartered by Distill to keep it simple,
Be own holy fool, own Myokonin, Atman beholden,
Through involved reckoned years,
Attending opponent weight of the world?

V

Allow, oh sign of things crossed. In the counsel of years
Anger rebukes accepted satiety, spread back-take of excuse!
Resistance, full fee, sets key to lock; and free! who
Omit full unquestionable sanity.
Essence of life is lengthening inquiry into God;
Certainly not unconstitute when separate into parts!

With civil tongue done then was canting veiled in curse.
And writer, nonce of books petitio principii had words for
bleed matter verse. Legacy stood merit,
not praise foul facile segregate;
So, like the mineralist in his Epigram, Venetian Thirty-fifth,
You 'Live and keep on writing friend,'!
St. Petersburg—your Cyrillic Rome, Walcott your Virgil.
What you do not understand of forms, virtues lost,
These beckon, answered, concerned, compt.

> Notes: Canthus: either of the angles formed by the meeting of the upper
> and lower eyelids; that slanting angle, that <-shape muscle group, 'the four
> Recti'!? that C–like, corner form!? Or, fully met, i.e. with eyes closed, as if.
> P/o Cant 2: a salient angle; a sudden movement that tilts or overturns a thing;
> tilted position; an oblique line or surface, as one formed by cutting off the
> corner of a square of cube; an oblique or slanting face of anything.
> Assination: for (my) asinine, stupid. Cerement: death cloths, etc. Oriel:
> a bay window. Distensible: swell, swollen, etc. Gadarene: The demon-possessed
> swine in Mt. 8:28 that rushed into the sea. Blandishment: something that tends
> to coax, cajole; allurement. Behoof(s): singular/personal of behoove(s). Myokonin:
> A Japanese Buddhist holy fool, "the wonderful kind people." Atman: In Hinduism
> = the self. Canting: affectedly pious or righteous. Nonce: the one, particular,
> or present occasion, purpose, or use (for the ~); the time being. Petitio principii:
> begging the question. Cyrillic: Slavic, Russian, Eastern European and Asian
> alphabet. Said to have been invented by St. Cyril. Virgil, Quintus of Smyrna
> (Izmir), our Milton...Heroes. Compt: archaic var. of count.

THE MOAT

Once, the scales of do and don't were known not equal,
could between the two distinguish.
Then counterbalance, selfish rush
and life no longer simple.

Seems some took the fruit,
killed kind tree to count its inner symbol;
parts not being wholes, danger loomed.
Entire lives stayed as at a signal.

Shall now I, this remove, entering the angle of evening's stare,
cross myself in wish and prayer and like to discovery in a poem's plan
much love find there,..... as all would wake and gleam cashes,
stayed by practical, selfish hands,
       un-learned in love, exulting the narrow, erring mind?
      Seems it wants to! And comes with a buyer's guide.

So, if here I linger stulted, near blind
    among the pulled flowers, broken rock,
    does that mean mean-men were right
    Life's a journey ready for mock?

By grace of life I smile as rivals meet their mend.
Blessed is he that lends like brook, allowing Life its wend.

EPIGRAM

Plato was wrong, Socrates right—
you will instruct the memory out of them.

Patience wants courtesies. But Patience will have to wait like the rest.

There is a young Werther moment here good Sir,
but I am too impatient to find it.

Folly and disaster are the sport of Implication.

The cup bears only what is poured.

In difficult times, the assistance one seeks seeks aid too.

The overall anxietal aspect of consciousness $\approx \pm 1/2$ the relative reality.

WAR

Dear Weary, Summer Dirty your aim—
rather what's left of man past histories dust bins
full of mold, twice as teary for the types of rolls
that can be done in empty spaces. They're all packed with air!

For our sunlit lives extend a furry for torching dark,
have threnodes lift by epodes as threadbare happy's flush.
Have a trove of tortured treasures winsome in lust
whet no applications that operate disgust.

Humanist-predecessor debunk should marry our will.
Now a low hum work in the still,
Priority has teeth to practice no kill.
File Rid! all this foul smell and blood in a bag (s)will!(?)

Note: Foul smell...—Old saw quoted by Marcus Aurelius, etc.

HOW TO DIE

Character is the wealth of nations
and no comic relief, Aristophanes.
Blood and water betrayal offer
to best men and better governments.

A secure position squares,
refuge will not, from that curtain cup.
His was a just pride in a good life and better dying.
Your Dad and Mom likely did that!

Try now to recall when you had a wisdom and loved it.
It was a comfort, and worry an evaporation.
Affection, when not disgust, was cheerful,
and with the line gave-up separation.

'Perfection licensed imperfection to prop;'
children drew better than a broken man's lot,
despair withered under the fallible net,
while deception faded not the precious pages of history.

Then the talk ran to silence. You drank your draught of quiet.
Love trained want—was there some backroom
you could operate from—and partition-master Death
paused in embarrassment.

AND ALL THESE MIRRORS MOTHER

A-wheel or chakra the fire, talk of timber wolf's sharp teeth
comes spoken on the breeze, through seethes.
How condor are shot about a hillock from here.
How fool hunter, empty poke, completes depletions,
while some anguish over ogre's stack.

Dollars mean to self-designate hosts,
have it some commentaries play best
when never viewed with a realistic mind or after the crime.
So, unlike Milosz who needs revelers add distance,
this broadside goes out tonight!

Byron and the Shelley's' 'abominations' at Lake Geneva
moved men resolve the name fright. And thou mother
art queen of days and all doings. I am,
because your purchase on subject kept straight apple value,
that now impugns present monsters see
what reflections in their mirrors actually look like,
and beyond the shrug sight.

AENEAS OR POETRYS' GOODLY EMPIRES

Rescued by Apollo, on Troy's plain, from god-tryer Tydeides.
"Not duly honoured by Priam. Second," that company, "only to Hector."
Among wonders seeing at Juno's temple, settlement to hero,
urged on by mother Venus, as he waited for the queen;
the Carthaginian mural tale-ing that terrible thing at Ilium.
That among many sights Virgil accounts pictured not only him, his exploits,
but Eoasque acies et nigri Memnonis arma; the Eastern ranks,
and swarthy Memnon's (Dawn's son. The Aethiopian ariston's) armour.

Now fleer, searcher, family carrier, finder, founder,
I would have carried my Dad had he wanted it
but the bones and clouds landed athwart and unrepresent.
Other weir also did not, so nearer the mothering women
he saw later part living, an honoured wish.
Mind! no words were sent, received that unspoken weren't,
but audibles fleet peer in the alt were;
where we'd been on an other day about similar circle and circus
up, un in the air, Atlas holding Uranus, Nut, weaving;
so, no need this time, with only the pull-away as agent.
I tried, or did I? Brother to tell, but I can't recall its
coming specifically through palisades now.
The Homer translation trolls and tolls, hailing-nicely!
I trill because want it know-ed!
Much good has come! Such speculate on-language run!
That call of Art, her distractions from! To Her seer work,
that needs em.

DEFENCES

Anticipatory resoluteness defines the even ground.
Over course of time, pa de tout,
with a moment of vision,
grip-hold on witling reality,
like surface fires in a hearth or sun firelight
seeing is believing on the high ground,
moments spent with you.

Note: Pa... not at all.

COUNTRY—PATRIOT?

Oh! Give your ruffled, your roar! Make a man perfect—
he wore his human on him!
Their Planet was still round; they made due for this often
and bred a bouncy breed just special like them.
Too, the shoo alcaic left heedless from areyard. "For the infant,
loving cards and stamps, The universe (is) equal to vast appetite wed.
Ah! And the world grand in its menu of lights!
Eyed the mind that world is brief!"
Give glance and dance, sororities answer...
I couldn't believe so much in my little self, Oh said—
and to it most assigned, someone slapped, mightily, a table,
Then left by the back door collapse, leap pod, off ebb enter.

Day, far from start, itself Spring-dressed if not Summer light....
coughs in coif. 'For wine a mirror is; shows
/ The image that is fair, / The friend of lightsome mirth; foe
/ Of shadow-haunting care.' Another: Care? Yet another,
curled copious her chariot, driving hard strong horses
Solicitude and Concern! Cura? Invented man jut his wholeness,
given only general charge.

Then! I think we must get on that horse! The bad-eying.
That very monster intercept with Love that flows arrant
through the best. No more bagatelle, if that means anything.
And if a citizen of wide worlds, surmise, as look, attend
and may every discussion make a regular civil servant of! Idinit!?

Notes: "For the infant..." From my Trans. of C. Baudelaire's Le Fleurs du mal;
La Mort; Le Voyage. First quatrain.
"For wine a mirror is..." From Autumn,
by Alcaeus. J.S. Easby-Smith trans.

REVOLUTION

As never-initiate, ravel administered,
belief in blind fairness came rarely a suitor to them.
Feet on divan, slack arm a chair-back slung,
fear covered tracks of how they got there.
Bold smiles tried un-smile eyes to hide,
spoke only the low truce deception had with rights—
more the restraint, and with other help, broke trust all sides.

Errors in patriot ears! Ah choice, made limp, decrepit,
falling away with each new appraisal,
the costly bind of Liberty's (our goddess!) new bandage
which she also jags liana a sling,
sights Disdains' simplest got that all are asked to bear:
hopes recessing separate ways out;
when not even a single bloom on cheeks,
toward in front rows' stump subsidence.

SCALE OF ANUBIS

Rush Erynius, a tree falls in the phat love forest.
The poet dreams of good everywhere
happiness throughout,
smiles the students' tone.
Music of the spheres blasts
tunes sacred where
plant and animal continue
with speeding stone and vernal soil
making mated worlds
to secure more happy men and women
to seed a heaven-heeded richly earth SHe gave,
started from down their line of decline
only a few evenings now from the balance.

Note: The Erinys: avenging deities. Upholders of natural and moral order.

MERIONES AND ACHILLES TO A CROWD

Obscure is this place! Oh, for a quiet bobbin of lace; peace of place—
Note—Life is in the instant. Lie not! it is a matter for Standing;
and the chance to assist? Highest reward and gift!
You will see then, we receive assignments equifactly.
Now then, you would, of weall, rampart, palisade.
So I, at this hole, by Maker's will, and guard sprite Theban Teiresias,
will, aside false attributes! of sieges you!
I remember, taking lead from Joshua, a wall-invincere downed;
being like you of all times and 'race', Ezry! At Timbuktu before,
and Plataea later. At shame-ridden Ishiyama Hongan-ji with Nobunaga;
we coaxed shy of error with those of merit at Port Hudson in The Louis Lands.
At Priam's, where the king's nephew with his Ethiopes came,
there was a wall, stout, the gods had fashioned
through mechanisms of the fire-keeper of that time;
coming and gone, guised in cloud, fogs, mists, as often they did.
Yet it and others we answered, and read south too. All of it,
under fault Duty, discounts of Just; proffered in this "confusion of face;"
things wouldn't want recalled, dredged as afflatus, from a drunken stupor up!
In fact, you might! dislodge yourself; compensation just!
As 'Publish these terrors to all,' that in the halls of slumber rummaging,
could not be stopped!

So, bared beard and branded: those days goodly numbers opposing,
from close at hand and far off, I with the bronze dispatched!
And few, save that fool first Roman, ever, had the temerity or prime-in-power
to call me Dancer! But like Aiacidao at this place before ar....—
(breaks in The Runner himself, rounding swirl about our previous speaker.)
"Her Guimige was his eeeverything! I, grandson of Aeacus rumble!
And say, take them then, men! Your broken end-zone dances.'
Transparent hands on cold chests the now late chill cover.
Unacknowledged by-heaven Yet surely to, praying in time;
'broken all-like, at the battered heal of Commerce,
and come to the top of your perils and solve! Every man an Atlas!
And Say what in your space and time you must make good,
before "Sorry!" slaying Goodness, brings the bad blood
slowing just-precedent to jamb, spanner in the works, moral starts
to disengage the terror-insistent man-killers now haunting thus!

"Further, witness and hear, how I, quickened, first in controversy,
maddest of madmen, against ire failed; and now,
how closed yet still un-harnessed life broke, bottled round in its delicate.
And how this somewhat deadly son of a sea goddess and mortal man,
presents to you remorses no longer secret, misplaced Duty and Honour list.
And say, all sin unmanaged is a shackle! Every uncontrolled rage, devil.

Every kill, failure; that in contemplation—unwise for battlers mid-battle—
reveals its inadequate sense of what could answer for
the so shriveled destructive nod that needs no skin, I prove it!
to reveal its discontents. And how I was insufficiently equipped to find one!

"Survey then, all the bile, upflow rile in indiscrete mouths; root-about,
add—'discipline' now called science, if gazed carefully,
that neither deserves, via unbiased works, nor gets, as here, the capitalization—
That honour, to the not knee bend nor head down to a very closed yore goes.
And prone on the devilry! to await Good's space;
where the few un-quay... And do proper battle!

"Away from kings insulted nigh, and princess's half-innocent unique
advertisements vow.
And neither by closed-interest on final numbers;
nor nods to not-very-fast Idomeneus's,
nor piqued dollars' in their wiggle Grant go!
And say your reveals, on your probable Ephyras, letting good virtues smile out.
'Cause one more delight attentioned the learning crowd as it paced, parted,
back and forth for blessed peripatete Protagoras—
his not 'loving the penny better than (their) whole lives,'
as across that porch; toward better reason went, upon better intents.
And this too may help in your knows where to start!
And where, if cannot to those helps immediate...
thrownout! cautlous word-cautions, their certainties serrate,
while staying within civil's bounderied strictures...
Dismissed! pride of place! dragging ego, eyely drugged;
consulting injuries, and your Histories... all this will go.
Yep! Same dumpheap of selfish behavior! But you know that.

"So feast dear thinker on your fire-breathers, spoken of by fire-breathers
mining, to impressions mold, and siding to a house hammer.
Pummel with justice brief-basic known, your selfish firstimers,
whence ruffian truth suffers no compromise on flat n worlds, alive.
Where measure victors humanist-thrust over who built to let fall, destroy.
That took a little or a lot from their majesties, with never gives back.
Whose toils are the days' Fates, according to works that will,
crucial balance, the salve and just desserts achieve, and yule over.

"At last aghast, drawn; jolt with as I recall, a recent read,
where one poet Illobserved another's work. Having panned,
he suggests, it was largely "...Illplanned..." But poet? Do you plan?
Sure, some eye and hand whirls in thought,
trace moves throughout natures' provides, which, possesses thus!
And yes! It's now! in need, in eyes on. Words nudge, and one sticks, adheres!
And Behold! In her arrogance, Hap may just have old Ignorance, out lain,
in her advantage still!

"Nor, will we leave un-exhaust in disequilibrium, and make back
to wall, serious, turn! Where thorough thought of a universalist,
between shelves redeem along the human chain,
that inherits to all species, no heresies ripe for a fall.
And avoid, by the work for good and selves, tired as it is, as it does,
saying that, 'bigness can only be achieved through the saintly search for small,'
as unencumbered souls might !

"Then. Yet unconvinced. Cry mystery! You are betrayed!
For few have had the fathom of ways; a way up, out.
Because agreed constructions among realities bounce;
and walled serendip nevertheless outs, and with sneaks
prepares clearwater for her mountain head, to receive, as now she does Truth,
because not she, mountain, but men lie!
That now, Earth, poetry and the Phoeban's light in her eyes,
from watcher-height gazes. A great height, a very large off/on manifold
that directs any hour, being topological and a thing of mass-energy equivalence.
So, detains the subject to her object suspect, as simple unit conversions take place.
And mass to energy and vice versa, the precious dimples of hydrogen with helium
dongle our universe."

Aiacidao finds something more interesting in the depts around him and flies off!
Meriones picks up. Have we gone off? Have I been over patient?
I believe I have! Yes? So back to old time.
False we were, and doomed, well before Aulis.
Storied better-half losses, fallen-in citizens, with riches-to-gain war'd.
Social critic, through philoverse of the time, boat and wave, as now, currently
allowed,
had at the loss said, it was not, when surely it was! Being in viridi observania
present to the minds of men, and in full force and operation,
a thing seen, for starters, etc., etc. Mr. Evident standing!!

Cynic then. I ask that with this company you do not assemble!
Nor crowd a city of hardheads weighing through hell in a Milgram Agentic,
the very nigh evils. (Which mind of my: Theory Angelic. Where men and women
designate Beauty (say of faces) with a general symmetry.
Too crooked-here or there—and one is put out of mind of Beauty,
and into that of revulsion. Crooked looking, crooked being! They think.
Which of course, can't be, in a diverse universe, at manic rest atop its maybe
quantic.
But the numbers, the numbers add up to intuition and
first impressions often being both debilitating and enough. And how not?
—This Angelic from efforts' repeat through reverent life after the Beatitudes,
Golden Rule, and every kindness exercised! Can in fact make one's beauty
in one's day and life; add, a certain practice.
So, no tenured priest, nor tripped-up convert will be let
to give about that a thing, a what, is what it is not.
That the practical Pope, of bishops suggests a wash,
dismiss of bare excuse and defense that, not much, expects of us.

One thing I should like to see, one day when Good's banner is up,
the archives at the Vatican, for truth and reconciliation, for mankind's eyes opened
up!
– Stray that! Tack courageous Indonesia, Brazil, Africa's centre,
'cause heavens turn to hells fast. And cold-still in bob, weave, bob, is hot,
weiring to catch soft flesh on a sticky ground. So, say, ask or think
something good of your own, and let the terrors stop!

I see, looking about, in every dreamy eye, the same dream is caught.
That over might, the seeming overnight, come. Bringing Green,
away from Brown, gazelle and hungry lion; and keep and leap its soft back,
for loose-leaf ground, soaked by rain, loosened! false-authority's ageless rule
and killer excess, kindly let down!

Then trepid! If you'll the make-over make round, hear!
Satellite images tell and told what the studious saw and see from Space.
The lull plead on the face of vengeful brown, for drought-less green,
that in photo, well documented does again come back round.

And as you, we gasp in the direction of distress, scene of which
once was glorious Green—whose nourish chanced against that flaming
market head, that greed, that now on to the broad-spread blindness feeds,
is the jewel that once crowned.

So! Students anywhere, do Not! to those word salads uncontrite that
their own long-range unjust hammering do, traitorous nsas, nasas, cias, fbis',
sterile in jumped-up blanko numbers, sans intuition—
in traitorous solidarity with destroying-because-can privilege lauded,
trying to hop off the planet, go!

But save resources for the 'next seven iterations,' as Native Fathers would.
That after duration, thick on thrice! Think! Is attacked head on, the problem,
with solutions tenacious, where lazy politicians, track no more of mars' solutions,
as the numbers-men shadow less, and retreat of GREEN is uncountenanced.
Or the ark veneer will secure delivery of evil throughout the timespace
and its never-learned magnanimity, on the Black Shoulder will efface.

Thereby, to repeat. Since you and I, at the big table glee.
Free-willing onto ruin, with The Maker and His All other othering.
Set Love, The Sane Note, a Notice, the sapien quarry among, par excellence.
That into The Likeness that saves, less slipped the first and every time
on the loose tripage or slide-right anchor of feign fully faulty ambition
that sends to weigh and drag down, and Look! The best for the Whole
Feels and Is righteous, alive; tingles approvingly in the gut.

WHAT MAKES THEM BETTER

Day after first meet before he reached the curb,
she watched and thought of way's he'd said he lived:

when first tall enough to palm a shovel (that was seven),
through most of boyhood, worked, pushed manhood,
kept prized by the lard-fired chicken wings (less capon)
and barbbie chips. The rest? To family
to curb short leash Dad & Mom had on that man.

'Ineluctable modality of the visible'?
What makes them better; as cold foot gets tooled:
"somethin's lost and can't be found!
Please St.Anthony, look around."
Shakespeare's speech in Bloom's dream:
Not much said, but whew! To manage a cringe,
a headache "Iagogo!"

Was understood could stand a bit a' company:
woman to match wits and genitals with
and that's where life in's, and art—
a reading out of words (which poet or philosopher?)
is path a dying star marble's its void.

Had a feeling that if anything, God must be thought:
idea and solid. Is beyond and must!? 'nor is nor is not.'
stand by! I have more!
Better landgrave, and fen match?
'Who thinks he knows, knows not,
who knows he knows, does not.'
Turns his collar 'round then to swim does.
Pitch's camp in a circle; rides bronc to eases.

Love of man, the race, is burden. Let go, watch, come,
gather phantasm and notwithstanding 'no-see-um's' spurl,
center comfortably, and shine minnesinger.

Note: capon: castrate male chicken.
"Iagogo..." James Joyce's Ulysses (Vintage Int'l, Vintage Books,
Division of Random House, Inc., New York, 1934
(Modern Library) 1961, 1990), 567-568.
Spurl: archaic for sprawl.

UNDER THE APPLE TREE

Well no, no cause so shelf-pie simple:
disobedience in a dimple.
No hermits' urge-certainty
via concuss discovery.

Neither dessert, nor transfix of eye.
But how the heavy roads ran, before, behind.
Too, what caught the manly drift
that as boy fed travels' itch.

That later went roar of pipe,
not un-Lion like, Ape-hanging on a bike
a whole continent aimed,
as rolled, went, came.

But let's be clear, it wasn't here
that without subsidy went
on trail, highway and surprised sidewalk.
Dad, Mom and Sis buoyed paying hind, delinquent rent.

So that now, all that escape and power
decades spent, down from its tower; we had our hooligan hour!
low, in comfy squat, quiet in no route,
under the apple tree staid, silent, does not romp.

RESOLUTION

Whereas wise Thespesion, on this issue,
doing what he was able to, to show the Greek Apollonius
what he could of the reverence of the ancients, even to worship
for the others in the animal kingdom,
and that surely it was not for him to disabuse same
of their thoughts, belief, when after-all
a Maker is in everything He makes,
and seeing futility as the new man, the Greek,
idle now his Pythagoras, repeated curses of stupid animals,
dumb beasts; sighs chest-tight following.
And whereas in such detractions old Eleusinian, Dionysian
and other cults and mysteries will stay and stand question.
And that even those who learn their whole lives and become wise,
their carried faults shine, and pride tosses within.
And further, since both, neither trying to convince nor deceive,
but tender true as they understood it were.
Be it hereby resolved that what a man makes has to be fallible.
If not, do they not mar lies upon themselves?

Note: I note here with no too little reservation, the likeness for me,
of the same old defacements some Euros' have wintered to fly the false notion
of nothing of worth in the higher realms of human endeavours coming, ever came
out of Africa, in the new (2005, 2012) translator of the Loeb Philostratus (Elder)
Apollonius of Tyana who in his dismissive introduction outright slanders the
Gymnosophists of Ethiopia as "petty and pretentious," 'perfect counterpoint
to the Wise men of India.' It has, for me, the familiar carried to the absurd allusion
of greed-stricken prefabricators sent on their never royal way assisted by smiling,
waving, playful under rod, scope, deceit, desert and barrel Africans.

TWILIGHT

With the ornament of evening passing long.
Table and wash what was said.
Because a more forthright 5th estate would have helped there,
lay all cards, each and every,
as by former lives and those to come bid able.

So, the binds that confuse inner-knows of good, harm,
and that cup-of-gain, disingenuous, ignore, let lie.
And you, stable—If I fulfill only myself
how will the whole advance?
It being enough to have made the distinction in a dread time.

Later that day, passing, as by the human road she sits,
ask close-cropped Charity if she'd always done her best.
But as she neither notices nor answers,
take those folded pleads and easy lacrimae home,
where gerry-found Hope still sets a table.

Pray then there to cleared skies, that their blue sear keep
and stay steps ahead of the too steep heat of ambition.
Be guard. For in tight, protective hunch, its corner filled with dust,
Necessity will repeal—forget petitioning Heaven, the long-flair universe
will match your wants. And thus! She lies.

EVENING 25,082 THEREABOUT

Father, your anvil molds in its tenancy,
wally wallrocket on its six
keeping the old grass company,
a close of pipe its clench.
I'll have it in before the rain!

A shield in battle, like you and Taliesin.
And thank You and many, when first sought to grip,
then learning grace,
grew to caress generous world.
A help it's been, ever present!

Unlike you, in Day's recede
I salute with something Mari-oughta
and image the stained eyes
of a splendid church
as the dust shrub, sun through, waves panes.

Not the Law fire bush of Moses, where
stood bloom of Justice this. But drear of men's terrors
that have disaster piled with more.
That sets pain and providence the un-sight to eye
one pandemic in its flyby.

I've been changed! Some have said, in garland
of acceptance of the virus in deadly attack. Pariah
of disease held admittance, that in recovery's timor
of return winter, I wish over for who have suffered
through. Be it over, for all ever, including you!

Logs, bad caretaker had, lounge lengths the loam lawn,
say only words signifying rest. Over! they say, And down!
Stretch your weight here, like us, on the cool brown grass
of the living ground and heal by!
It's been the loss of nothing, the gain of everything.

STILL NOT

How display Her wares precious other than have?
Spinning spun on, stride silic yarn?
Seems doing without a tree was torture too, for our young Keats!
a philosophic imagery that could train men, late,
all out of anthropocene, that banks the evil in.

When as the fat lady had not,
Time, the arc, unbent whether on or off
laughed, and languish slid cupis.
Still flop, clop, man insists
about ... what-the-fluck, any dent! he's right, it's his! Isn't!

Notes: *First line A thing to go back to...?*
Something left to its timing? Yes!?
Silic, for silvan.
Cupis, for Cupid.

A REMINISCE AND SORROW IS THERE

(Owing To A Wordsworth Line In A Version Of The Prelude
Where He Is Speaking—A Carefree Childhood And It Is "not"!
"...and sorrow is not there..." But I seem to speak of the sorrow
of necessarily losing childhood's wisdom.)

A blessed activation—youth,
that from low, dark brow of early death
and distress un-account of ancient accident
that startles, high time, did cull.

It was certainly a life of privilege.
Enfranchised, went for a stretch,
arms out, bent palms Blakean, dance full,
restriction, little. They were such traditional parents
and simpler times.

Choke sky, so often a dirty fit of we then,
the not-sharing blind, on their fortunes-lost,
in losing a world to a rise of self
skipped merrily by. .)

I had thought—of the special notice.
Ego stuff—self for self—Life stays at
on open board of given-so-much and taken-more, against
that trust put-in by The Maker, Lord of flesh and dust.

Where care for round-home and?
Where leaves of Life's notice, animal pride in being one?
Was taught?—truly good behavior—
at kitchen table, kirk and dodgeball "think shop?"

Do we know, complicit, we were killing us?
No!
Life led by the growing-up, left concern for long, good life
to the near, awake adults to lift, carry and huff.

We drank the Wind's water, ate what it called fallen,
and generally went forward like swell-head
tofts of an abundant rhyme, that set climbs
on easy hills to rough.

Trouble took the seat hind.
Rosy rhetorics, deceptive hunch
and we-can't-see-that now! tremble some,
off the weight of their Tom, Dick, and Harry tucks

that flattered racists, terrorists and Patience
to give traitors another chance to kill the populous—
we tried to hold upright tomorrow's tombstones—
"We were only livering as our parents had done!"—

Being scandalous to regale in the midden of righteous anger
and vengeance full vent upon generations that,
the sacred covenant broke to desert destinies, befuddled,
hot, ported, that never got out, seems excessive. Or not!

On! *harvest scowl,* leanings sound, strews of hate by,
literature, like summer's windfall — oh! bare interaction!
purports imperfection! passed on. In autumn,
whiled, sharp-eyed and blessings after.
So, hurry storm! gray to blue, like Du Bois we're:
study and assertion Are poets' duty; whose *visions last,*
race-y Walt. *Who speaks true speaks shadows,*
and who is a pirate! Celan, 'Is to make known *and* let be'
emotion, opinion, sensation. No intuition harbour out.

Now, Ant, I see you iron with the skin, and bind—
how many difficulties have I balanced, how many blessings brought in?
(→ There's a blade propeller propped pine needle/twig
Bly-matter Wind by – gone coincidence active,
with a between noon and five-to, and five-after sway... 'till woops!
Handler Wind! Loose the gather.)
But why not, like that grass, How *always* under resolve — muse follow
not only in spring snows of pollen, or mystery, but in witching, tiger,
even 'Violet Hour?' Why not 'Cross at the ford,'
'study all things with no teacher,' Musashi? Let have for a song?
"See into the heart of things" Homer, "make what the hand falls to"
Cohen, like the grateful fed? And "a privilege so awful" race-y Emily is!
Happens most as *you* said, "in banishment from native eyes,
in sight of native air," yet becomes "Such necessary sugar,
such goings on," Ann ... "doing reverence work in sin."

Roll out then, watch hulks grow on your mountain.
Star intaglio, frame perfect, dark in dense Sub-Machina,
marches mist-flat backdrop. Soft ranks fleet across.
And Day, not so hot, Doves in exercise or poorly roused, showing ... What?
So much vista cloud? *We Love you!* And to knees drop.

Hail! Good praise! Come not! destroyer in, flutter insect to stomp!
Life — gives, receives, takes, no sure contract. You?
Only that known!? Do not go blindly among!? Are Green enough?
Proper balance? Intend you that river, Barrymore to ask for sober back,
And still destroy the man?
Well, better than print, scratch and line mark Sudan/Egypt, Pentaur!
Shakespeare is grouping his 'broken syntax,' Lowell!
Fanon and Du Bois proper schooling, while Blake and his Catherine,
dub, dot, light on their daubes;
and many 'asked to be obsessed with writing. And were.'
Now Fire, the words of Ellison lost?!

I think I will 'wake to sleep and take my waking slow' Roethke!
'Learn by going where I have to go!' God Bless! Like Pop!
And Dickens' Sloppy "good at the papers we too

"Do The Police In Different Voices," As Serious Drenched moves,
prods Eliot, like many, sensing what that Greatest Generation had to do,
before they had to do it.

An open window, let me let what wants to, when it wants to come in or go out—
as *All writing* indeed, *is hearing yourself*, Chomsky.
Leaving to eternity the mope, majest, wait-swill in repeats the bio-soup likes;
living with uncertainty, unknown reliefs in the rear sphere,
nates accurate if watching how squat, run — healings on the way where.

About, as falters twist in nights' errants; silence at shore,
broken by first trucks' drifts, safely welcome wealth
that is in the truth having! And shout — grow silence!
We name you friend! As ale'd, unlike our island Dylan,
because 'they expected it,' have not broken that poet body.
But express mainly Love — as strife, the ricochet bullet of life,
hits anything, any time, killing fragile man,
wonderous woman, studious soldier, ferocious poet.

So, *Bose-Einstein condensation** and the stimulated emissions*
at the origin of lasers, Have to look At&t closer at! Even as
that concern's management, along with jet fuel sinks, ejects,
flight paths have had to live with, go no passing Christ-like,
even as I align *Burden 2*, or *Oh! Days*
from gained-time's many numbered *Evenings*
recent in the poles, *Cold Nighs* on *the way with,*
and prepare with salt, the Humanist feel!

For like Phyton, young fool, I did mean to near-insult, climb, drool,
feet flex in Father, Mother (Nut) Air, root, Serapis, Uranus, reasoning not light,
that from that lighted back, who is lengthening, as brother to enormity,
meropes anthropoi, ask: hold hand double-talk agent!
Sing, rejoice! for the suit and stagger on! As cheer whole, gut out,
bottom-filler breaths and the fair air breathe, which, some days,
is so clear, a man here, could climb the far hills there.

So! also maybe: too-much-waste-to-leave-alive, throes, owes
for exclusion of the known manifests in very panting air,
and says we shall never man them, men have better to accomplish.

But *you, you* are brimopatre mighty fathered. And will harm nascent
break, not be like. And there with ©dodeka tuning© to Dasein
(*shepherd of being*) here, there heart-feeler to maneater,
dip das man, the they-self as, in, and cinch sweetwater,
circle air's rich particularity. That like the rest,
ready sometime even insulae of a city to alloy,
as "A new world order, a brand-new day, a change of mind (comes)
for the human race," Curtis Mayfield! Cast selves again ascets among — Who
the Gates of Heaven, contingent joining, the gates of harm would storm.

Notes: Harvest scowl — Hypodra idon — from under brow.
Dodeka: twelve.
Bose-Einstein condensation ... see for example Vitelli, Fruchart
Hanai, Littlewood, U. Chicago, etc.
©Dodeka Tuning© = Ala, Equivalent this Twelve American Dances.

QUIET TWO-STEP

Leucothea sprang slight leap to riiise rested here this morning.
A down-elevener night, then
two pages of Amplier from Fathers Non Meek,
under sun to translate, as revisit of (fri)end), a work toing.

A-nonce! joint test desire's run. Poor Petronius,
Tired soon from that! Besides, severity laid:
Breath Is no passerby in vitae
but still and pillar when, whether/if.

In that once, operations decay to antic;
cease derivative dust 'round, sand in eye;
and men, known to paste urbid for health watch,
close, at home, soft on lifeless shell previous worn,
in modern time, uncoil reverse caduces,
medical crime aligns with infamy;
and many fixed-superstructure-early-enough,
very democracy republic, both, go participatory compact.

But not enough!—The Simple back in!! crenel edge prehend:
toothy wedge beg no merlon arrest disgrunts why'd.
Still, ties do lament, thick brume o conflict preen, decamp.
Life has for so long affirmed conventional, mankiller battle
under, such hard, shy lie, long (this was education)
having no leg to land on. While too many
ignore the agency of recklessness,
make no knowledge of self-watch in calm round fathers' future fates
that no troubles eye. And among the awful there was no imagination.
A hellish-sweet in cast habitus.

But released: the realized pass of death to oblivion, maid right
a wrecking planet. Graves end: but safe! awful's infamy
of ever hate and ill wish, if they think, pre/per arrival,
sits pretentious.

Why not live bountiful forever if life's a dream you steer by?
Citizens it is! and
Having thought'n much on: make it pediment of good
could honest work find, after which even hut of toothpicks
moniker's a Bliss, luxurious quiet evenings come with—
Birthing a fine recovery, and finer vigour to live and work by!

As eagle's talons for yet to come (that's posterity)
akin gift griptures, which are not needed, of Aikido,
with joys in literature—pass the days and all shy canon of Just,
join in patriot work in sympathy with love of country proper,
country of men, just 'by heaven, in their place, having shone
where Wordsworth led: be indeed Content.
Have say of, and mean it!'

Notes: Leucothea — in Homer's Odyssey; Bk 5, line 334.
And Lit. light goddess/morning in John Milton's Paradise Lost (Most texts);
Bk XI, lines 133-135.

'ANOTHER BEAUTIFUL DAY IN THE NEIGHBOR HOOD'

All, doing what they're doing, crew Life's dance,
opt with their opposite.
So, we bring the snake, the aloe, zz, small peace lily,
faux calathea orbifolia in
and take out the double lucky bamboo,
tangled in choice, having tried true's travails!

The you're-in-my-space bees—
busy wild-flower high-yellow spikes of
some cousin of good rosemary, that tries consistently
to crowd the walk, sun conscious—see, and don't see me.
I do and see them not. So we get along.

Squirrel? Less keen, less civil. It's taken longer,
this relative—territories to agree—
being specie(which is specious)-simple, to come to:
Stay clear of me, and I'll do same for you!
Since we spy, scramble, same bounty.

Jays, Stellar and Brush patrol siren or hush.
Crows swish racket as go by the air.
Doves heave chests deep, wide butterfly wap
as they speed wings pushing pact,
front then full press back and out again.

October, and the longed for, thank God committee
of hardly-assured vultures have nighted in the near trees.
That pinion really swipes the air.
You hear a Caw! You look up, that's Hawk!
Stern. Amused. Splicing thermals to get Her beak wet.
When you look through the pine, Voila!
Love, Heaven, Mercy, One.

THE OLDEST AND THE STRONGEST

(Abraham channeling on 90.7)

What beauty that blessed alignment:
there death can not.
Here, happy—astute,
enters the race and wins
though it assists all others
and no finishing line has mark,
since eternity is molding.

Once have-a-mind-to is breach its pass,
Round-about selves, specific
in pluck manifestation restored—
comes, squeeze of hands; everywhere
souls compass space and time...
As the making effort theirs:
oldest and strongest joined.
Old: new, strong: pliant.
Oh! intention stalwart,
you, are building, spread!

JEWEL

Of all the lights in heaven
none has had the brightness
of our Mother.
Her care for us—
the height of lightness,
a heart that soul held weightless,
had nothing missing there.

Please pass along the gift
and let your loved ones hear
the sound that comes
of simple rightness—
a kindness void of fear;
the jewel of many facets,
and nothing missing there.

TO THE HOUSE QUIET

Back with Frost, in from florid fields on knee,
as there are innocents to be defended!
South of easy injury
some say must be Good's amused mirror,
we found a second act to lives.
Foment no gall, ship no discontent,
lead-out where sense went.
There and in that that is
a cool bench, no fire under it,
contrasts are for all governing all,
without 'professionals' whose misuse
had not the stage-set
as in every falling away century.

Januarily, a rambunctious flush to storied faces;
wildfire that knows faraud logic of selfish-lost;
disembodied yells in years' greedy silence
and Old Yeller melt his porch,
guard 'a living!' with doubt.

But breeze in this, clears her evening throat
and comfort, like it or not,
is not wondering on the last trees
and about to disturb baby's caroling field.
Right has stopped carnage.
Men had try and savor,
reenter the house, quiet.

Notes: Faraud: a species of man marked by coarseness and effrontery.

Apple, Sun & Sky

END NOTES

* The Secret Life of a Hat, Starting Back, Reunion Fancy, posted to/ Published, if memory serves, on poetry.com in roughly the 1997-2003 time frame.

*Song appeared on ahapoetry.com (Encore III) Dec. 2002

*Adherence Crafted, Wide-Eyed, Heraldic, Legacy, The Work, Going to Ground, Moving Earth, Can Meadows Sing, Shee, Posted to/Published on daypoems.net 2002-2003. Note that Day poems 'harvested' I think, some earlier work published at various sites on the web back then 1998—Early 2000's, like Missing A Love, And and others picked up, apparently, by such as poem hunter, poem ist, and the like.

*The World Left its Own Devices, For Pauline and William, Potash and Coal Dust, To Mum, Dad, Non Gun, Holy, Behave, Non-knowing, Privilege, Too Soon, Judgment, posted to/Published on allpoetry.com 2002-2005 and elsewhere.

*Everything Old to: Yahoo Timecapsule on-line.

*ΟΜΕΡΩ Homer or Omar to wikimaps on-line.

*The Silk Tree, to a British News comment, on-line (The Guardian!?), I forget which site.

*All Book Reviews published to amazon dot com through the years.

*Some Poems appeared on Dragonconversation.com.

*And some here, were published on Joeduvernay.com through the years.

GENERAL BIOGRAPHY
Joseph Marcel Duvernay

Born Feb. 1952. Parochial school 1-9th grades (he thanks his Ma and Pa!), High Schooled in the public schools, and with one month off after high school graduation in June of 1970, hired-on in August of that year with Western Electric Co. of the then Bell System, where, after thirty years, ten months and 28 days of service—through various company re-namings, etc. Joseph retired in July of 2001.

During that time Joseph attended various Community Colleges in the Los Angeles area, and had a quarter or two at Cal. State University Los Angeles and Long Beach when assigned to night-shifts on the job, centered around Mathematics and Technologies. During his years on the job, Joseph was fortunate to receive many Electronics and Management courses at Western Electric, AT&T Network Systems and Lucent Technologies, Bell Labs Innovations and went from Entry level (Inside plant) 1-Index Installer to 5-Index Installer, Tester and In-Charge (Foreman), to Field Engineer, to Supervisor, to Project/Implementation Manager, and did several projects for Bell Labs specifically.

He also somewhat pursued his love of the wild, by attending two or more U.C. Davis and one other University's Wild Horse viewing and Mule-packing Extension courses in the California and Nevada wild areas.

He married his High School sweetheart, this did not last with the need to work the many 12 hour / 7 day-a-week / double shifts, etc. he felt was necessary to stay on good terms with management through the early and later years. But he has five wonderful children, eight wonderful grandchildren, and three books of poetry published preceding this: *Twelve American Dances*.

His interests remain: The Peoples of the world and fair play administered to them. Hiking, camping, reading, writing, study and translation.